what did you eat yesterday? 4
fumi yoshinaga

VERTICAL.

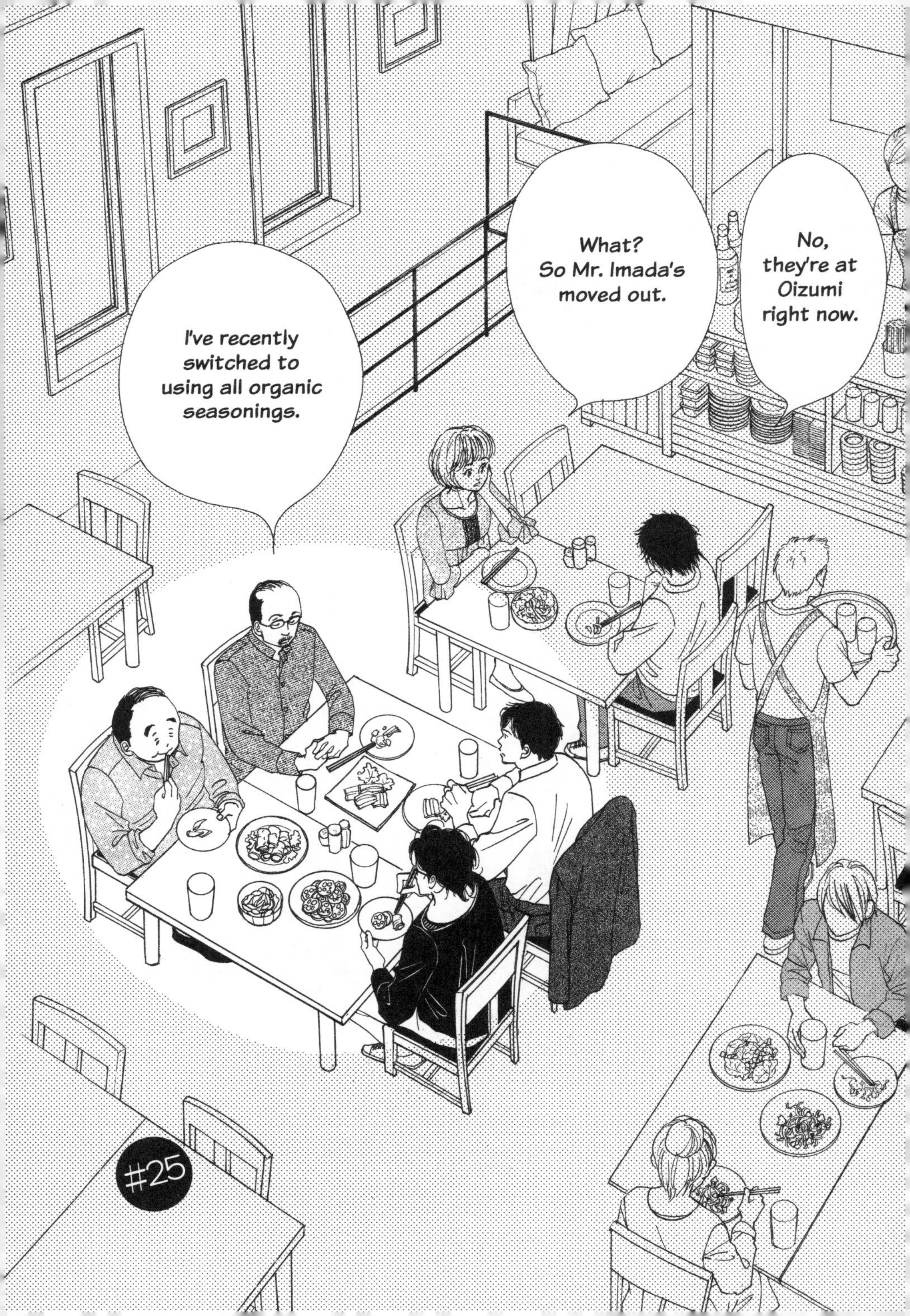
No, they're at Oizumi right now.
What? So Mr. Imada's moved out.
I've recently switched to using all organic seasonings.
#25

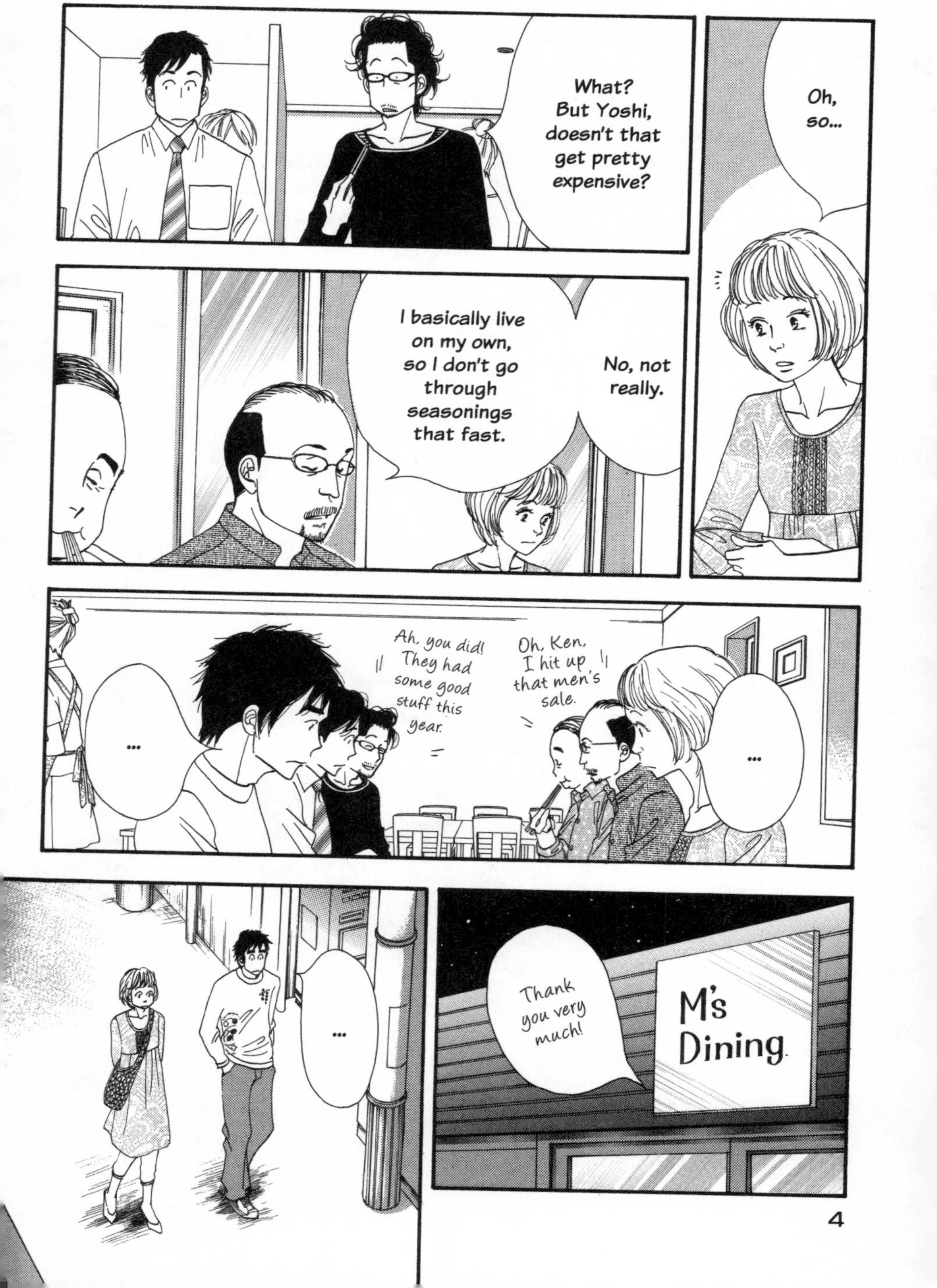
Oh, so...
What? But Yoshi, doesn't that get pretty expensive?
No, not really.
I basically live on my own, so I don't go through seasonings that fast.
...
Oh, Ken, I hit up that men's sale.
Ah, you did! They had some good stuff this year.
...
M's Dining
Thank you very much!
...

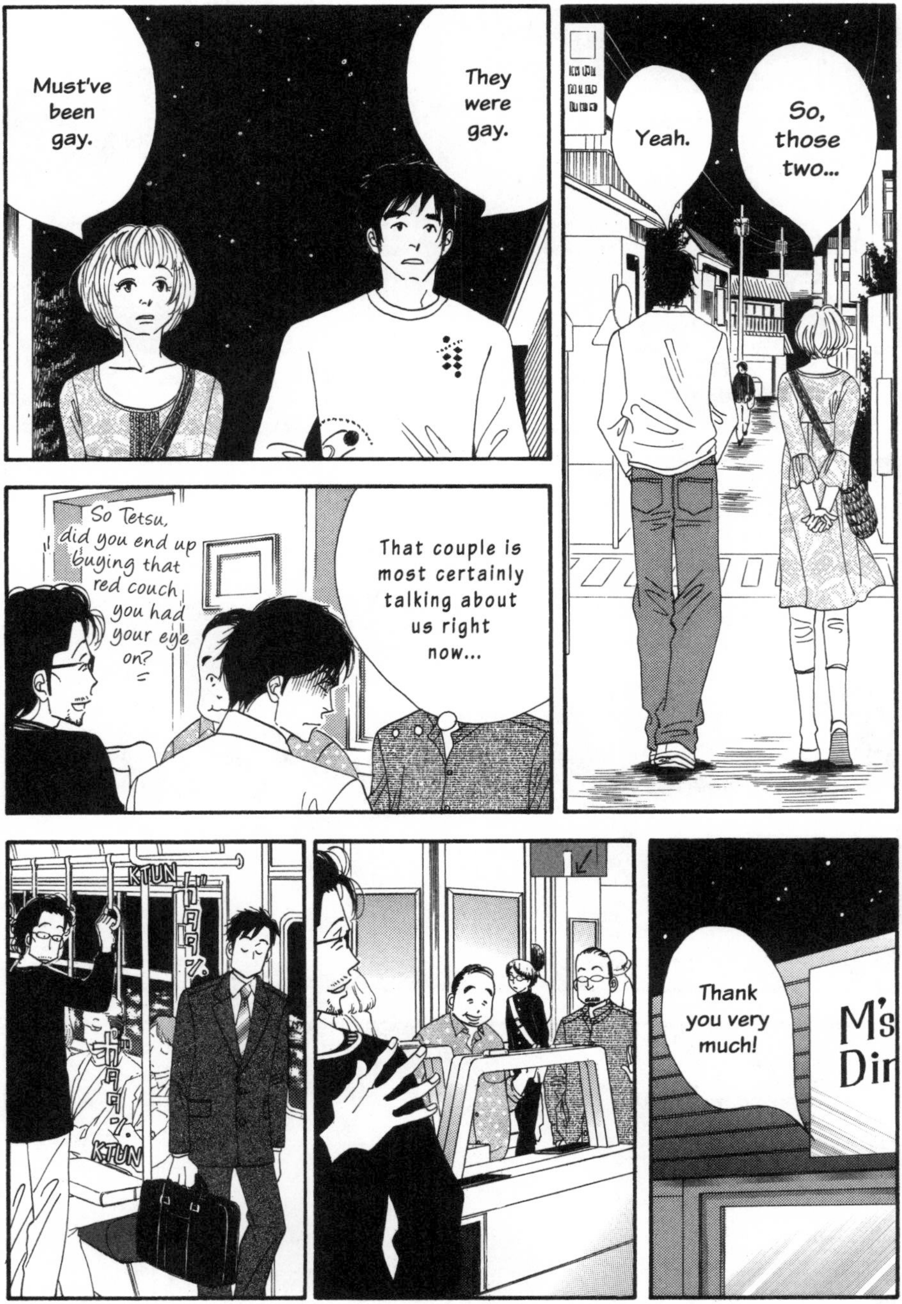
So, those two...
Yeah.
They were gay.
Must've been gay.
That couple is most certainly talking about us right now...
So Tetsu, did you end up buying that red couch you had your eye on?
Thank you very much!
M's
KTUN
KTUN

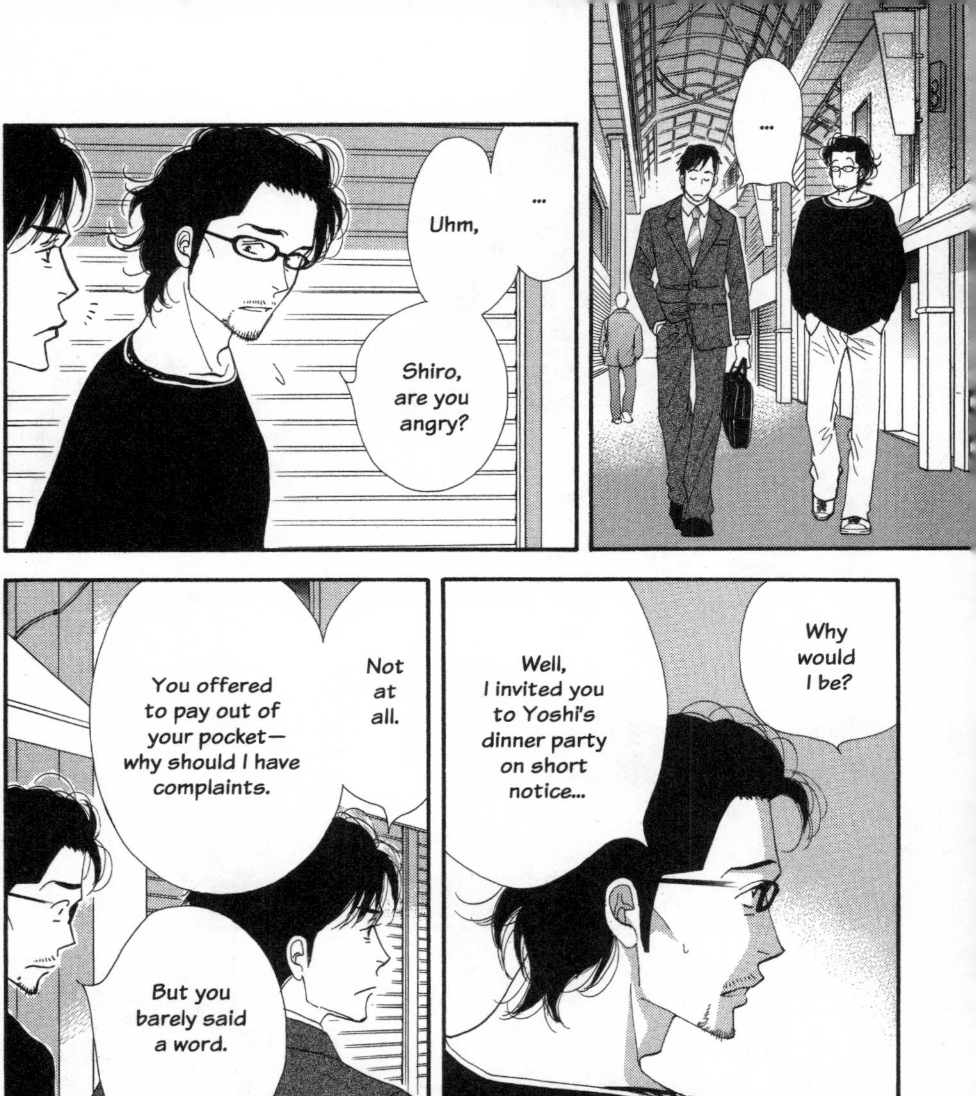
...
...
Uhm,
Shiro, are you angry?
Why would I be?
Well, I invited you to Yoshi's dinner party on short notice...
Not at all.
You offered to pay out of your pocket— why should I have complaints.
But you barely said a word.
That's not true.
And we talked about all sorts of gay stuff... Food seasonings, interior design, clothes...

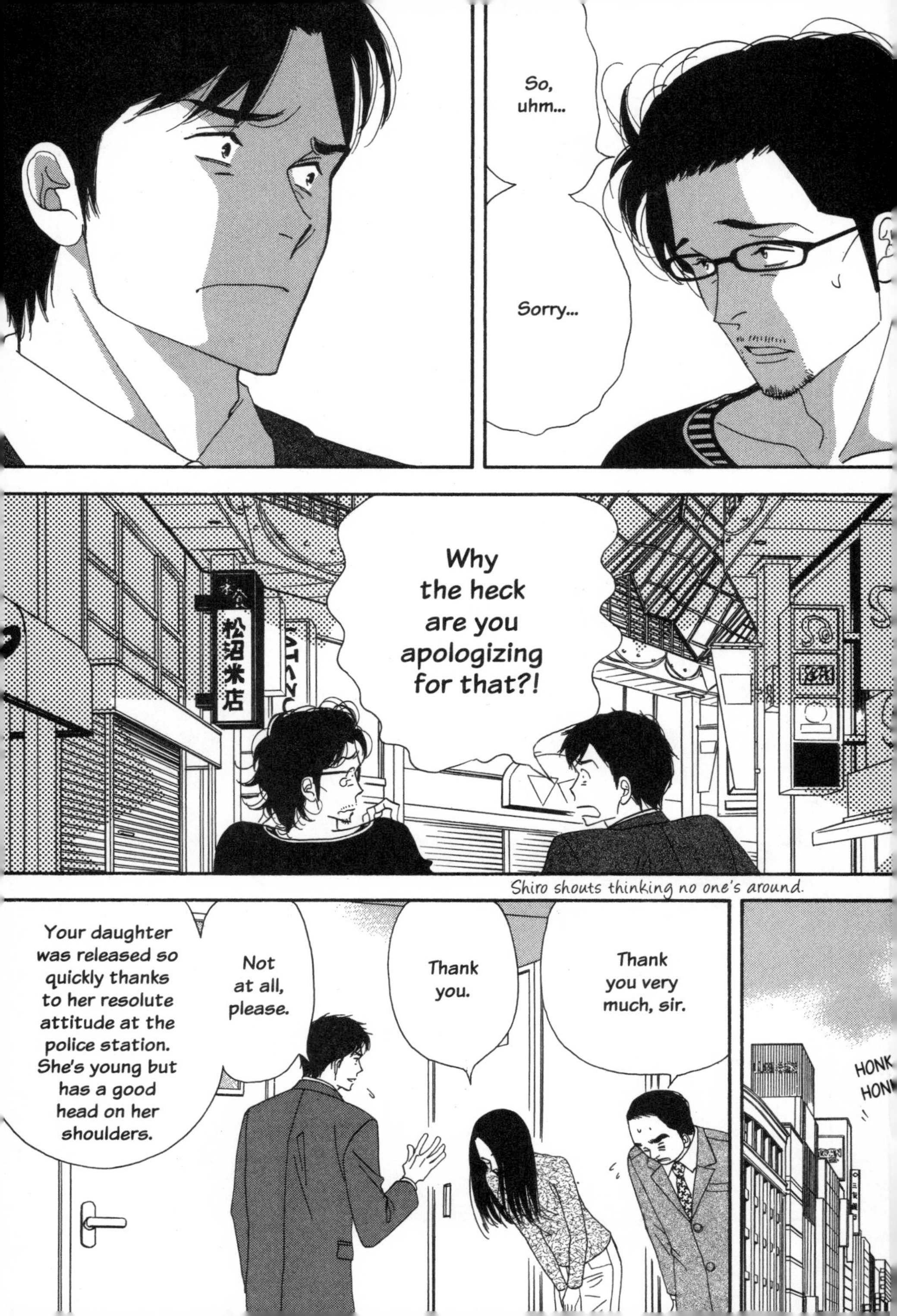
So, uhm...
Sorry...
Why the heck are you apologizing for that?!
松沼米店
Shiro shouts thinking no one's around.
HONK HONK
Thank you very much, sir.
Thank you.
Not at all, please.
Your daughter was released so quickly thanks to her resolute attitude at the police station. She's young but has a good head on her shoulders.

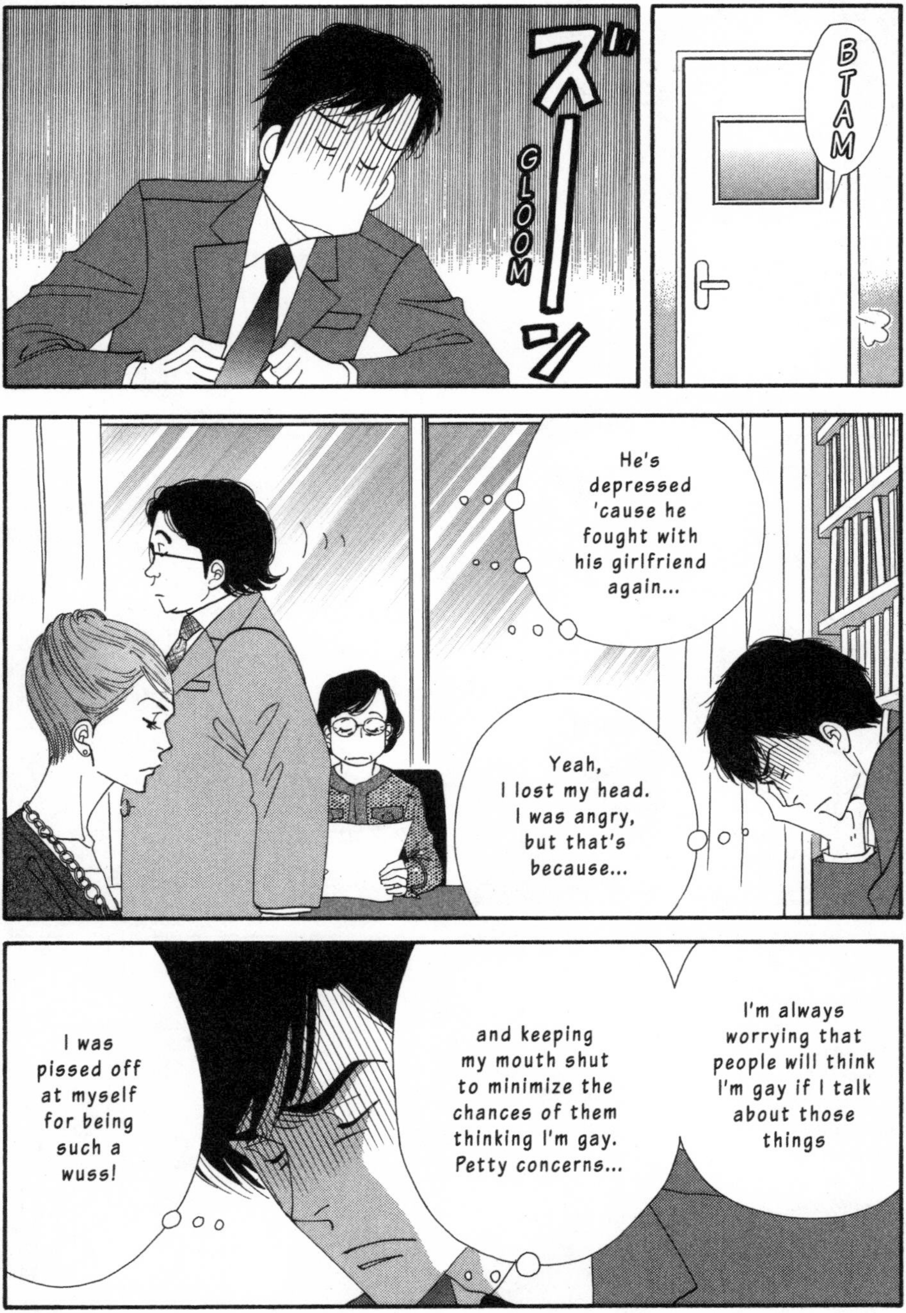
BTAM
ズーン
GLOOM
He's depressed 'cause he fought with his girlfriend again...
Yeah, I lost my head. I was angry, but that's because...
I'm always worrying that people will think I'm gay if I talk about those things
and keeping my mouth shut to minimize the chances of them thinking I'm gay. Petty concerns...
I was pissed off at myself for being such a wuss!

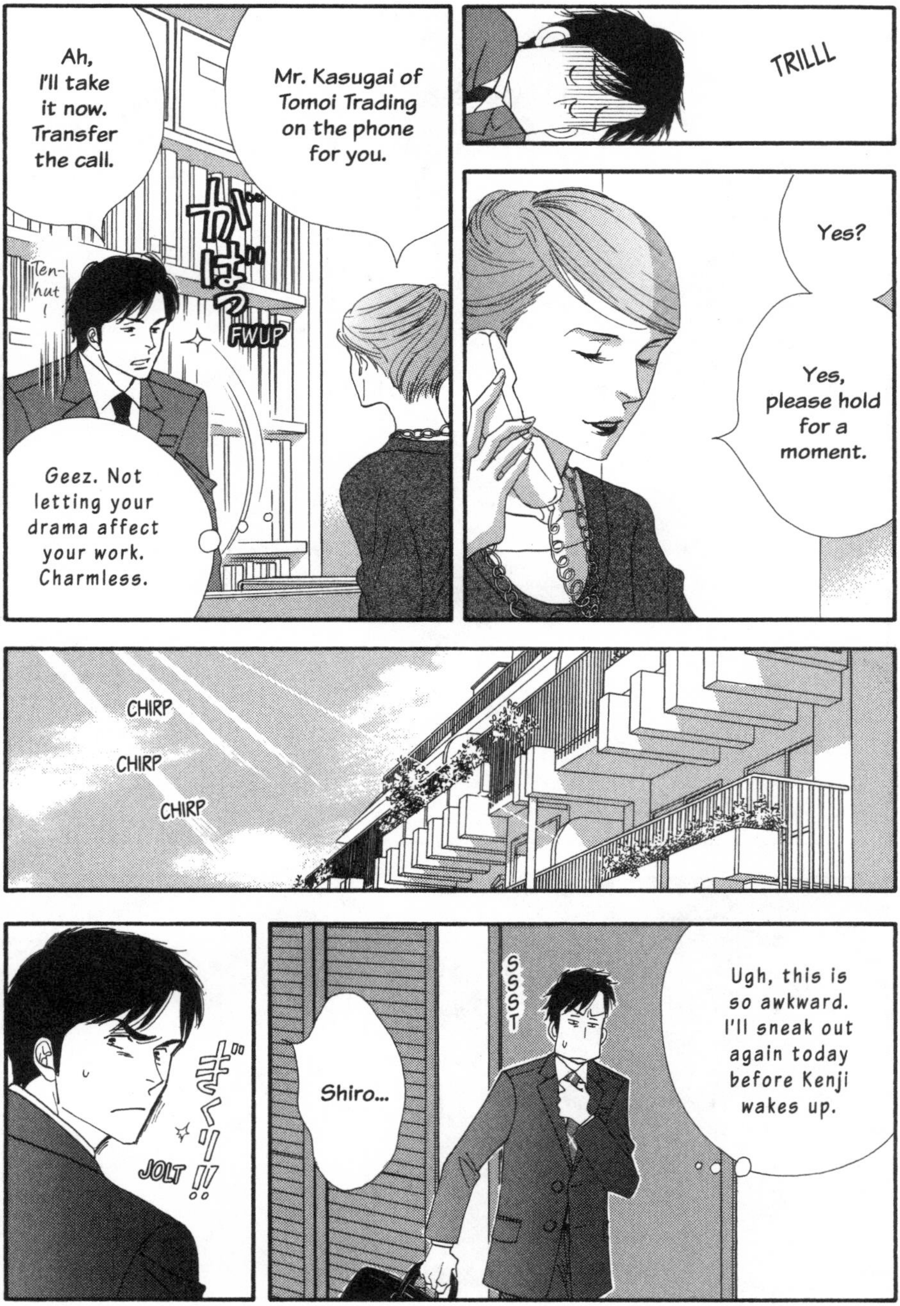
TRILLL
Yes?
Yes, please hold for a moment.
Mr. Kasugai of Tomoi Trading on the phone for you.
Ah, I'll take it now. Transfer the call.
がばっ
FWUP
Ten-hut!
Geez. Not letting your drama affect your work. Charmless.
CHIRP
CHIRP
CHIRP
Ugh, this is so awkward. I'll sneak out again today before Kenji wakes up.
SSST
Shiro...
ぎくーっ
JOLT!!

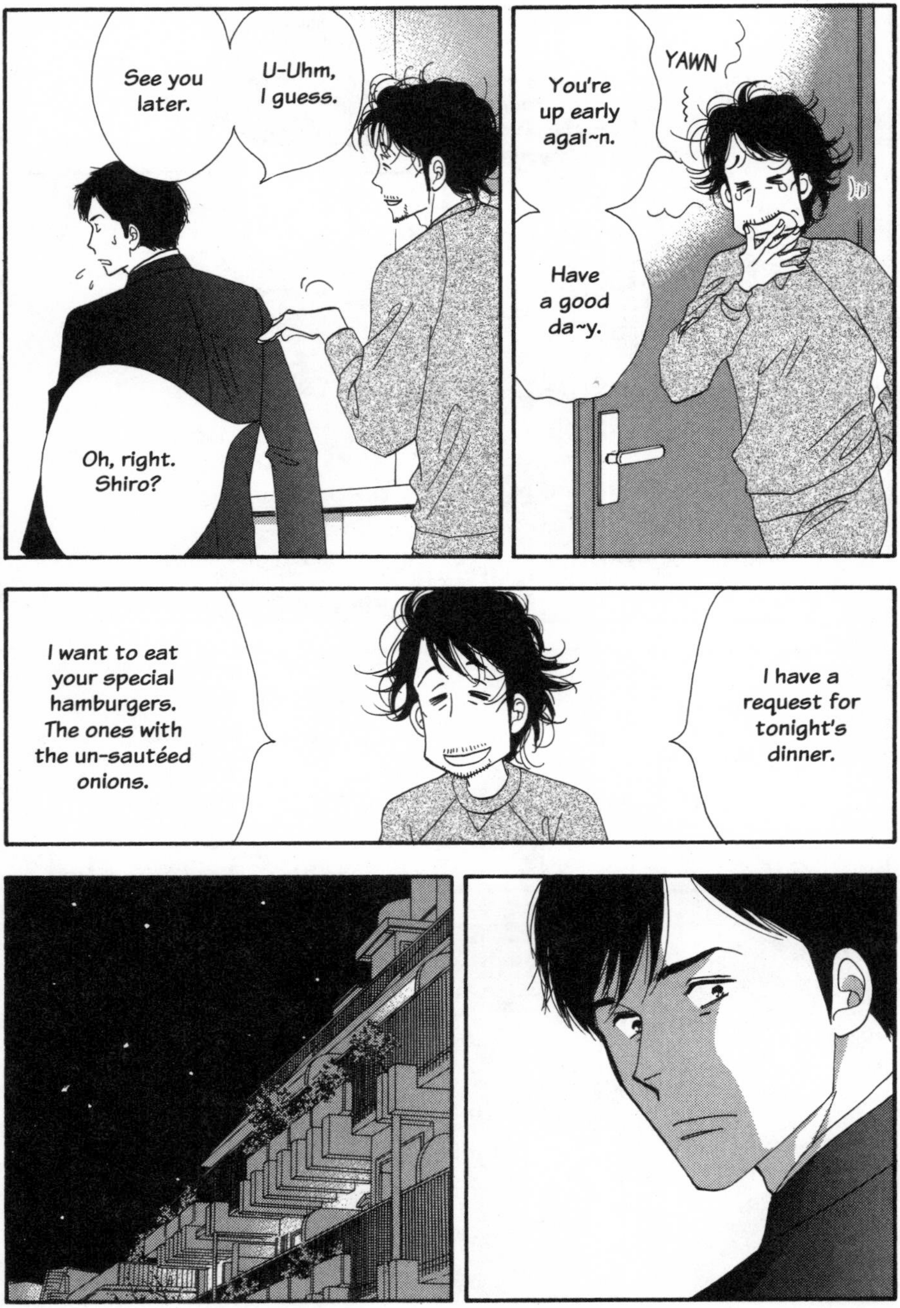
YAWN
You're up early agai~n.
Have a good da~y.
U-Uhm, I guess.
See you later.
Oh, right. Shiro?
I have a request for tonight's dinner.
I want to eat your special hamburgers. The ones with the un-sautéed onions.

Now then...
CHOP CHOP
THOK THOK
BLUB BLUB
Bring 2 small bowls' worth of water to a boil.
TMP
SHFF SHFF
TOK TOK TOK TOK
Miso soup with eggplant, thin fried tofu and fall-harvest ginger buds—done.
Keep ginger buds in the bowls.

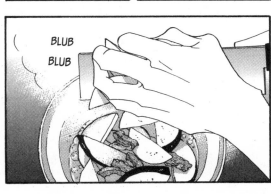

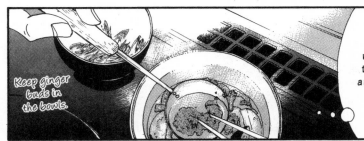

Next: Slice 5 cm of *daikon* into slender quarters, 1/4 large carrot into half-moons, and 1 small cucumber into thin slices on the bias...
Sprinkle with 1 tsp salt and let sit...
In the mean-time...
RIP
WSHH
SPLOSH
PLOSH
CHOP
The root ends of leafy greens are usually muddy, so rinse the ends thoroughly...
Roughly chop a 1/2 bunch of mustard spinach, rinse bean sprouts and let drain in a strainer.

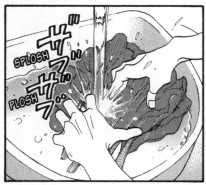

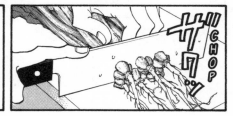

The *daikon*, cucumbers and carrots should be tender by now so press out excess liquid...
SQUEEZE
Dust with 1 tsp powdered kelp tea, season with vinegar to taste and a dash of sugar, and the lightly-pickled veggies are ready.
THOK
Leaving the root end intact, thinly slice onion, then cut crosswise to mince.
THOK
TOK
TOK
TOK
Ah... Chopping onions makes me cry.
STRIP
Combine 1 minced onion with about 1 lb ground mixed beef and pork.
If you are sautéing the onions beforehand, hamburgers are pretty simple.
WHOP

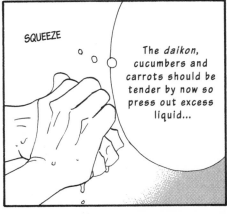

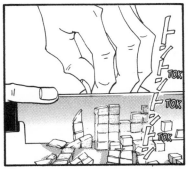

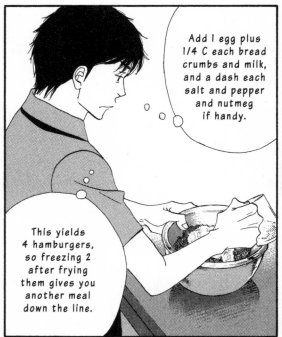

KRAK
SHFF
Add 1 egg plus 1/4 C each bread crumbs and milk, and a dash each salt and pepper and nutmeg if handy.
This yields 4 hamburgers, so freezing 2 after frying them gives you another meal down the line.
SMAK
SMAK
Knead well until sticky.
SPLICH
SPLICH
SLAP
SLAP
Shape into 4 patties.
Pack the patties tightly as if playing catch to expel air and keep them from crumbling when fried. Indent the center to ensure even cooking.

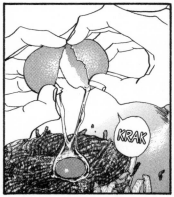

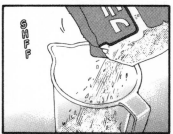

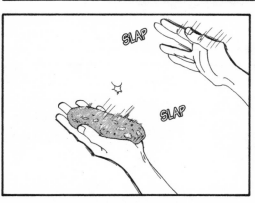

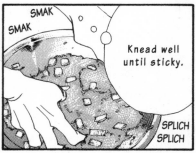

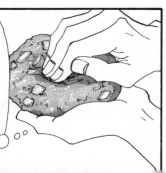

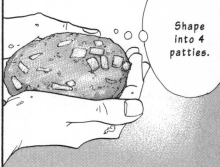

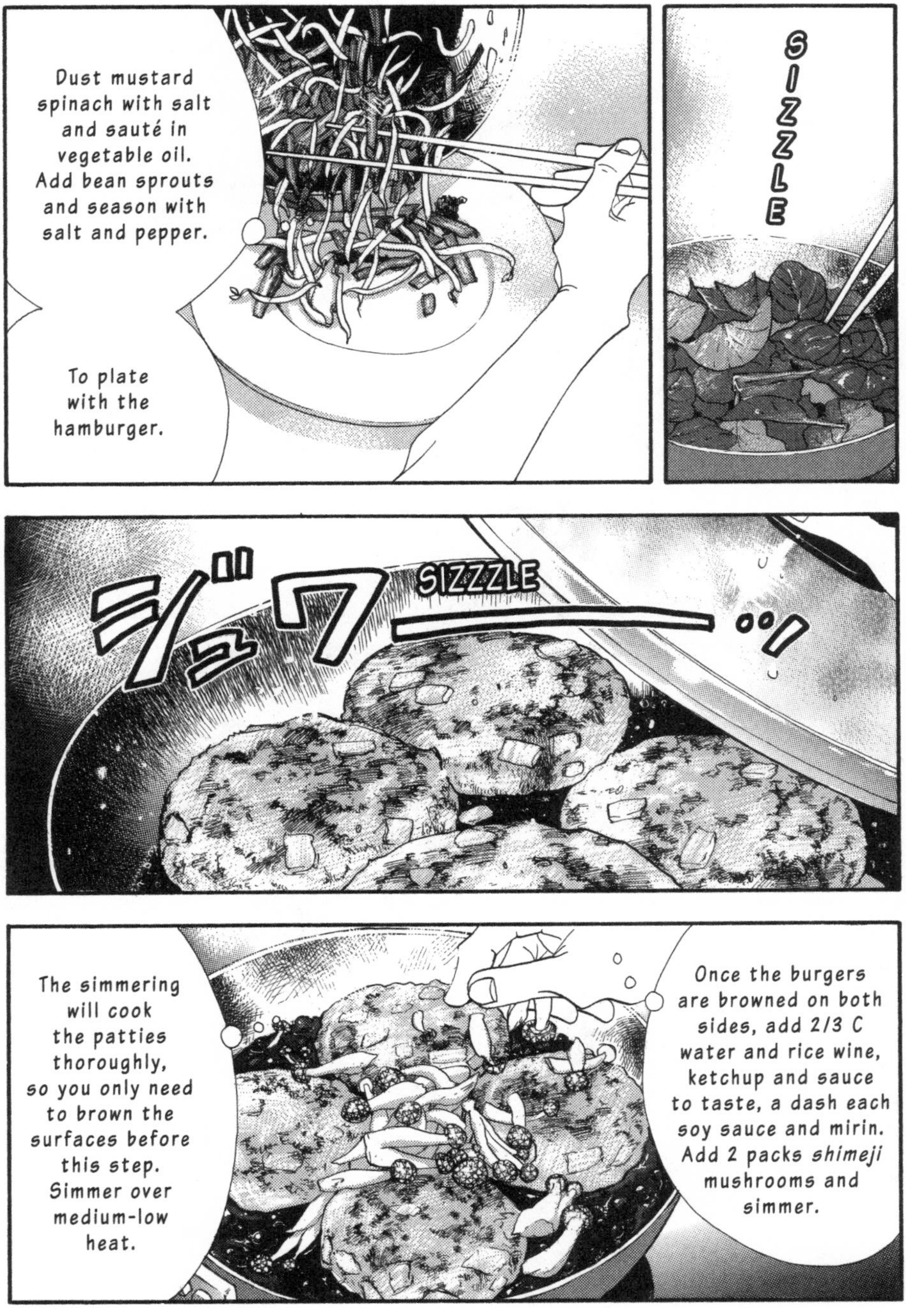
SIZZLE
Dust mustard spinach with salt and sauté in vegetable oil. Add bean sprouts and season with salt and pepper.
To plate with the hamburger.
ジュワーッ
SIZZLE
Once the burgers are browned on both sides, add 2/3 C water and rice wine, ketchup and sauce to taste, a dash each soy sauce and mirin. Add 2 packs *shimeji* mushrooms and simmer.
The simmering will cook the patties thoroughly, so you only need to brown the surfaces before this step. Simmer over medium-low heat.

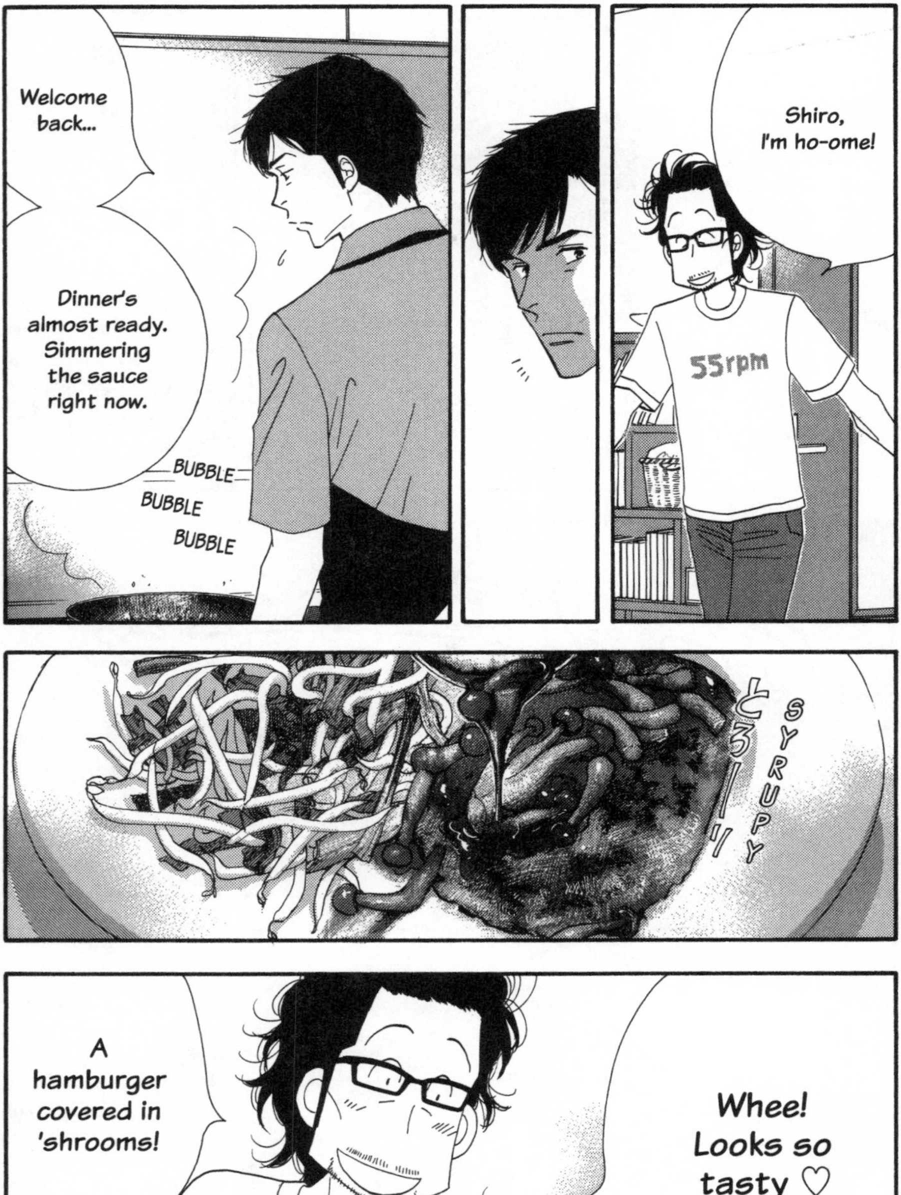
Shiro, I'm ho-ome!
55rpm
Welcome back...
Dinner's almost ready. Simmering the sauce right now.
BUBBLE
BUBBLE
BUBBLE
とろーり
SYRUPY
Whee! Looks so tasty ♡
A hamburger covered in 'shrooms!

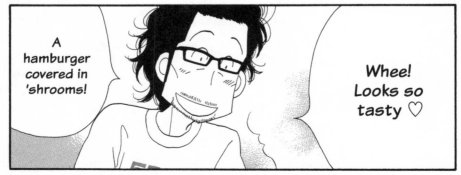

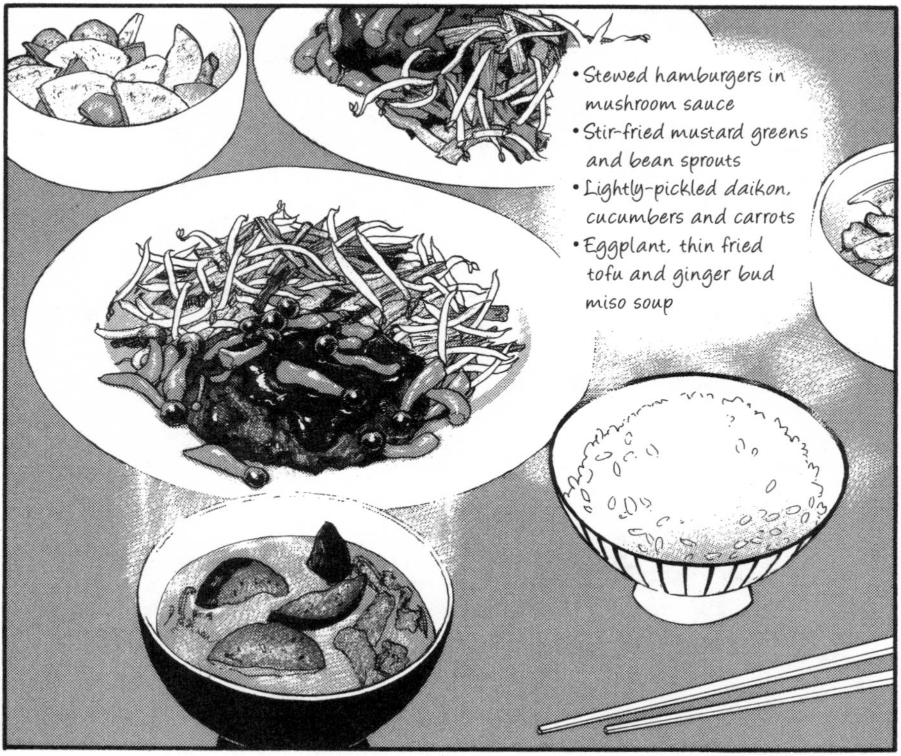
•Stewed hamburgers in mushroom sauce
•Stir-fried mustard greens and bean sprouts
•Lightly-pickled daikon, cucumbers and carrots
•Eggplant, thin fried tofu and ginger bud miso soup

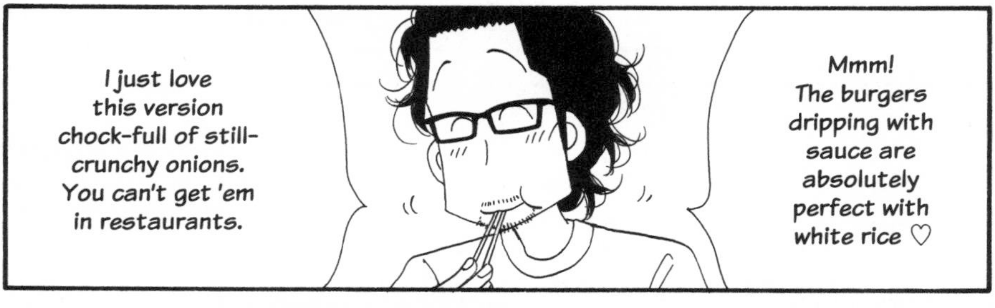
Mmm! The burgers dripping with sauce are absolutely perfect with white rice ♡
I just love this version chock-full of still-crunchy onions. You can't get 'em in restaurants.

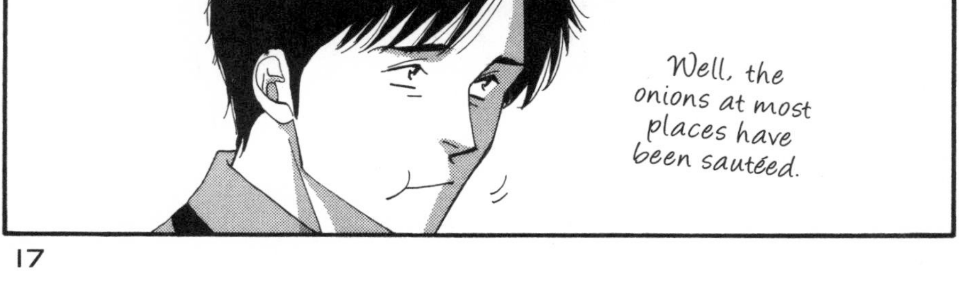
Well, the onions at most places have been sautéed.

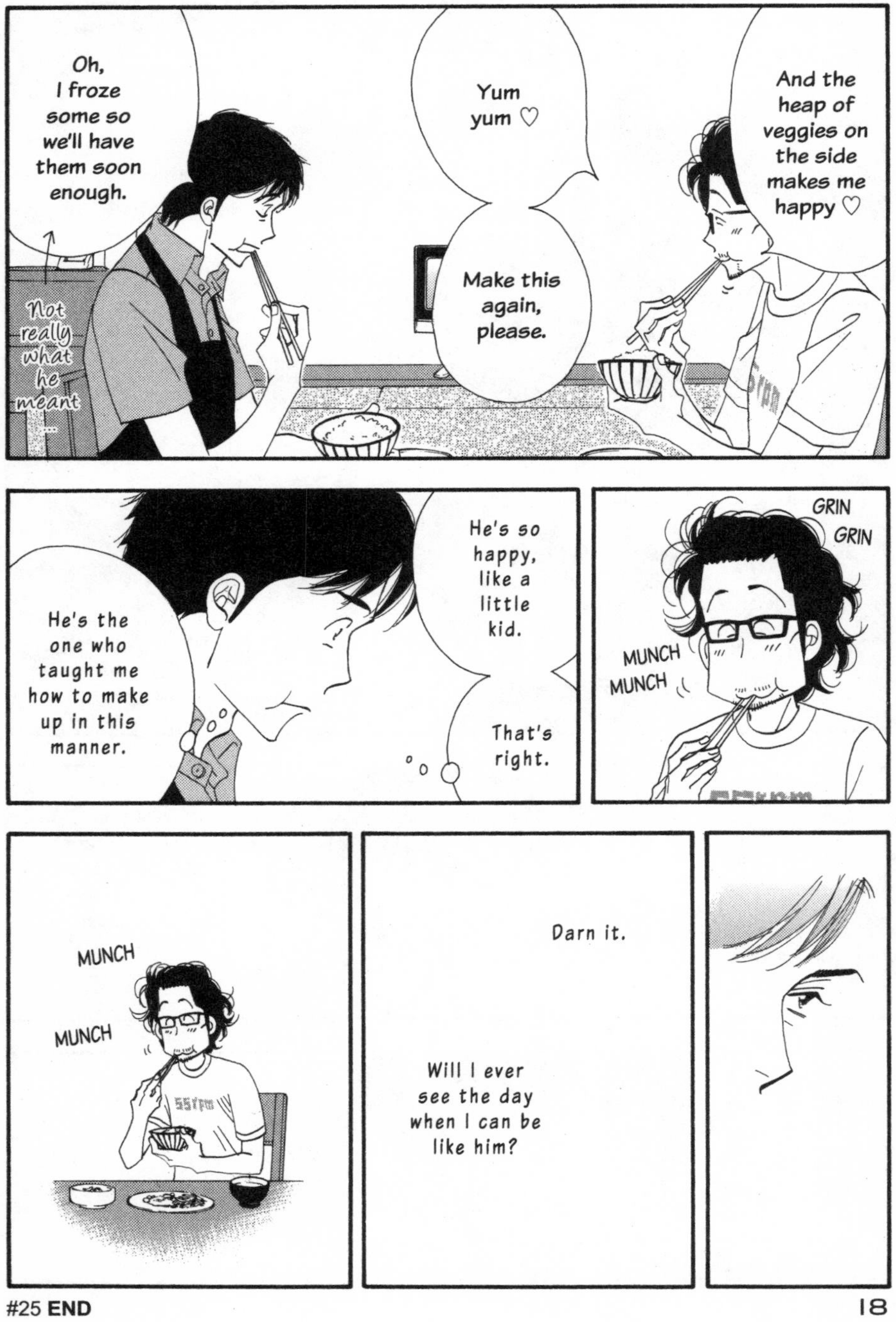
And the heap of veggies on the side makes me happy ♡
Yum yum ♡
Make this again, please.
Oh, I froze some so we'll have them soon enough.
Not really what he meant...
GRIN
GRIN
MUNCH
MUNCH
He's so happy, like a little kid.
That's right.
He's the one who taught me how to make up in this manner.
Darn it.
Will I ever see the day when I can be like him?
MUNCH
MUNCH

#25 **END**

The sauce for the **stewed burgers** is pretty rich,
so keep the seasoning for the sautéed mustard
greens and bean sprouts on the lighter side.
Having boiled broccolis with just the hamburger
sauce is even healthier and tasty.
Dicing the onions for the burgers in a
food processor will sap out the moisture,
so please mince by hand instead.
Roughly is fine since they'll be simmered.

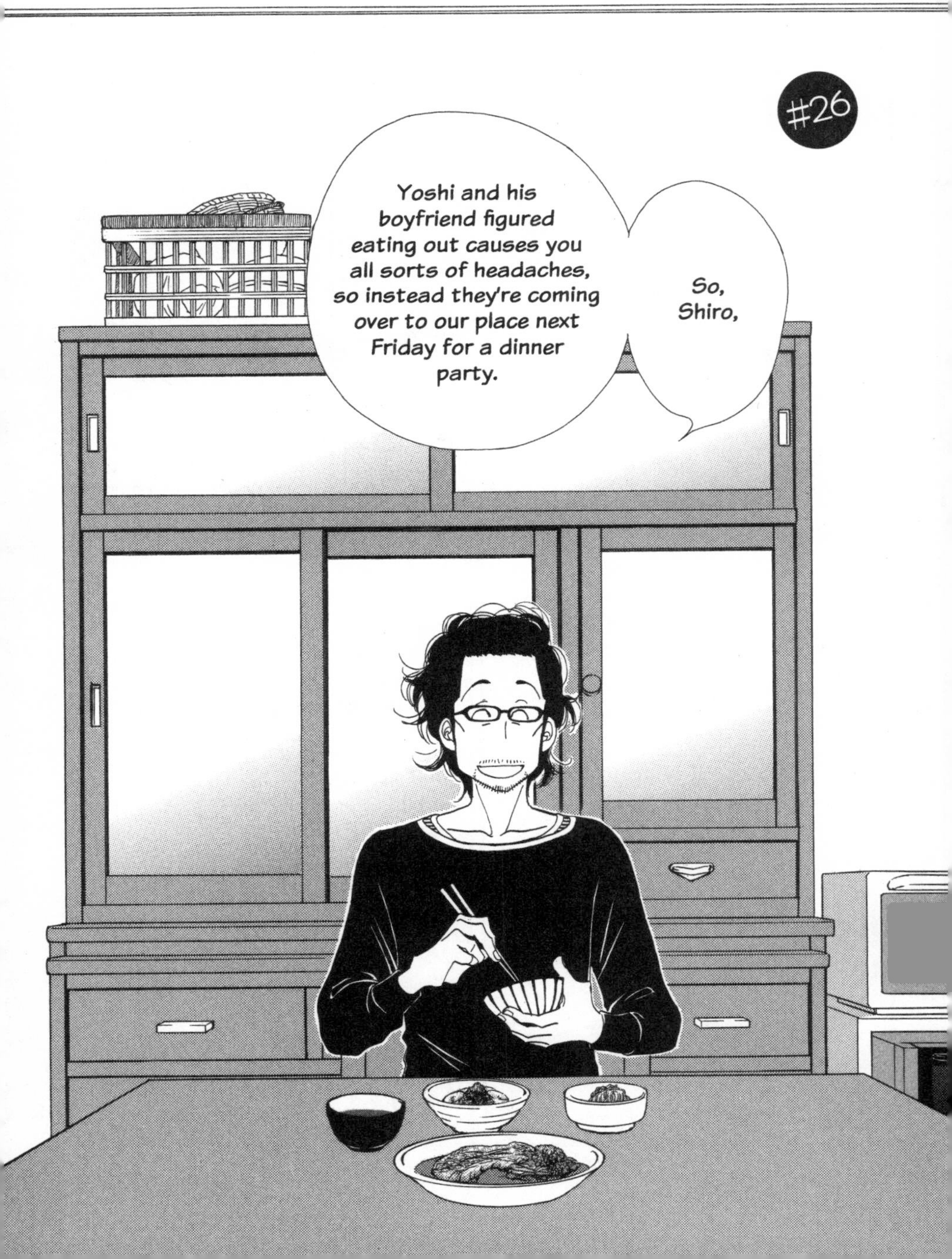
#26
So, Shiro,
Yoshi and his boyfriend figured eating out causes you all sorts of headaches, so instead they're coming over to our place next Friday for a dinner party.

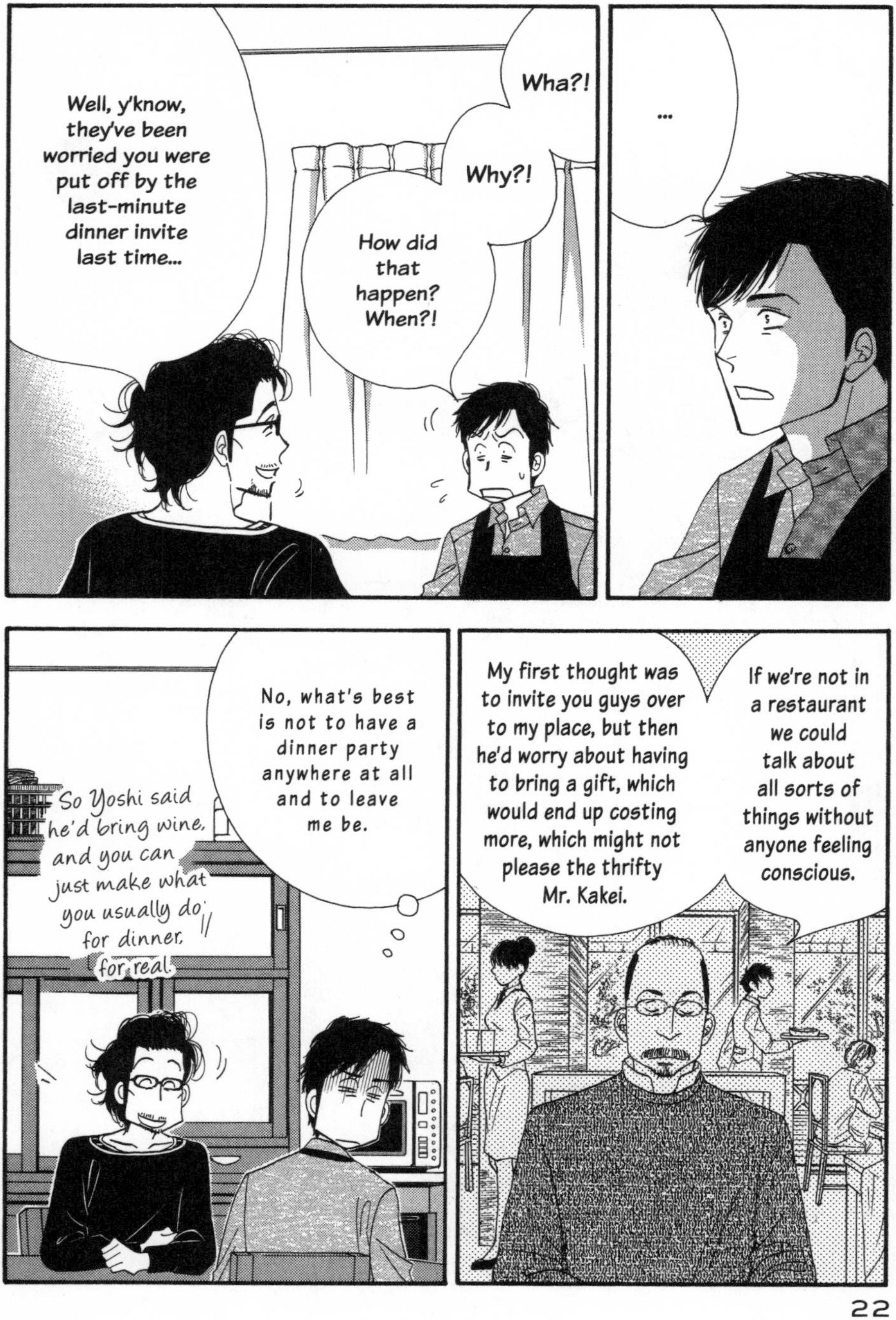
...
Well, y'know, they've been worried you were put off by the last-minute dinner invite last time...
Wha?!
Why?!
How did that happen? When?!
My first thought was to invite you guys over to my place, but then he'd worry about having to bring a gift, which would end up costing more, which might not please the thrifty Mr. Kakei.
If we're not in a restaurant we could talk about all sorts of things without anyone feeling conscious.
So Yoshi said he'd bring wine, and you can just make what you usually do for dinner. for real.
No, what's best is not to have a dinner party anywhere at all and to leave me be.

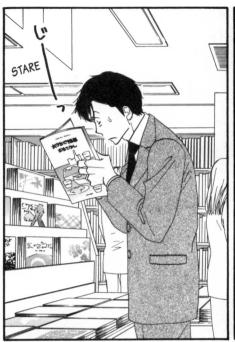

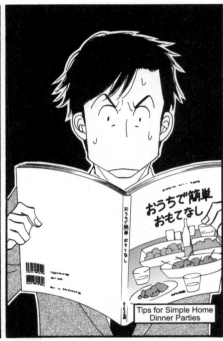

おうちで簡単
おもてなし
Tips for Simple Home Dinner Parties
じー
STARE
YOSHI'S COOKING SKILLS ARE EXPERT-LEVEL.
He eats couscous with broth using so much bonito flakes that you could stick chopsticks in them and they'd stand up. Cooks en *flambé*, has a tajine...
That's the kind of man he is!
What could I, a humble working househusband who only cooks daily out of necessity, serve him?!
SPLISH
FWASH!

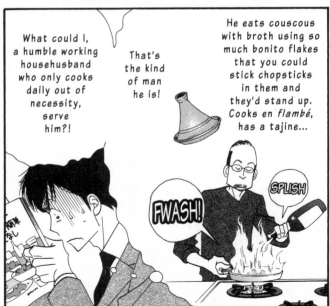

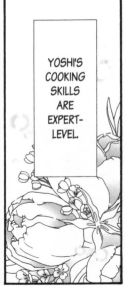

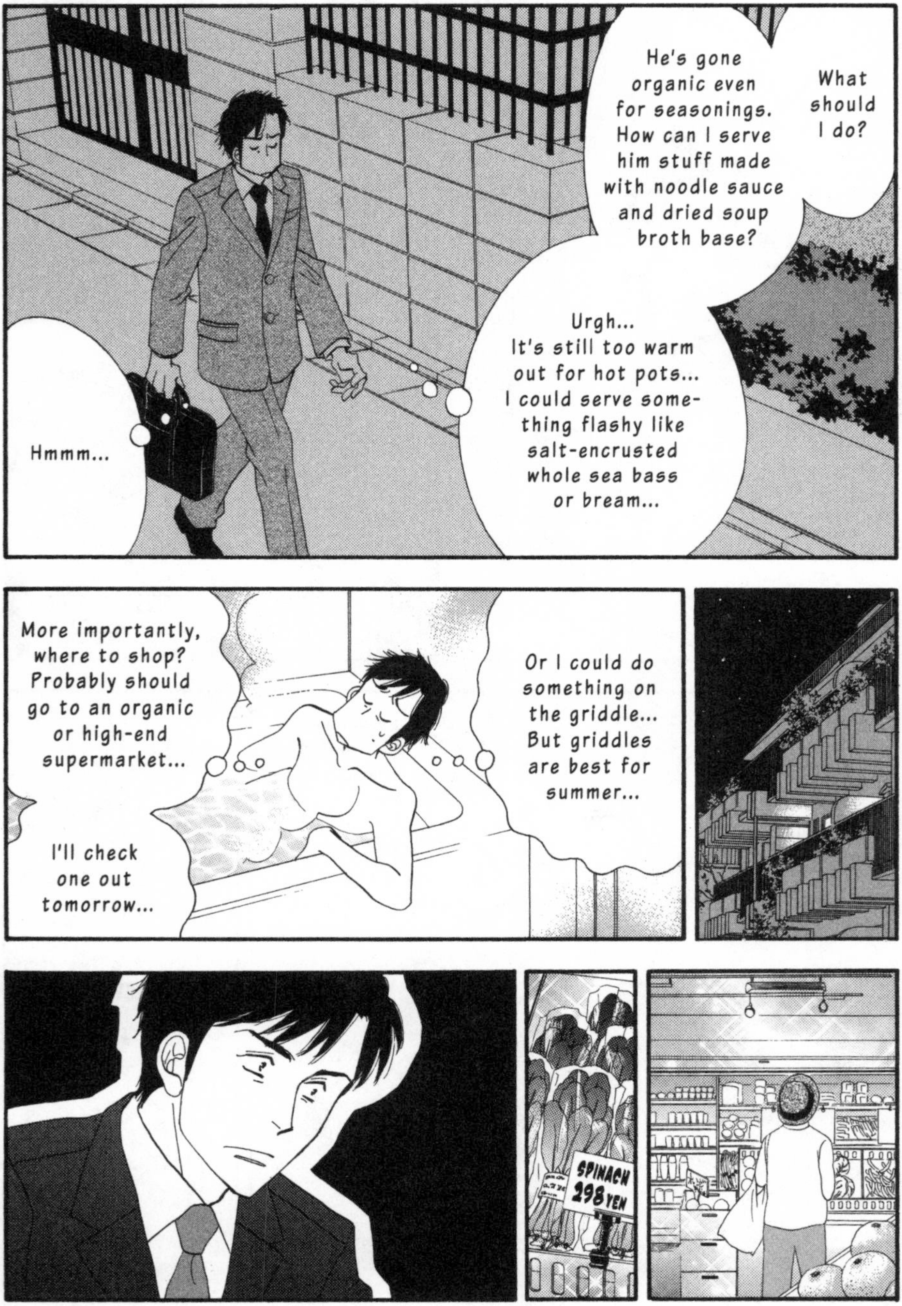
What should I do?
He's gone organic even for seasonings. How can I serve him stuff made with noodle sauce and dried soup broth base?
Urgh... It's still too warm out for hot pots... I could serve some-thing flashy like salt-encrusted whole sea bass or bream...
Hmmm...
Or I could do something on the griddle... But griddles are best for summer...
More importantly, where to shop? Probably should go to an organic or high-end supermarket...
I'll check one out tomorrow...
SPINACH 298 YEN

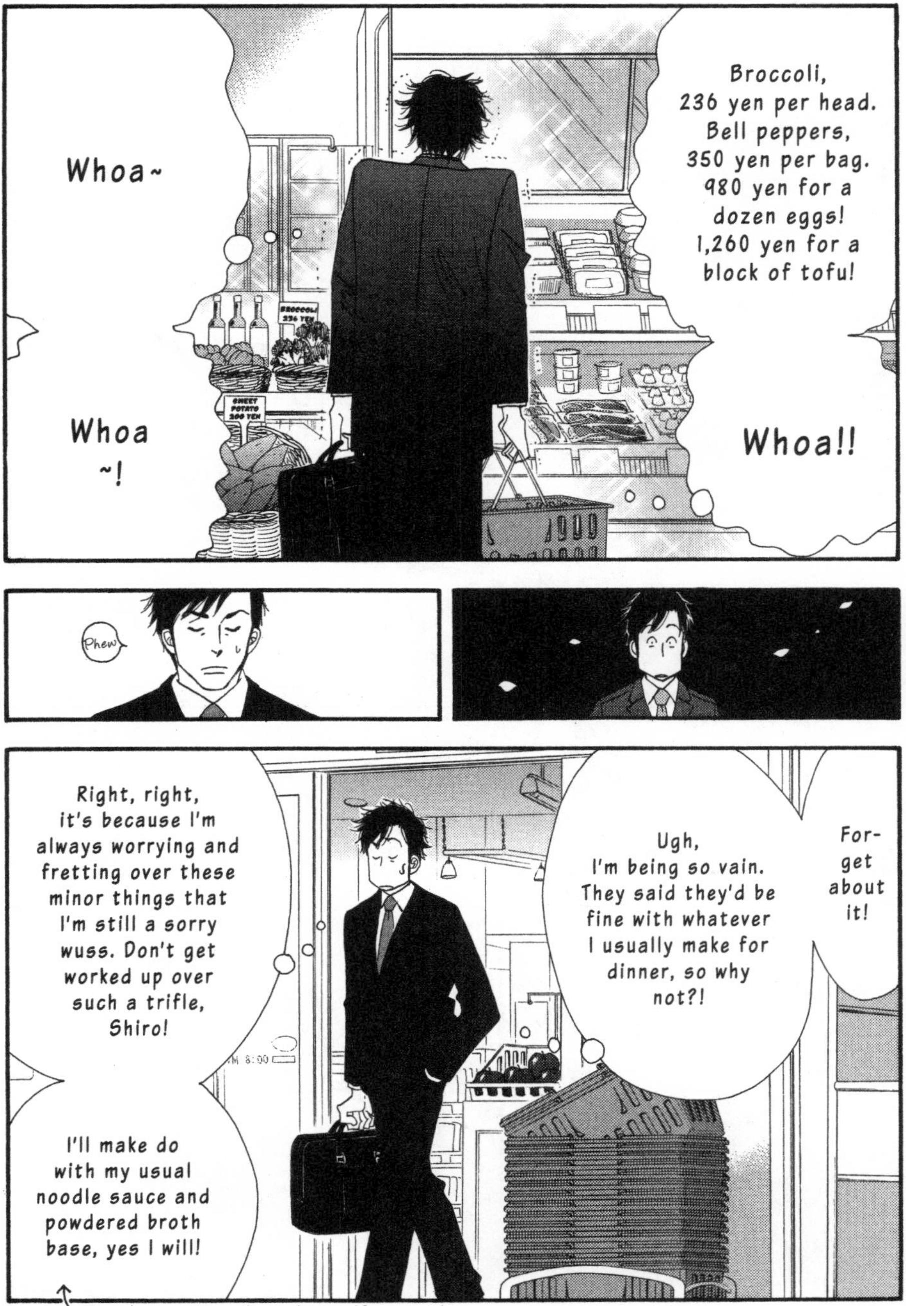
Broccoli, 236 yen per head. Bell peppers, 350 yen per bag. 980 yen for a dozen eggs! 1,260 yen for a block of tofu!
Whoa!!
Whoa~
Whoa ~!
Phew
For-get about it!
Ugh, I'm being so vain. They said they'd be fine with whatever I usually make for dinner, so why not?!
Right, right, it's because I'm always worrying and fretting over these minor things that I'm still a sorry wuss. Don't get worked up over such a trifle, Shiro!
I'll make do with my usual noodle sauce and powdered broth base, yes I will!

But he's gotta cheer himself on to do so.

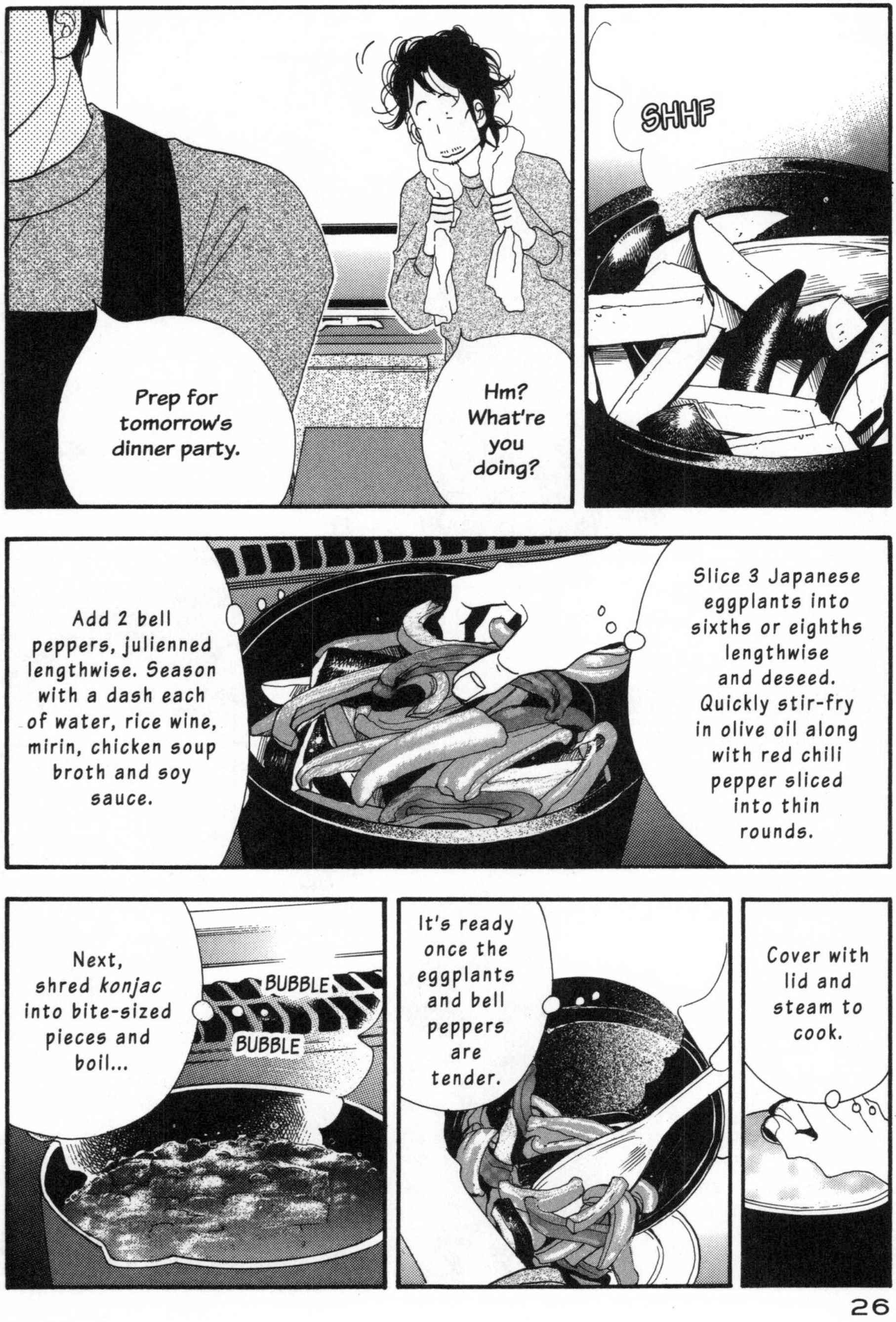
SHHF
Hm? What're you doing?
Prep for tomorrow's dinner party.
Slice 3 Japanese eggplants into sixths or eighths lengthwise and deseed. Quickly stir-fry in olive oil along with red chili pepper sliced into thin rounds.
Add 2 bell peppers, julienned lengthwise. Season with a dash each of water, rice wine, mirin, chicken soup broth and soy sauce.
Cover with lid and steam to cook.
It's ready once the eggplants and bell peppers are tender.
Next, shred *konjac* into bite-sized pieces and boil...
BUBBLE
BUBBLE

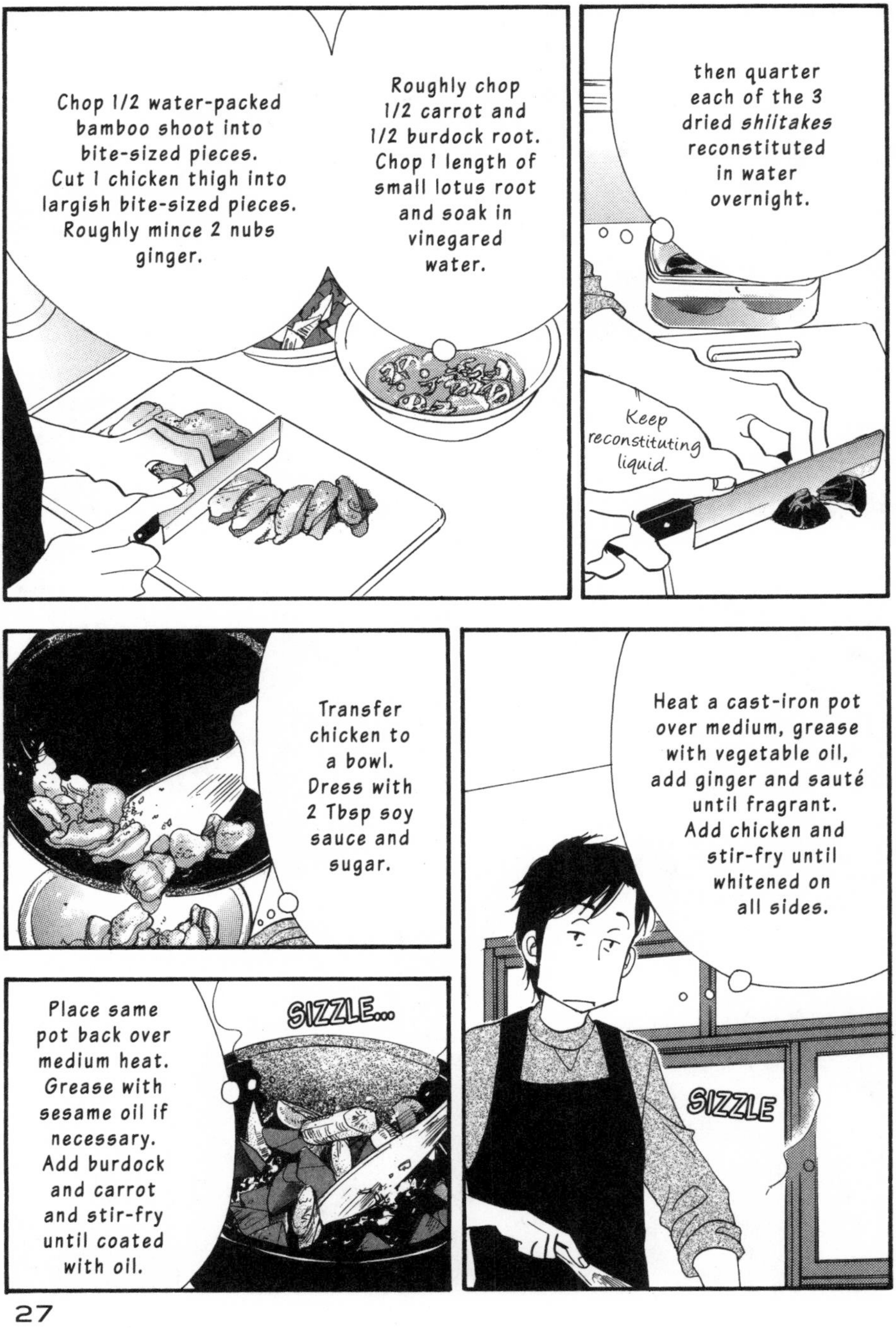
Chop 1/2 water-packed bamboo shoot into bite-sized pieces. Cut 1 chicken thigh into largish bite-sized pieces. Roughly mince 2 nubs ginger.
Roughly chop 1/2 carrot and 1/2 burdock root. Chop 1 length of small lotus root and soak in vinegared water.
then quarter each of the 3 dried *shiitakes* reconstituted in water overnight.
Keep reconstituting liquid.
Heat a cast-iron pot over medium, grease with vegetable oil, add ginger and sauté until fragrant. Add chicken and stir-fry until whitened on all sides.
SIZZLE
Transfer chicken to a bowl. Dress with 2 Tbsp soy sauce and sugar.
Place same pot back over medium heat. Grease with sesame oil if necessary. Add burdock and carrot and stir-fry until coated with oil.
SIZZLE...

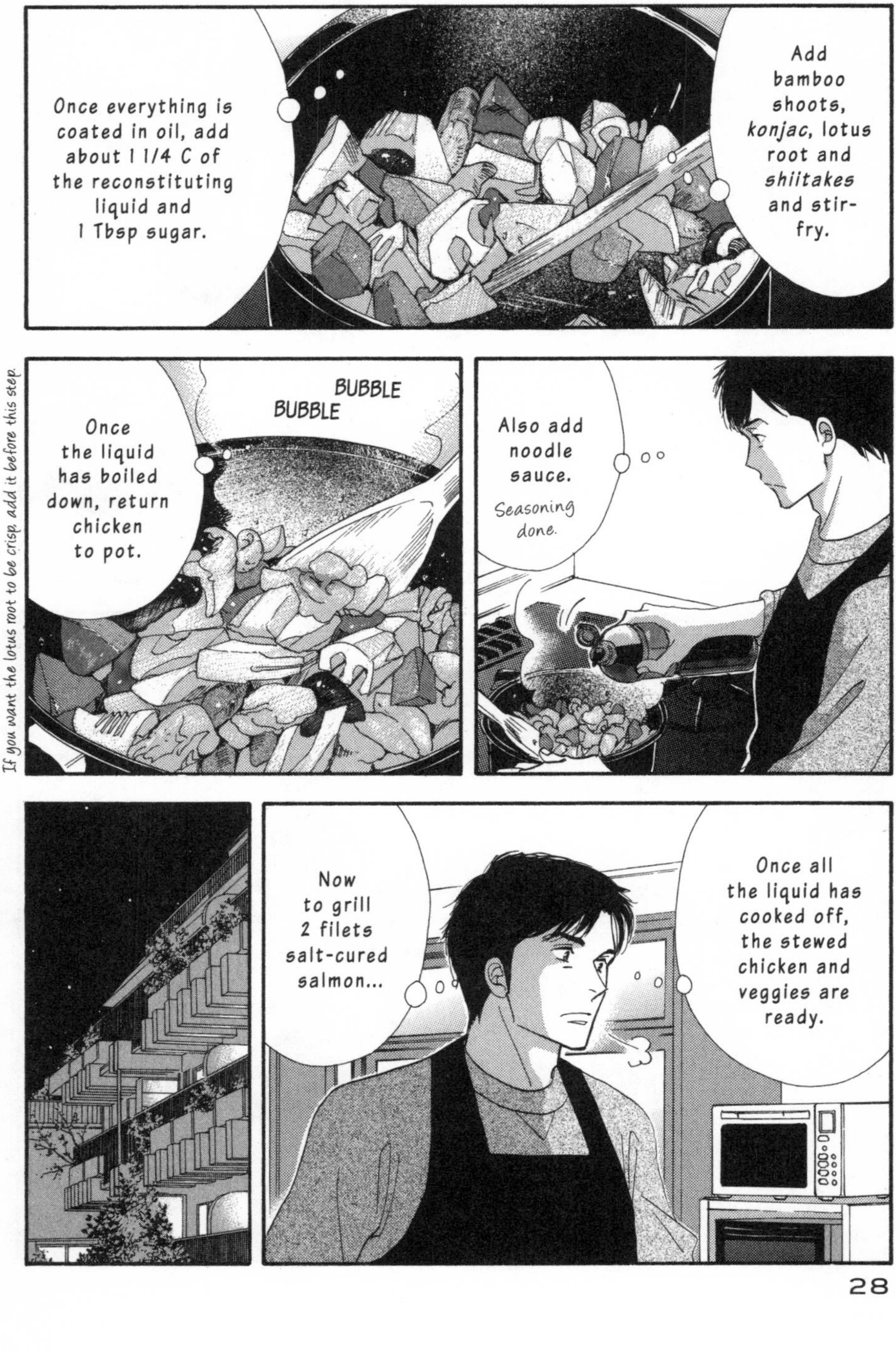
Add bamboo shoots, *konjac*, lotus root and *shiitakes* and stir-fry.
Once everything is coated in oil, add about 1 1/4 C of the reconstituting liquid and 1 Tbsp sugar.
Also add noodle sauce.
Seasoning done.
BUBBLE BUBBLE
Once the liquid has boiled down, return chicken to pot.
If you want the lotus root to be crisp, add it before this step.
Once all the liquid has cooked off, the stewed chicken and veggies are ready.
Now to grill 2 filets salt-cured salmon...

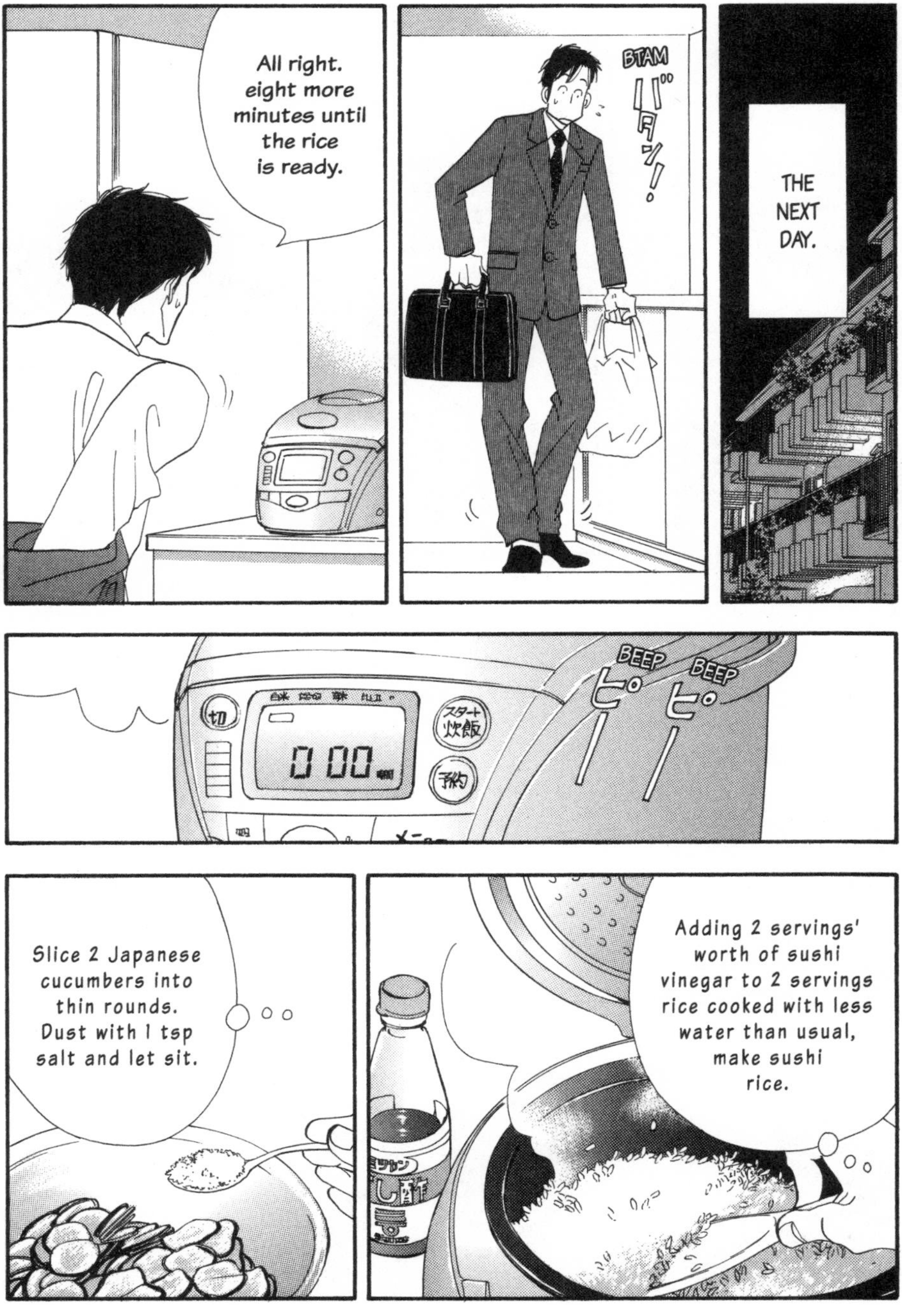
THE NEXT DAY.
BTAM
All right. eight more minutes until the rice is ready.
BEEP
BEEP
Adding 2 servings' worth of sushi vinegar to 2 servings rice cooked with less water than usual, make sushi rice.
Slice 2 Japanese cucumbers into thin rounds. Dust with 1 tsp salt and let sit.

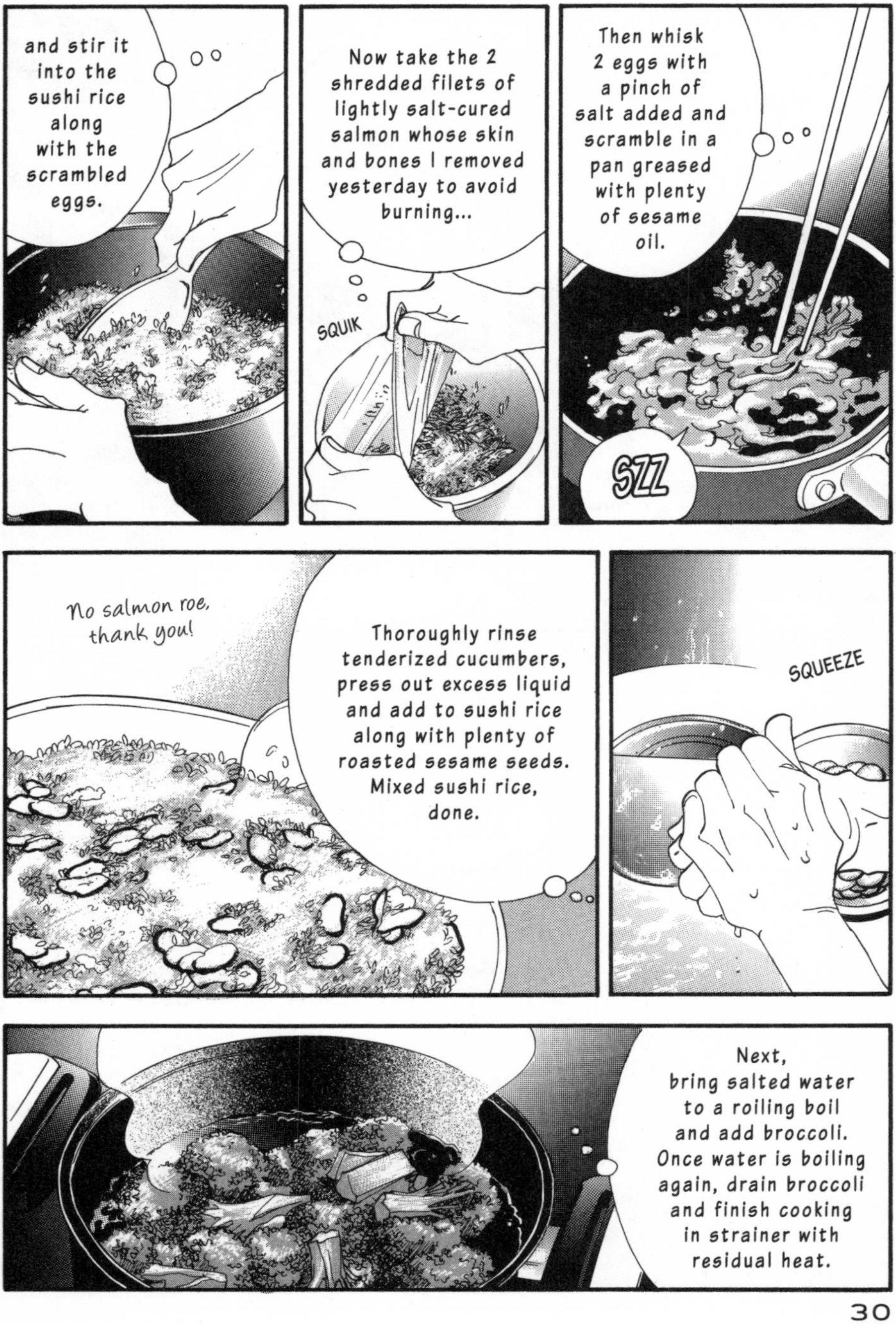
Then whisk 2 eggs with a pinch of salt added and scramble in a pan greased with plenty of sesame oil.
SZZ
Now take the 2 shredded filets of lightly salt-cured salmon whose skin and bones I removed yesterday to avoid burning...
SQUIK
and stir it into the sushi rice along with the scrambled eggs.
SQUEEZE
Thoroughly rinse tenderized cucumbers, press out excess liquid and add to sushi rice along with plenty of roasted sesame seeds. Mixed sushi rice, done.
No salmon roe, thank you!
Next, bring salted water to a roiling boil and add broccoli. Once water is boiling again, drain broccoli and finish cooking in strainer with residual heat.

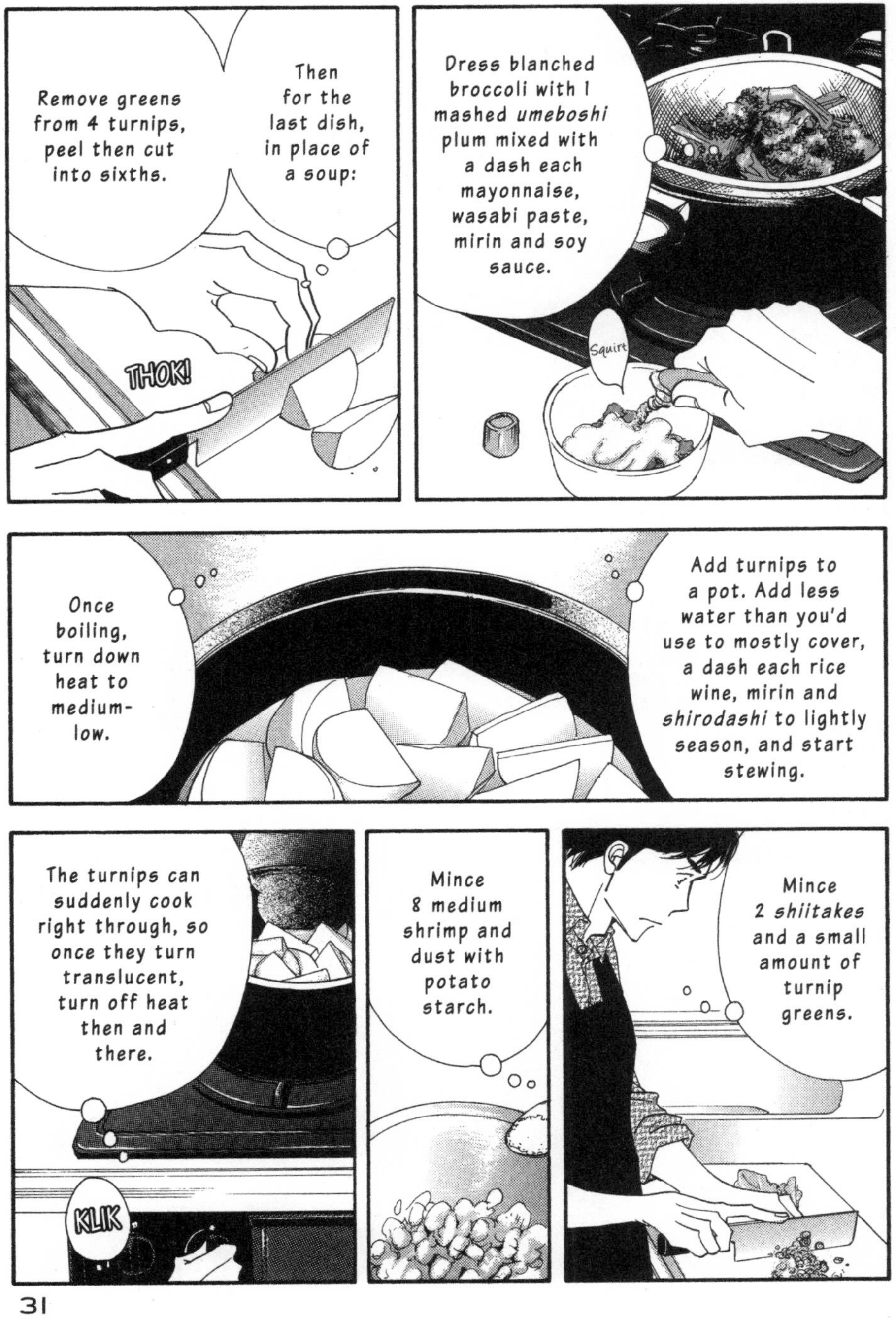
Dress blanched broccoli with 1 mashed *umeboshi* plum mixed with a dash each mayonnaise, wasabi paste, mirin and soy sauce.
Squirt
Then for the last dish, in place of a soup:
Remove greens from 4 turnips, peel then cut into sixths.
THOK!
Add turnips to a pot. Add less water than you'd use to mostly cover, a dash each rice wine, mirin and *shirodashi* to lightly season, and start stewing.
Once boiling, turn down heat to medium-low.
Mince 2 *shiitakes* and a small amount of turnip greens.
Mince 8 medium shrimp and dust with potato starch.
The turnips can suddenly cook right through, so once they turn translucent, turn off heat then and there.
KLIK

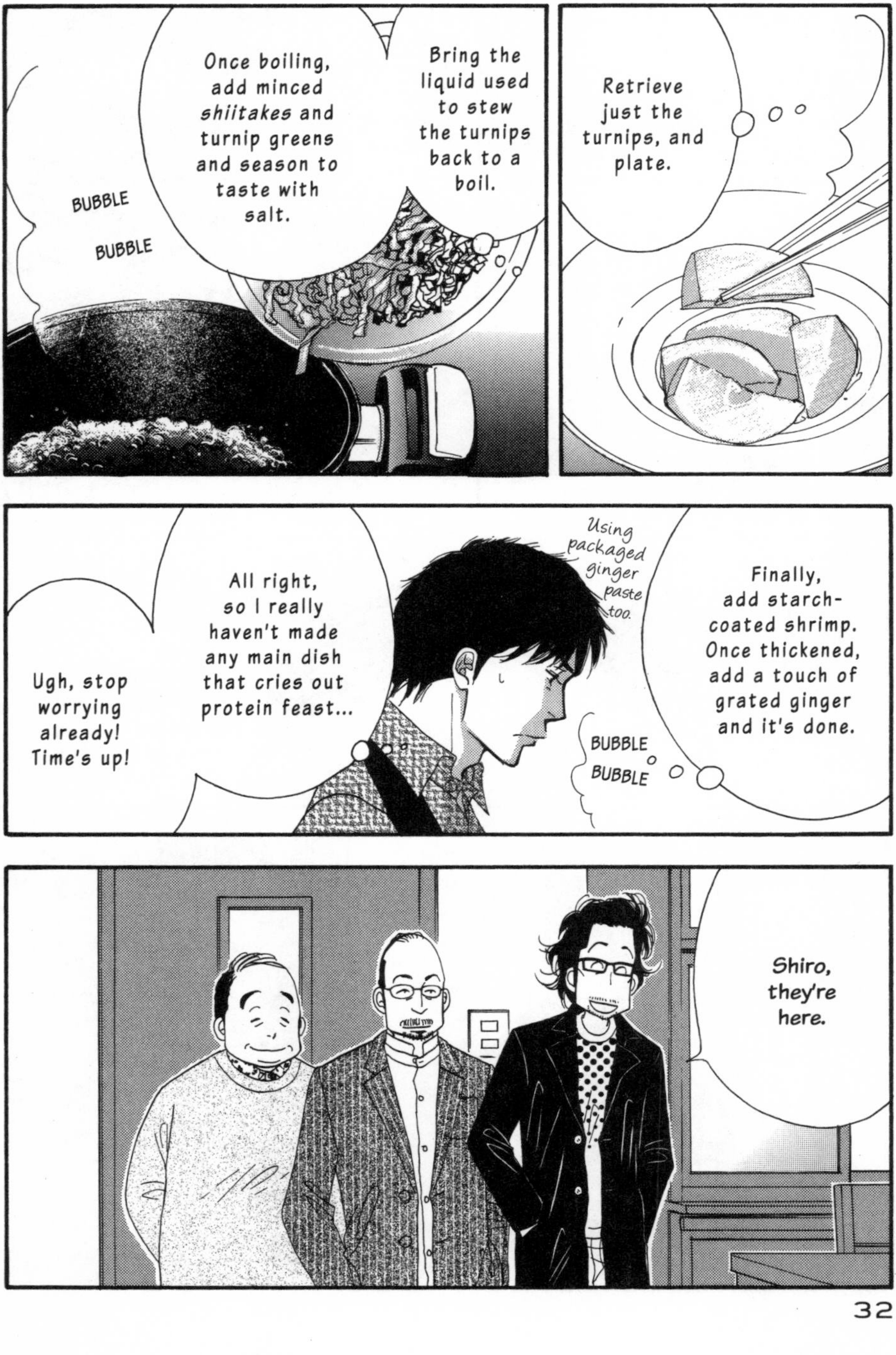
Retrieve just the turnips, and plate.
Bring the liquid used to stew the turnips back to a boil.
Once boiling, add minced *shiitakes* and turnip greens and season to taste with salt.
BUBBLE
BUBBLE
Finally, add starch-coated shrimp. Once thickened, add a touch of grated ginger and it's done.
BUBBLE
BUBBLE
Using packaged ginger paste too.
All right, so I really haven't made any main dish that cries out protein feast...
Ugh, stop worrying already! Time's up!
Shiro, they're here.

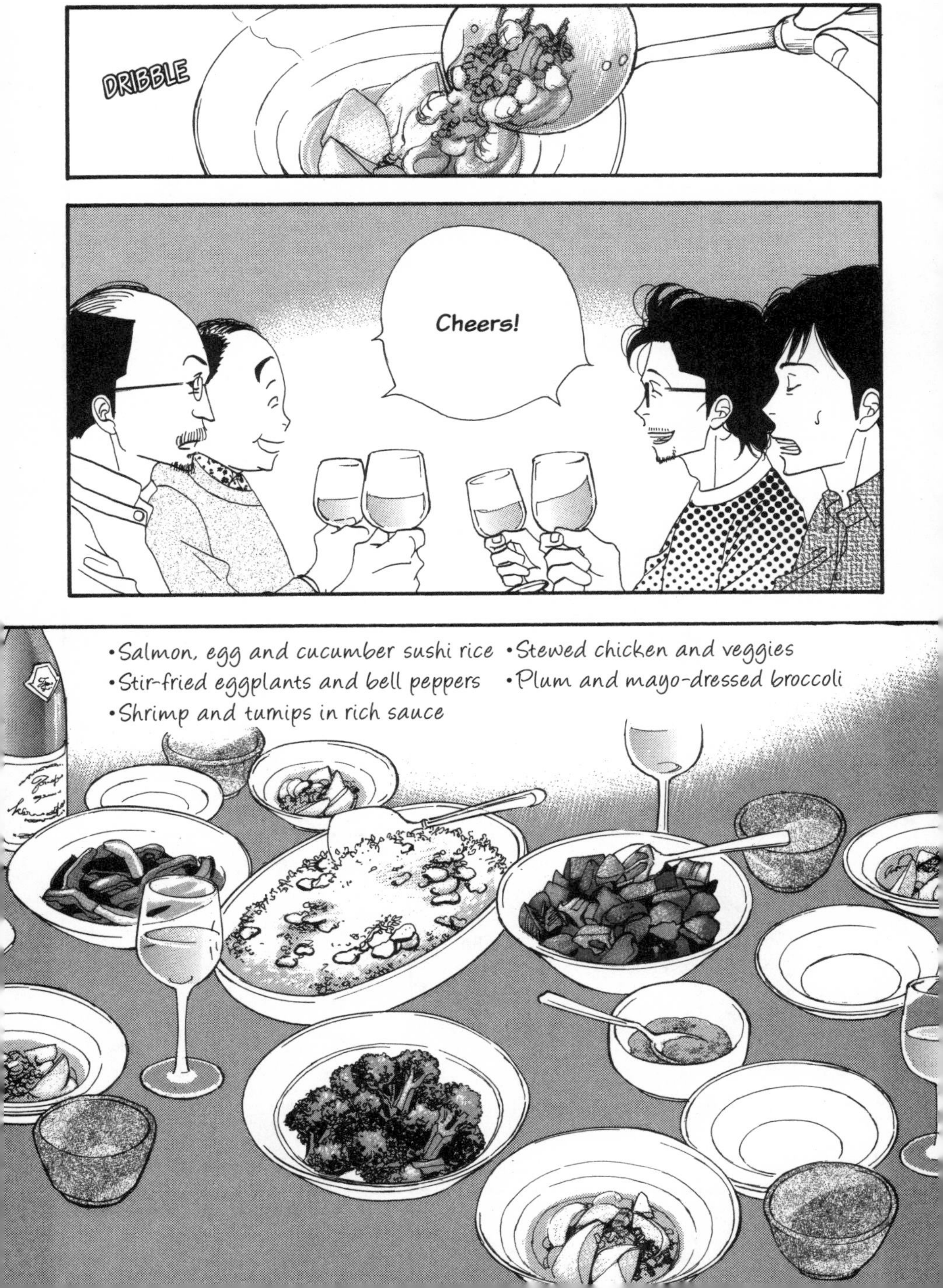
DRIBBLE
Cheers!
•Salmon, egg and cucumber sushi rice
•Stir-fried eggplants and bell peppers
•Shrimp and turnips in rich sauce
•Stewed chicken and veggies
•Plum and mayo-dressed broccoli

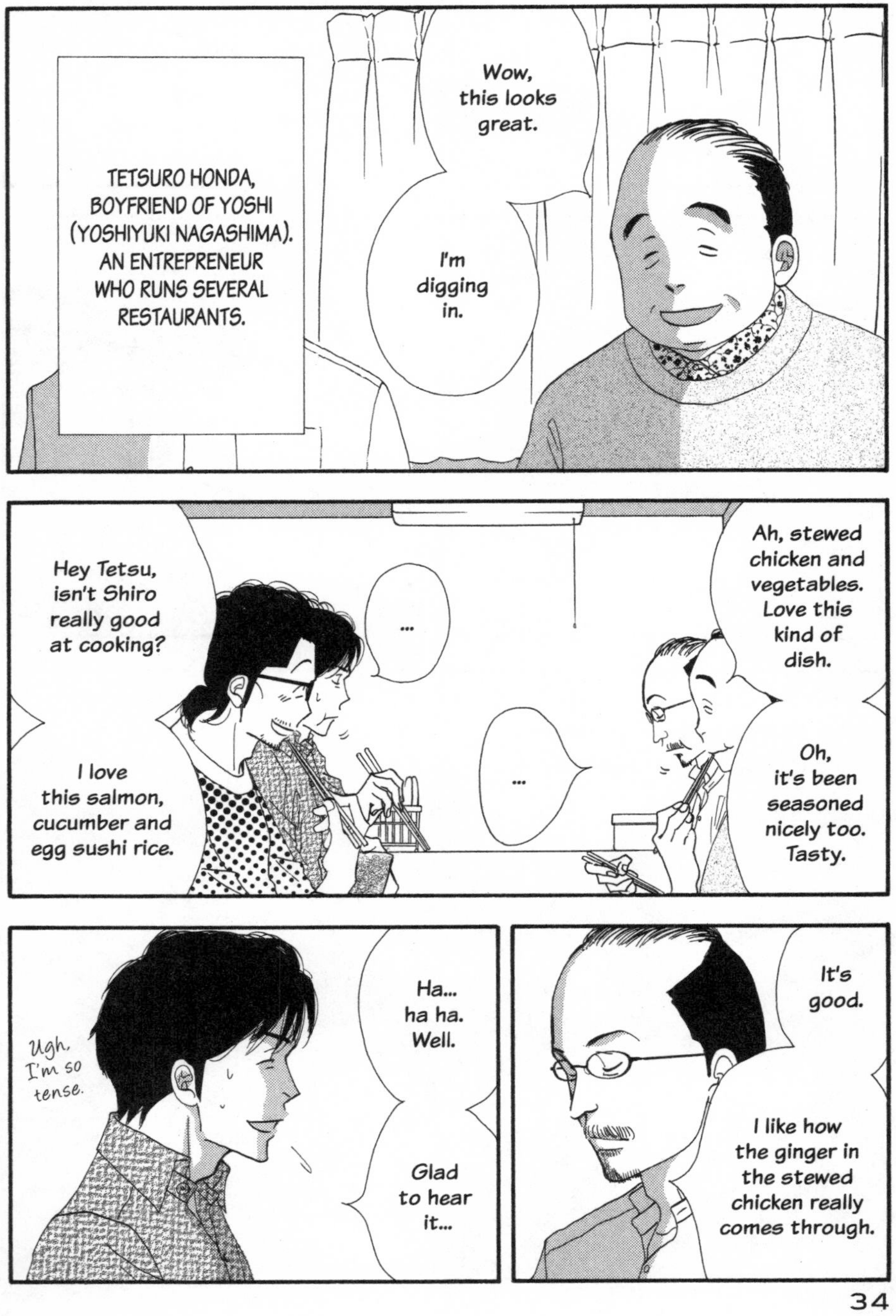
Wow, this looks great.
I'm digging in.
TETSURO HONDA, BOYFRIEND OF YOSHI (YOSHIYUKI NAGASHIMA). AN ENTREPRENEUR WHO RUNS SEVERAL RESTAURANTS.
Ah, stewed chicken and vegetables. Love this kind of dish.
Oh, it's been seasoned nicely too. Tasty.
...
...
Hey Tetsu, isn't Shiro really good at cooking?
I love this salmon, cucumber and egg sushi rice.
It's good.
I like how the ginger in the stewed chicken really comes through.
Ha... ha ha. Well.
Glad to hear it...
Ugh, I'm so tense.

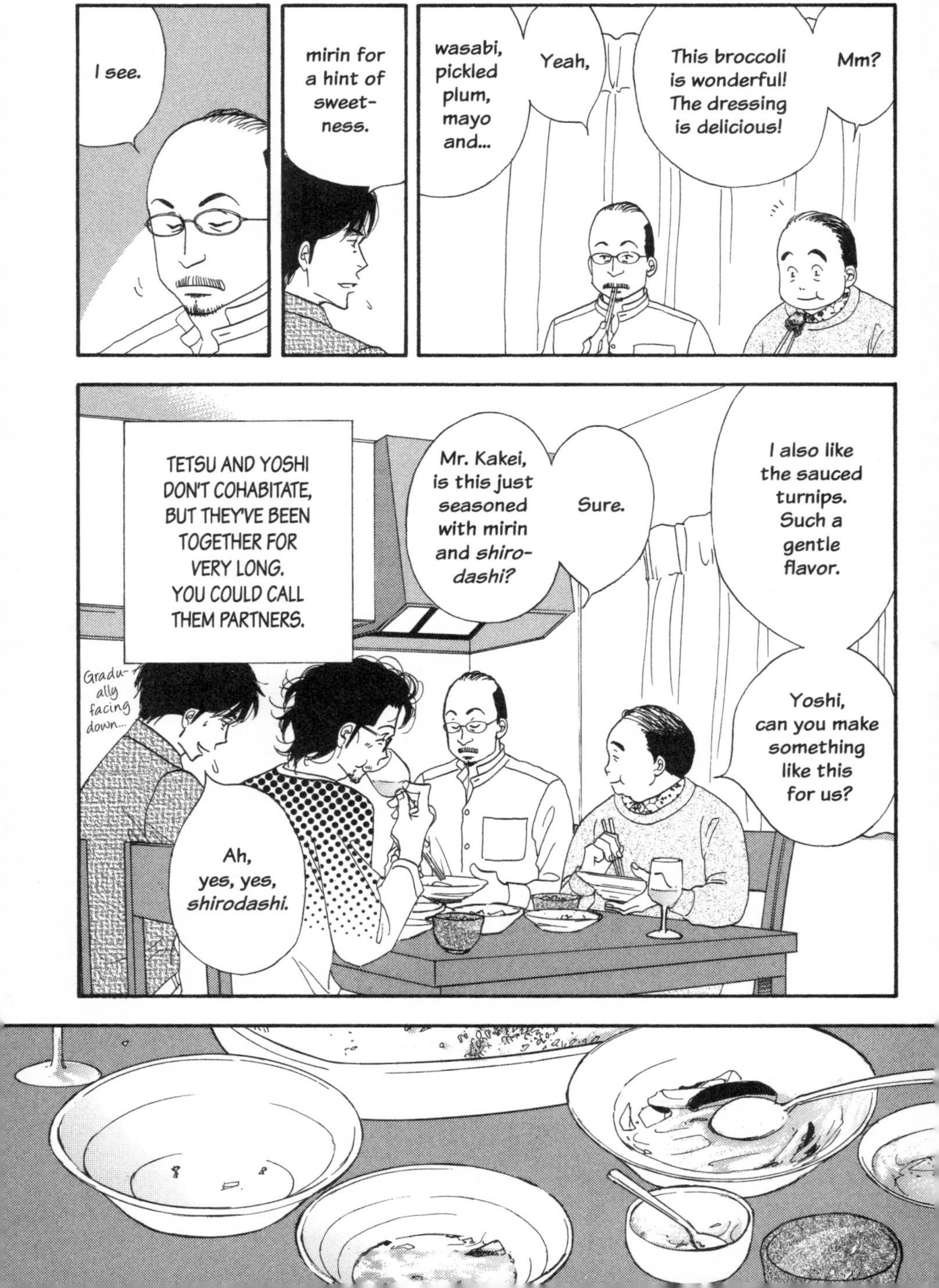
Mm?
This broccoli is wonderful! The dressing is delicious!
Yeah,
wasabi, pickled plum, mayo and...
mirin for a hint of sweet-ness.
I see.
I also like the sauced turnips. Such a gentle flavor.
Sure.
Mr. Kakei, is this just seasoned with mirin and *shiro-dashi*?
TETSU AND YOSHI DON'T COHABITATE, BUT THEY'VE BEEN TOGETHER FOR VERY LONG. YOU COULD CALL THEM PARTNERS.
Yoshi, can you make something like this for us?
Gradu-ally facing down...
Ah, yes, yes, *shirodashi*.

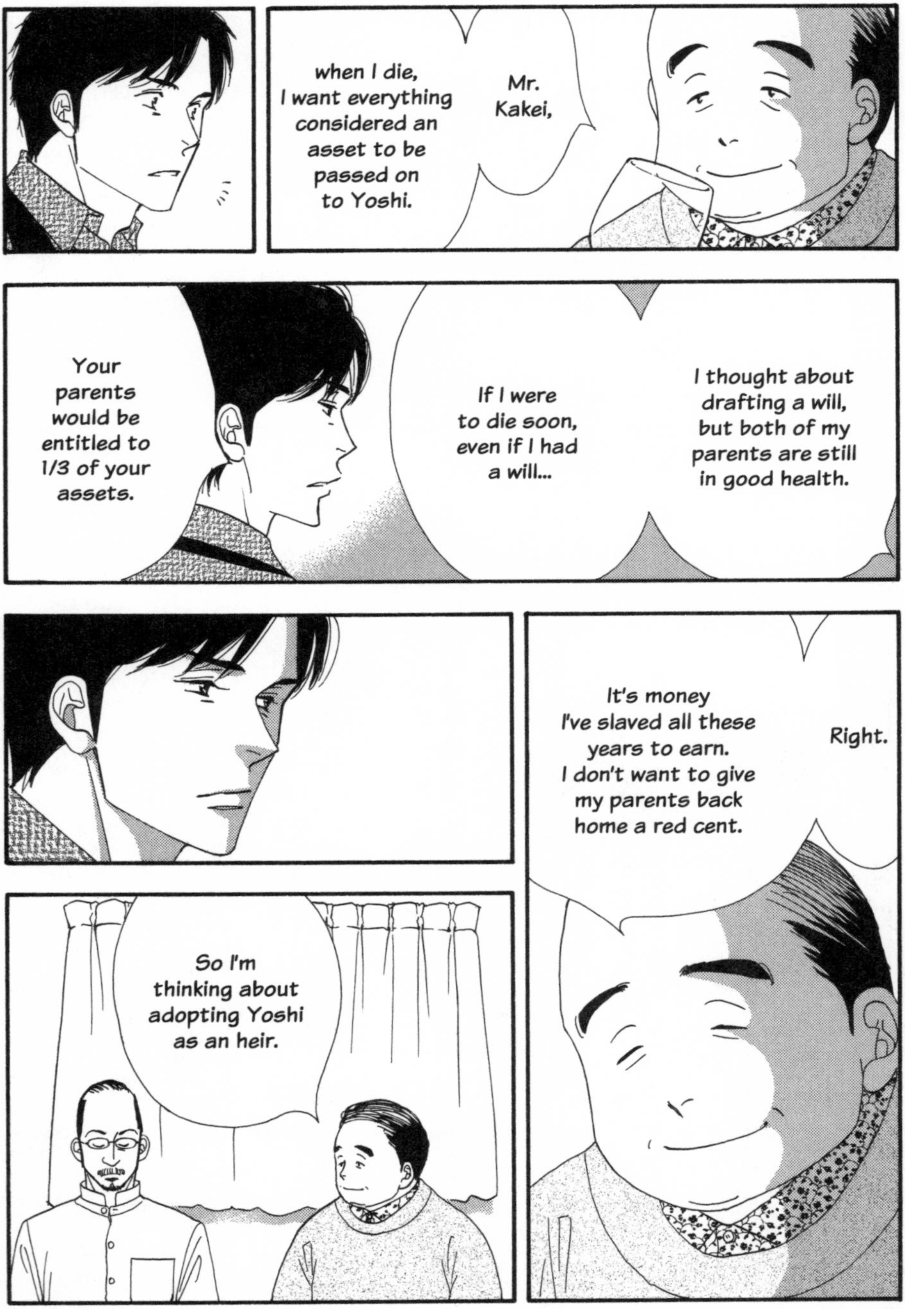
Mr. Kakei,
when I die, I want everything considered an asset to be passed on to Yoshi.
I thought about drafting a will, but both of my parents are still in good health.
If I were to die soon, even if I had a will...
Your parents would be entitled to 1/3 of your assets.
Right.
It's money I've slaved all these years to earn. I don't want to give my parents back home a red cent.
So I'm thinking about adopting Yoshi as an heir.

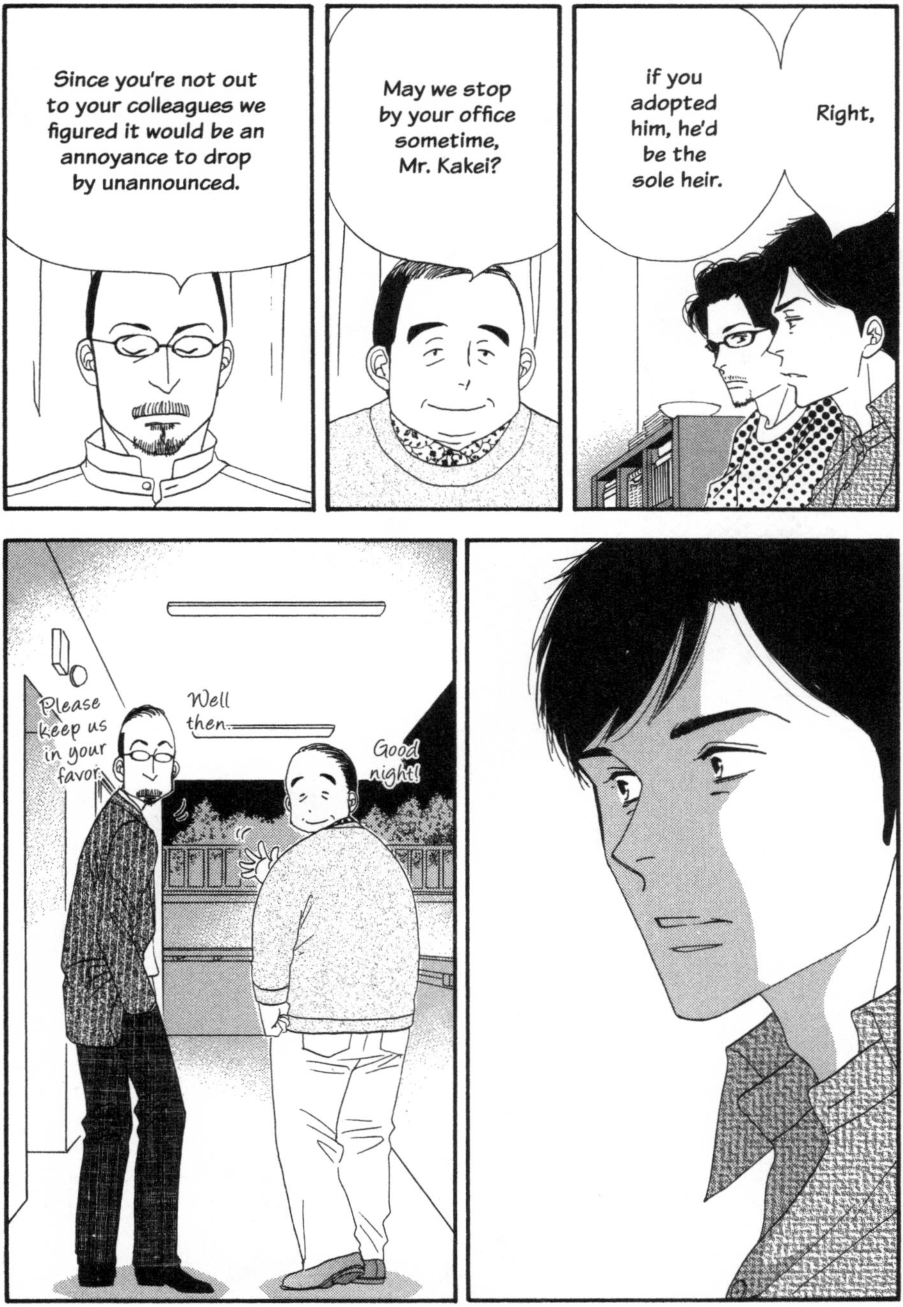
Right,
if you adopted him, he'd be the sole heir.
May we stop by your office sometime, Mr. Kakei?
Since you're not out to your colleagues we figured it would be an annoyance to drop by unannounced.
Good night!
Well then...
Please keep us in your favor.

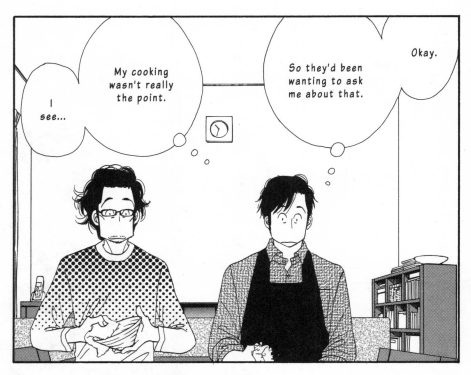

Okay.
So they'd been wanting to ask me about that.
My cooking wasn't really the point.
I see...
Uh huh...
HONK HONK
BUT THREE DAYS LATER, A TEXT FROM TETSU.
"Yoshi made the 'shrimp and turnips in rich sauce' and it was delicious."
I'm sure it cost four times what mine did...

#26 END

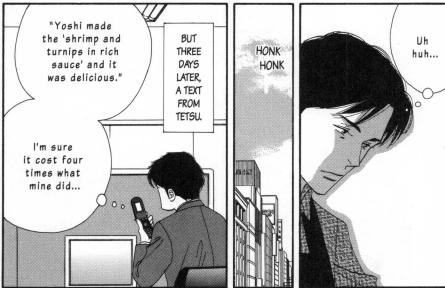

Top warm tofu with the
shrimp and *shiitake* sauce–
very tasty.
In which case top with wasabi too
if you'd like.

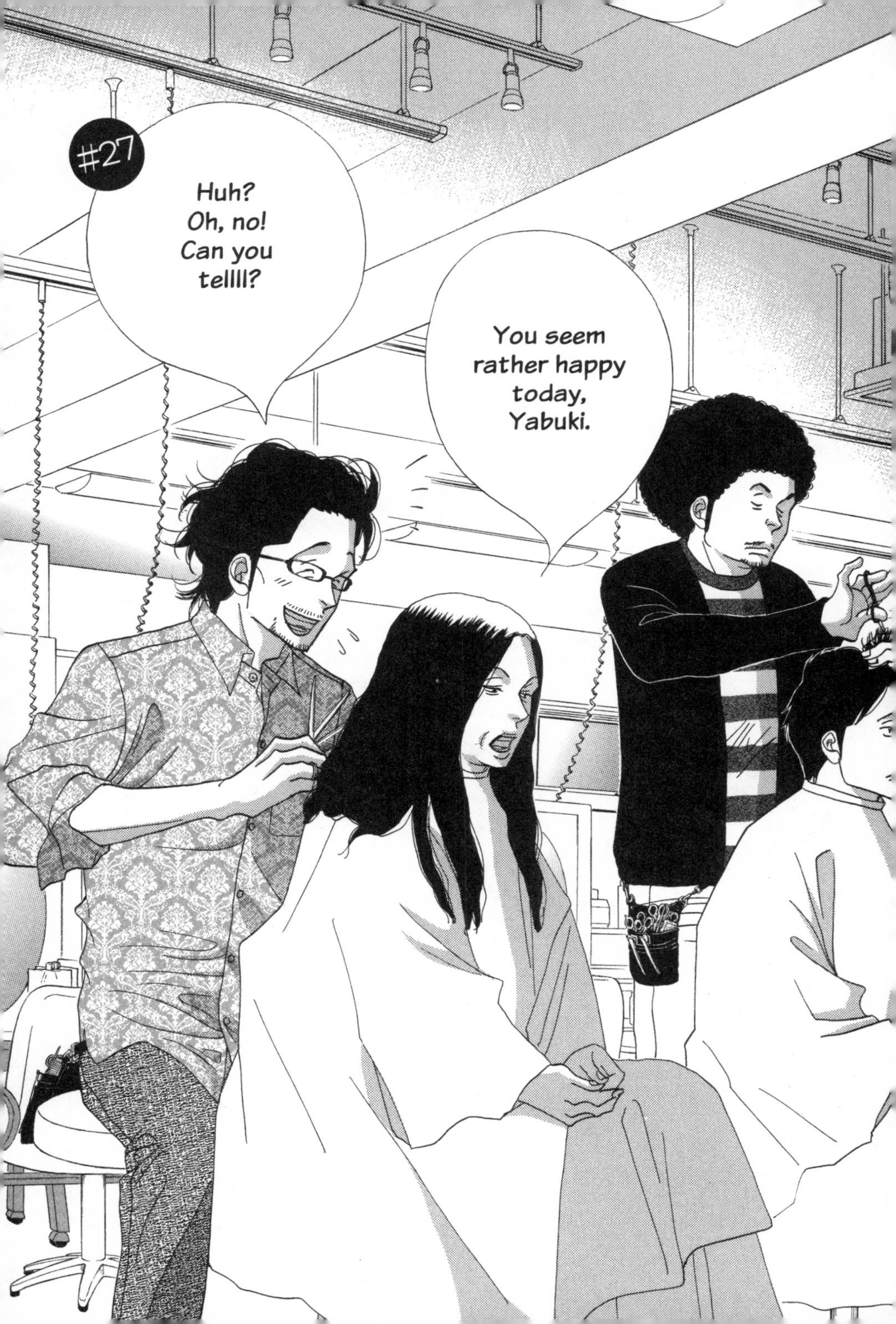
#27
You seem rather happy today, Yabuki.
Huh? Oh, no! Can you tellll?

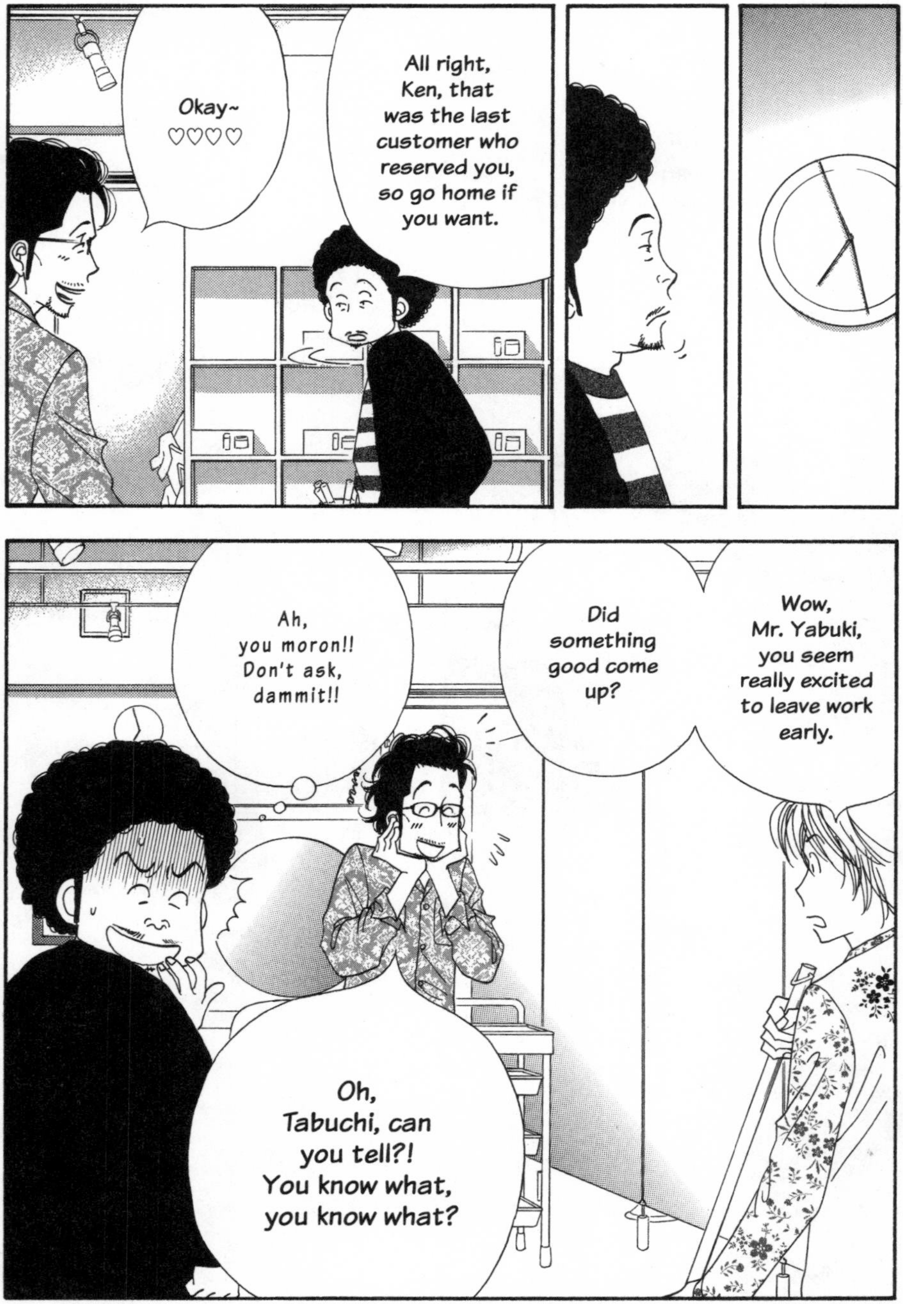
All right, Ken, that was the last customer who reserved you, so go home if you want.
Okay~ ♡♡♡♡
Wow, Mr. Yabuki, you seem really excited to leave work early.
Did something good come up?
Ah, you moron!! Don't ask, dammit!!
Oh, Tabuchi, can you tell?! You know what, you know what?

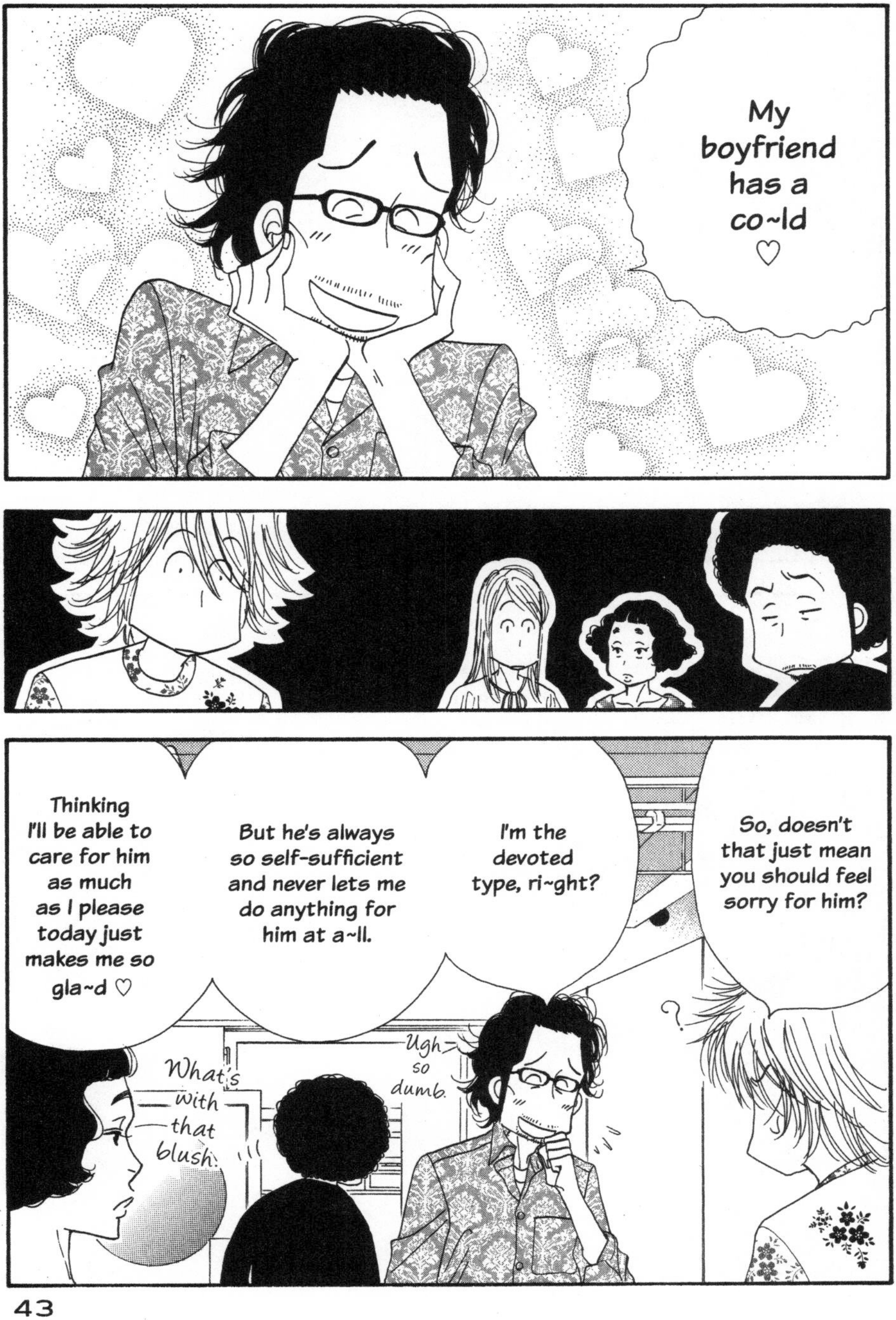

My boyfriend has a co~ld ♡
Thinking I'll be able to care for him as much as I please today just makes me so gla~d ♡
But he's always so self-sufficient and never lets me do anything for him at a~ll.
I'm the devoted type, ri~ght?
So, doesn't that just mean you should feel sorry for him?
Ugh— so dumb.
What's with that blush.

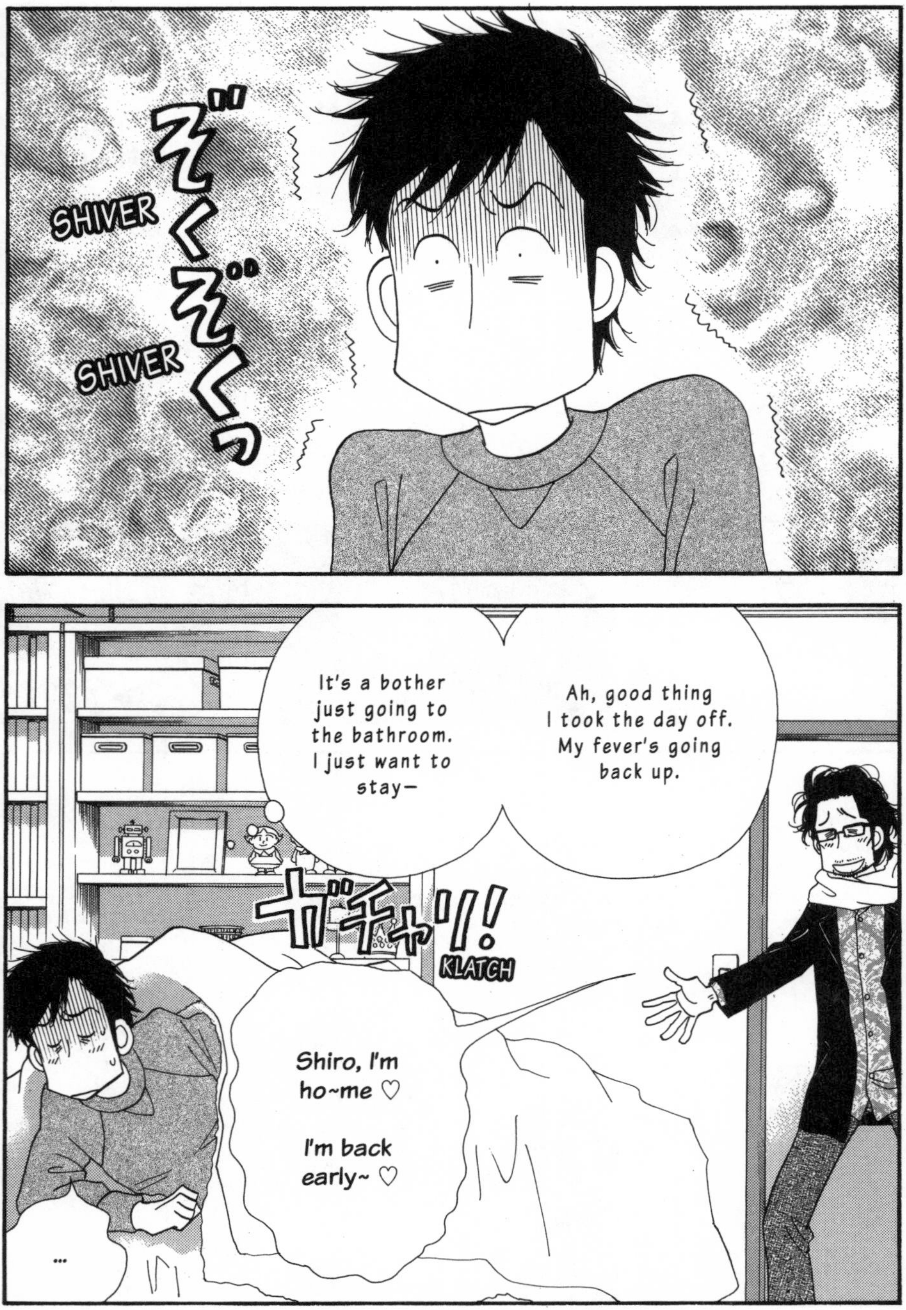
ぞくぞくっ
SHIVER
SHIVER
Ah, good thing I took the day off. My fever's going back up.
It's a bother just going to the bathroom. I just want to stay—
ガチャリ!
KLATCH
Shiro, I'm ho~me ♡
I'm back early~ ♡
...

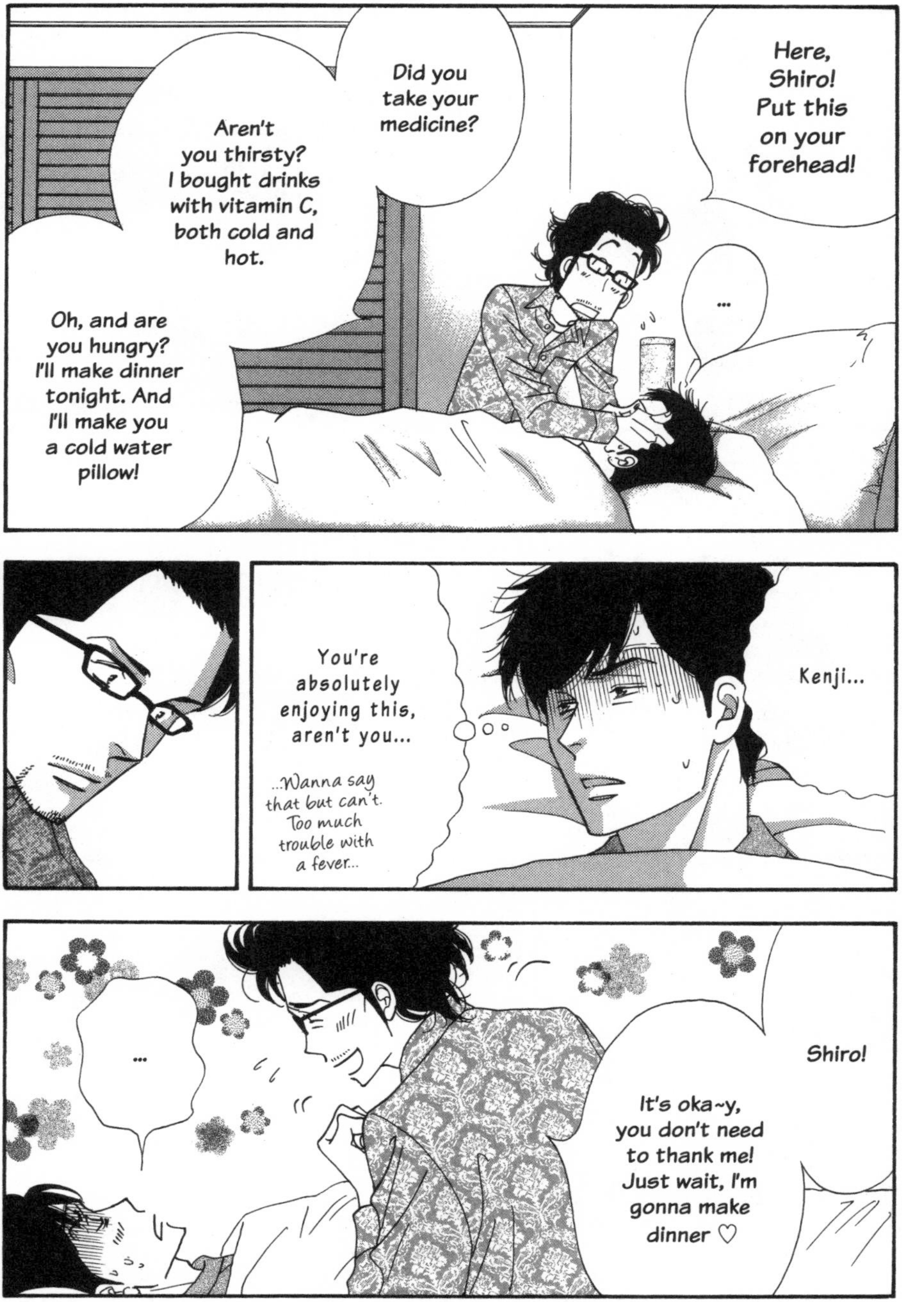
Here, Shiro! Put this on your forehead!
...
Did you take your medicine?
Aren't you thirsty? I bought drinks with vitamin C, both cold and hot.
Oh, and are you hungry? I'll make dinner tonight. And I'll make you a cold water pillow!
Kenji...
You're absolutely enjoying this, aren't you...
...Wanna say that but can't. Too much trouble with a fever...
Shiro!
It's oka~y, you don't need to thank me! Just wait, I'm gonna make dinner ♡
...

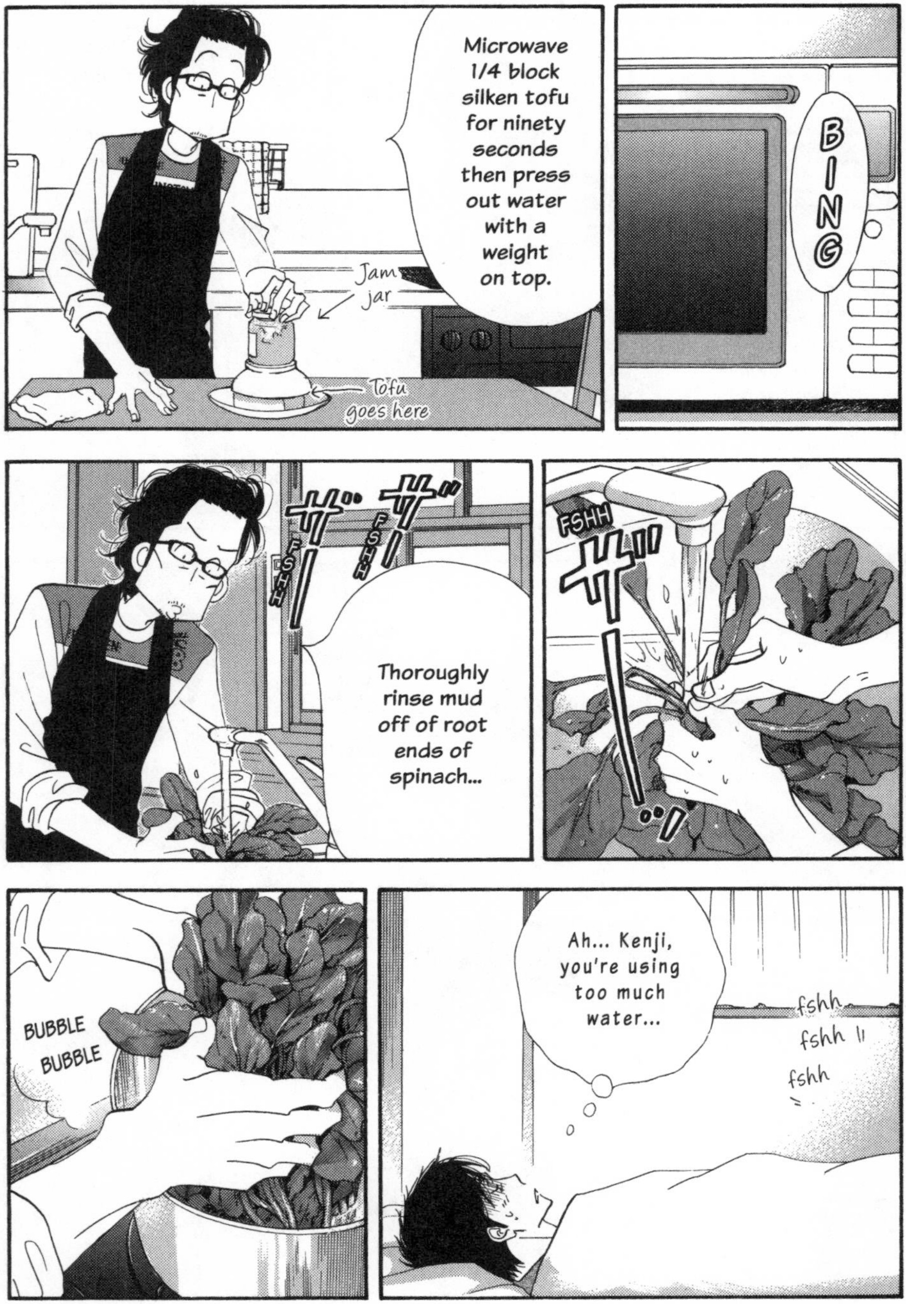
BING
Microwave 1/4 block silken tofu for ninety seconds then press out water with a weight on top.
Jam jar
Tofu goes here
FSHH
FSHH
FSHH
Thoroughly rinse mud off of root ends of spinach...
Ah... Kenji, you're using too much water...
fshh
fshh
fshh
BUBBLE BUBBLE

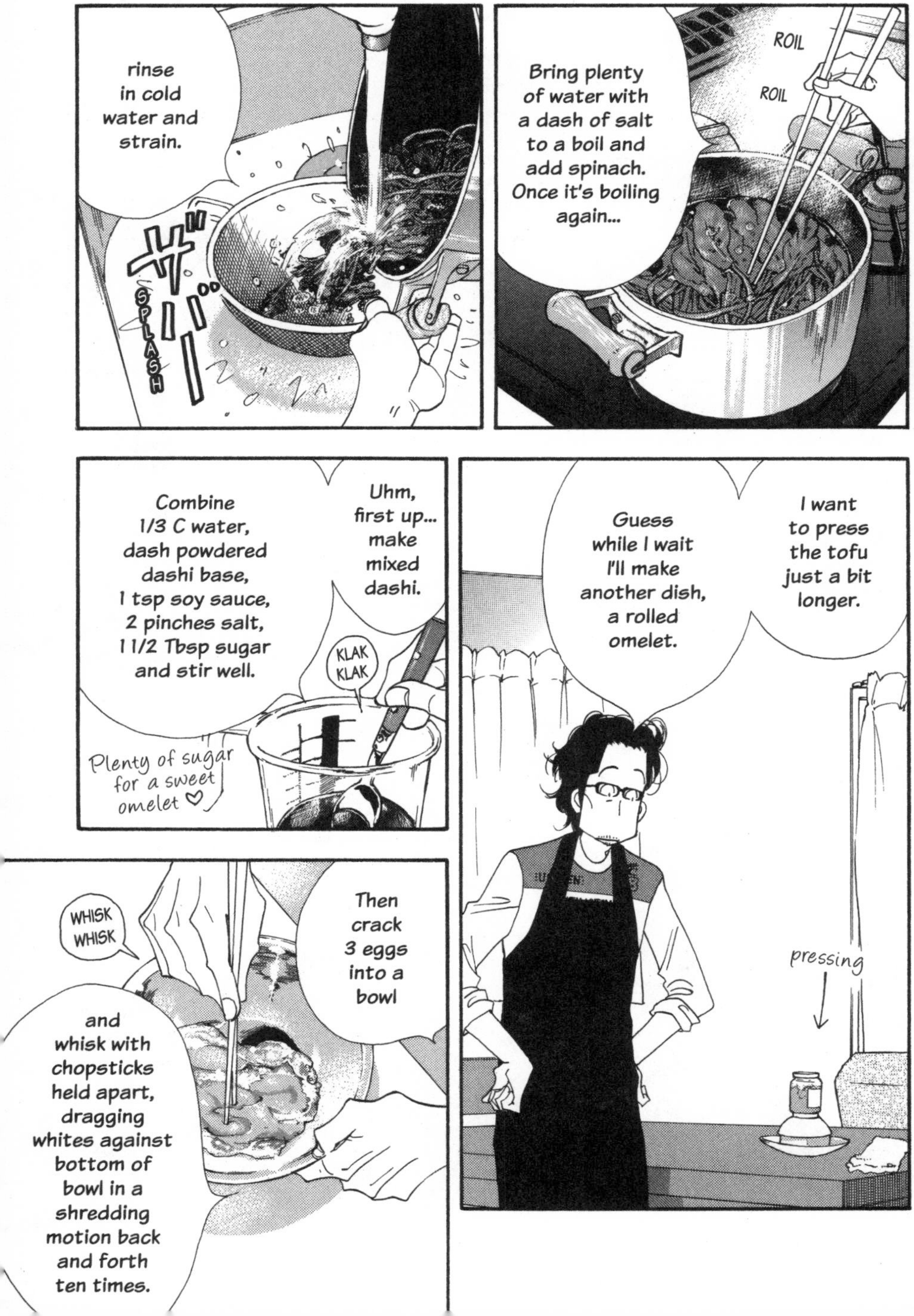
Bring plenty of water with a dash of salt to a boil and add spinach. Once it's boiling again...
ROIL
ROIL
rinse in cold water and strain.
SPLASH
I want to press the tofu just a bit longer.
Guess while I wait I'll make another dish, a rolled omelet.
pressing
Uhm, first up... make mixed dashi.
Combine 1/3 C water, dash powdered dashi base, 1 tsp soy sauce, 2 pinches salt, 1 1/2 Tbsp sugar and stir well.
KLAK KLAK
Plenty of sugar for a sweet omelet ♡
Then crack 3 eggs into a bowl
and whisk with chopsticks held apart, dragging whites against bottom of bowl in a shredding motion back and forth ten times.
WHISK WHISK

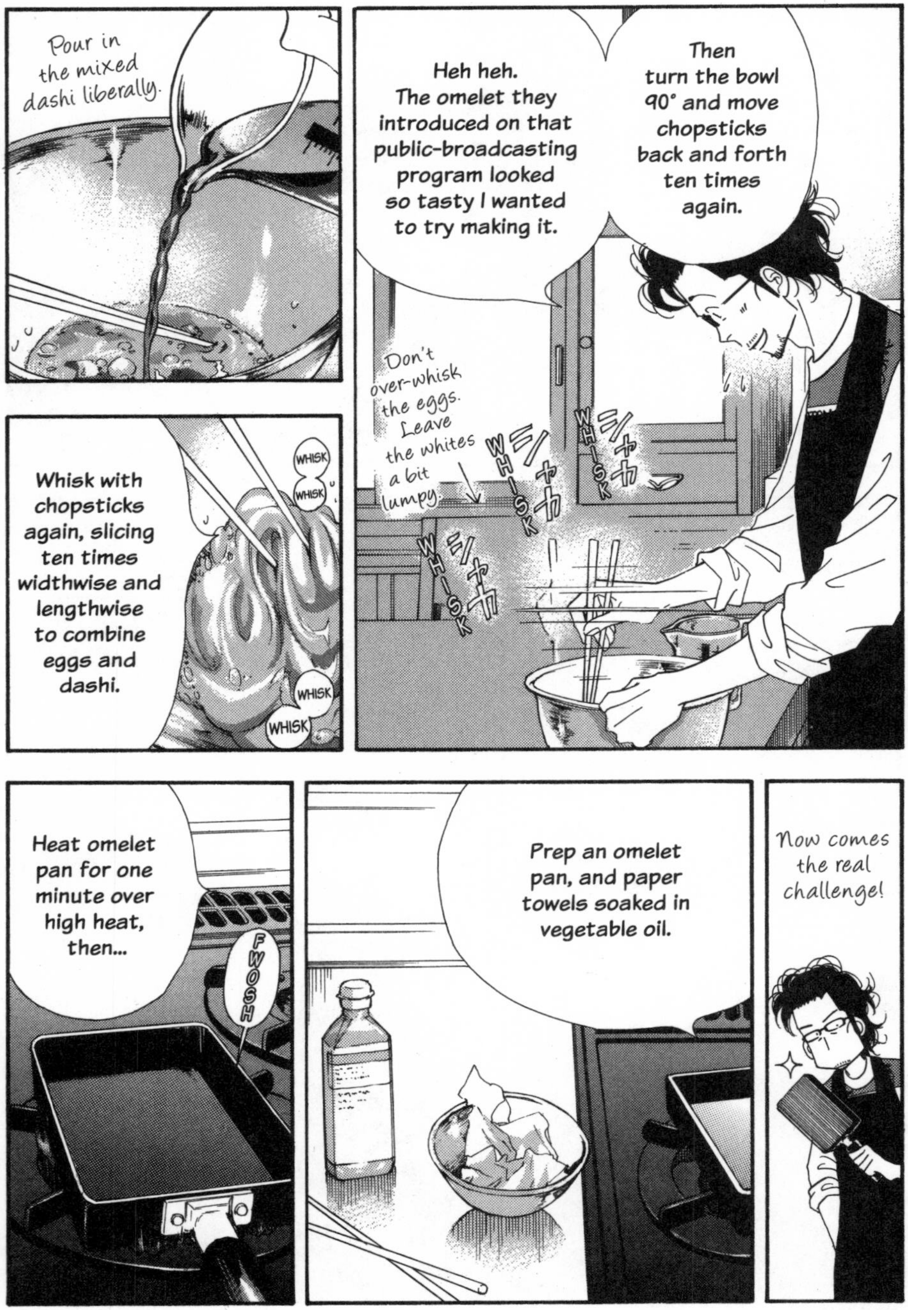
Then turn the bowl 90° and move chopsticks back and forth ten times again.
Heh heh. The omelet they introduced on that public-broadcasting program looked so tasty I wanted to try making it.
Don't over-whisk the eggs. Leave the whites a bit lumpy.
WHISK
WHISK
WHISK
Pour in the mixed dashi liberally.
WHISK
WHISK
Whisk with chopsticks again, slicing ten times widthwise and lengthwise to combine eggs and dashi.
WHISK
WHISK
Now comes the real challenge!
Prep an omelet pan, and paper towels soaked in vegetable oil.
Heat omelet pan for one minute over high heat, then...
FWOSH

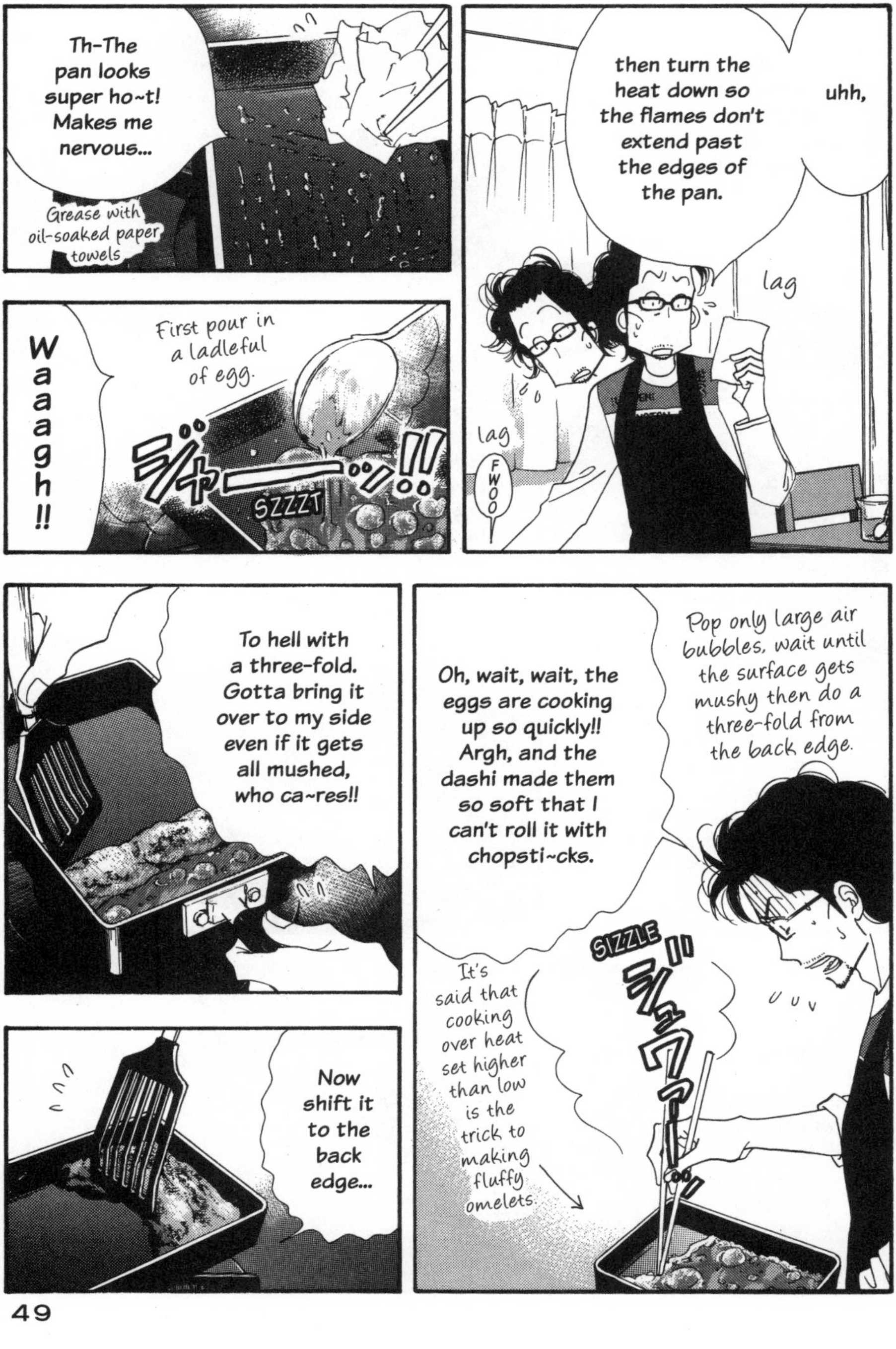
uhh,
then turn the heat down so the flames don't extend past the edges of the pan.
lag
lag
FWOO
Th-The pan looks super ho~t! Makes me nervous...
Grease with oil-soaked paper towels
First pour in a ladleful of egg.
Waaaagh!!
SZZZT
Pop only large air bubbles, wait until the surface gets mushy then do a three-fold from the back edge.
Oh, wait, wait, the eggs are cooking up so quickly!! Argh, and the dashi made them so soft that I can't roll it with chopsti~cks.
SIZZLE
It's said that cooking over heat set higher than low is the trick to making fluffy omelets.
To hell with a three-fold. Gotta bring it over to my side even if it gets all mushed, who ca~res!!
Now shift it to the back edge...

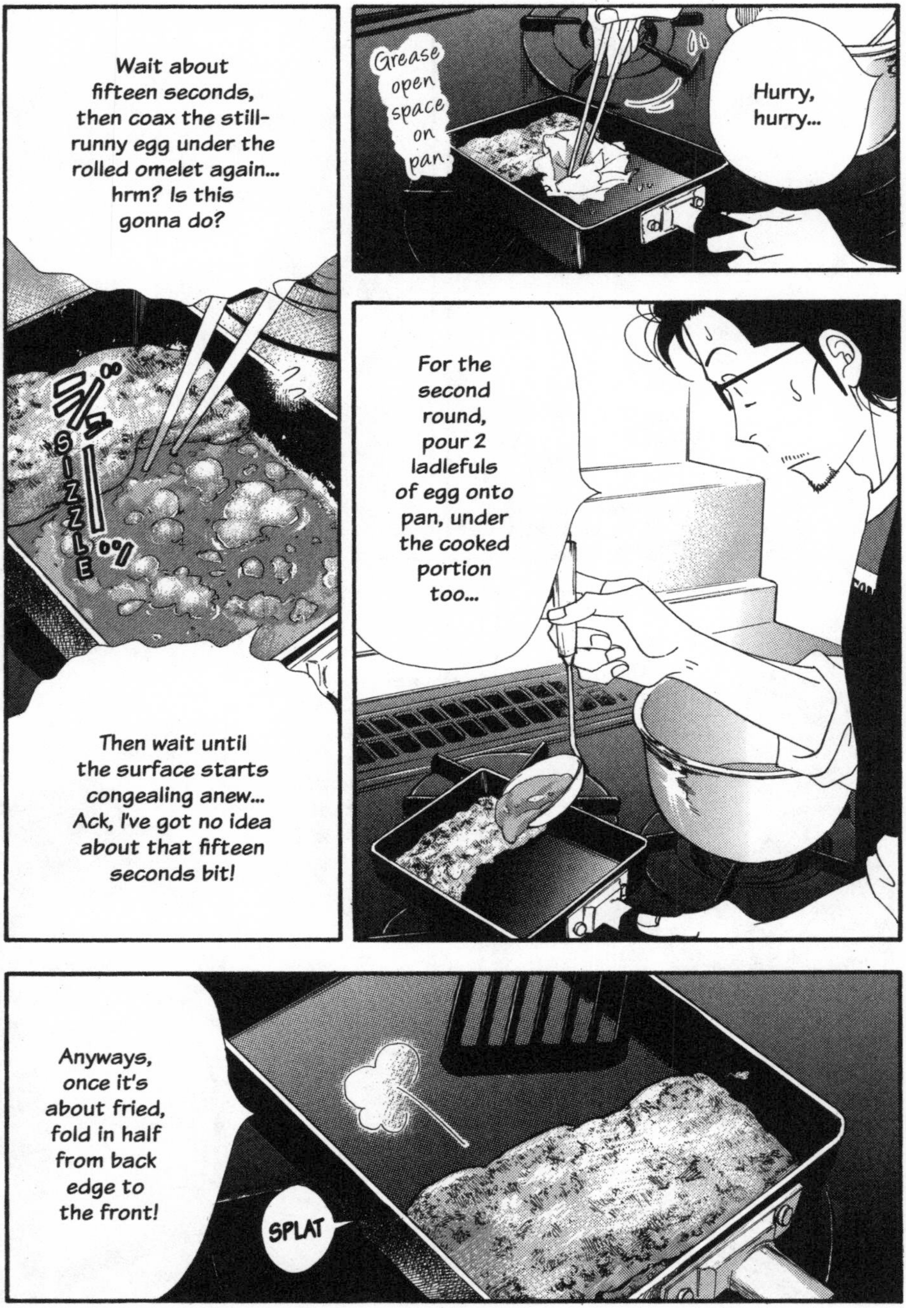
Hurry, hurry...
Grease open space on pan.
For the second round, pour 2 ladlefuls of egg onto pan, under the cooked portion too...
Wait about fifteen seconds, then coax the still-runny egg under the rolled omelet again... hrm? Is this gonna do?
SIZZLE
Then wait until the surface starts congealing anew... Ack, I've got no idea about that fifteen seconds bit!
Anyways, once it's about fried, fold in half from back edge to the front!
SPLAT

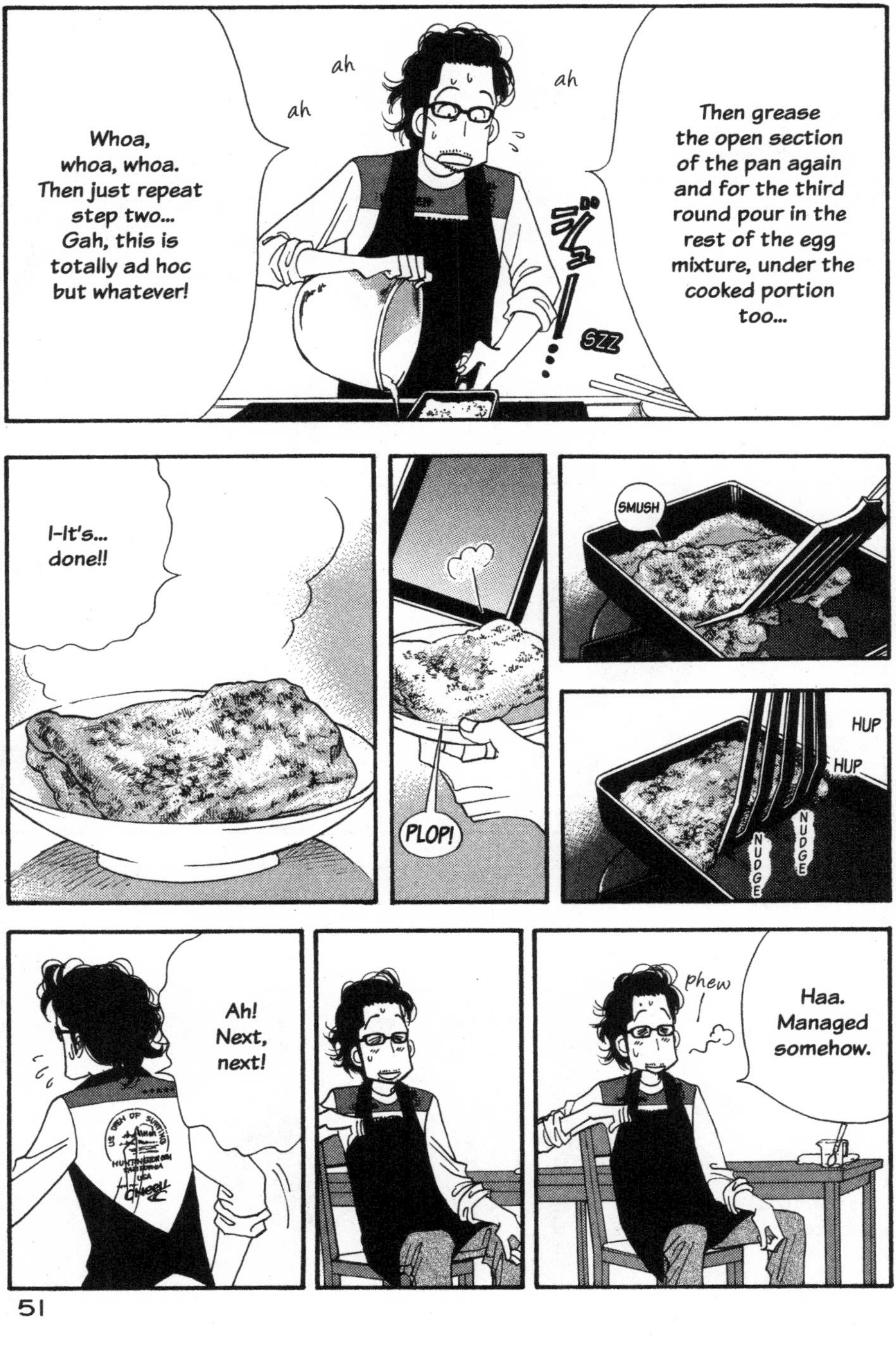
Then grease the open section of the pan again and for the third round pour in the rest of the egg mixture, under the cooked portion too...
ah
ah
ah
Whoa, whoa, whoa. Then just repeat step two... Gah, this is totally ad hoc but whatever!
DO
SZZ
SMUSH
HUP
HUP
NUDGE
NUDGE
PLOP!
I-It's... done!!
phew
Haa. Managed somehow.
Ah! Next, next!

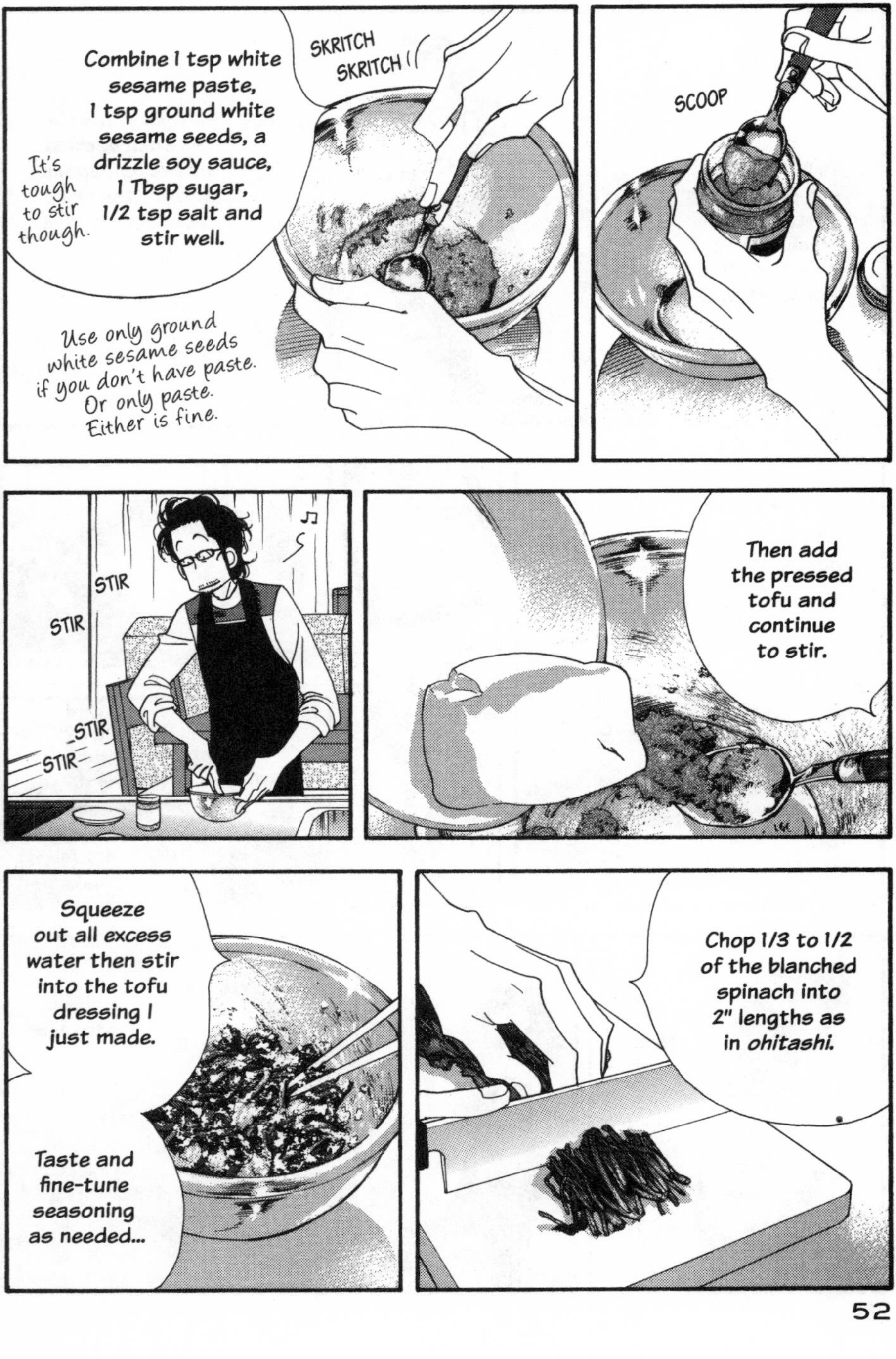
SCOOP
SKRITCH
SKRITCH
Combine 1 tsp white sesame paste, 1 tsp ground white sesame seeds, a drizzle soy sauce, 1 Tbsp sugar, 1/2 tsp salt and stir well.
It's tough to stir though.
Use only ground white sesame seeds if you don't have paste. Or only paste. Either is fine.
Then add the pressed tofu and continue to stir.
STIR
STIR
STIR
STIR
Chop 1/3 to 1/2 of the blanched spinach into 2" lengths as in *ohitashi.*
Squeeze out all excess water then stir into the tofu dressing I just made.
Taste and fine-tune seasoning as needed...

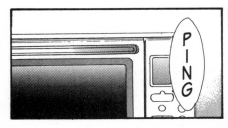

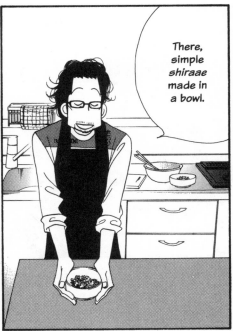

There, simple *shiraae* made in a bowl.
PING
Microwave 2 small servings of frozen cooked rice then rinse briefly.
FSHH
I'm gonna cook this rinsed rice with plenty of water and an arbitrary amount of *shirodashi* to make a porridge ♡
KLANK!
Chop chicken.
BUBBLE BUBBLE BUBBLE
Once the water has boiled and the rice has puffed up, add bite-sized chicken thigh pieces.

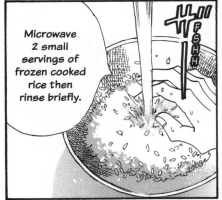

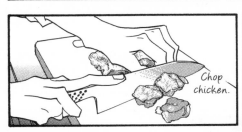

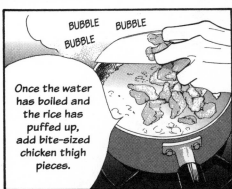

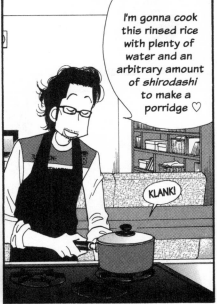

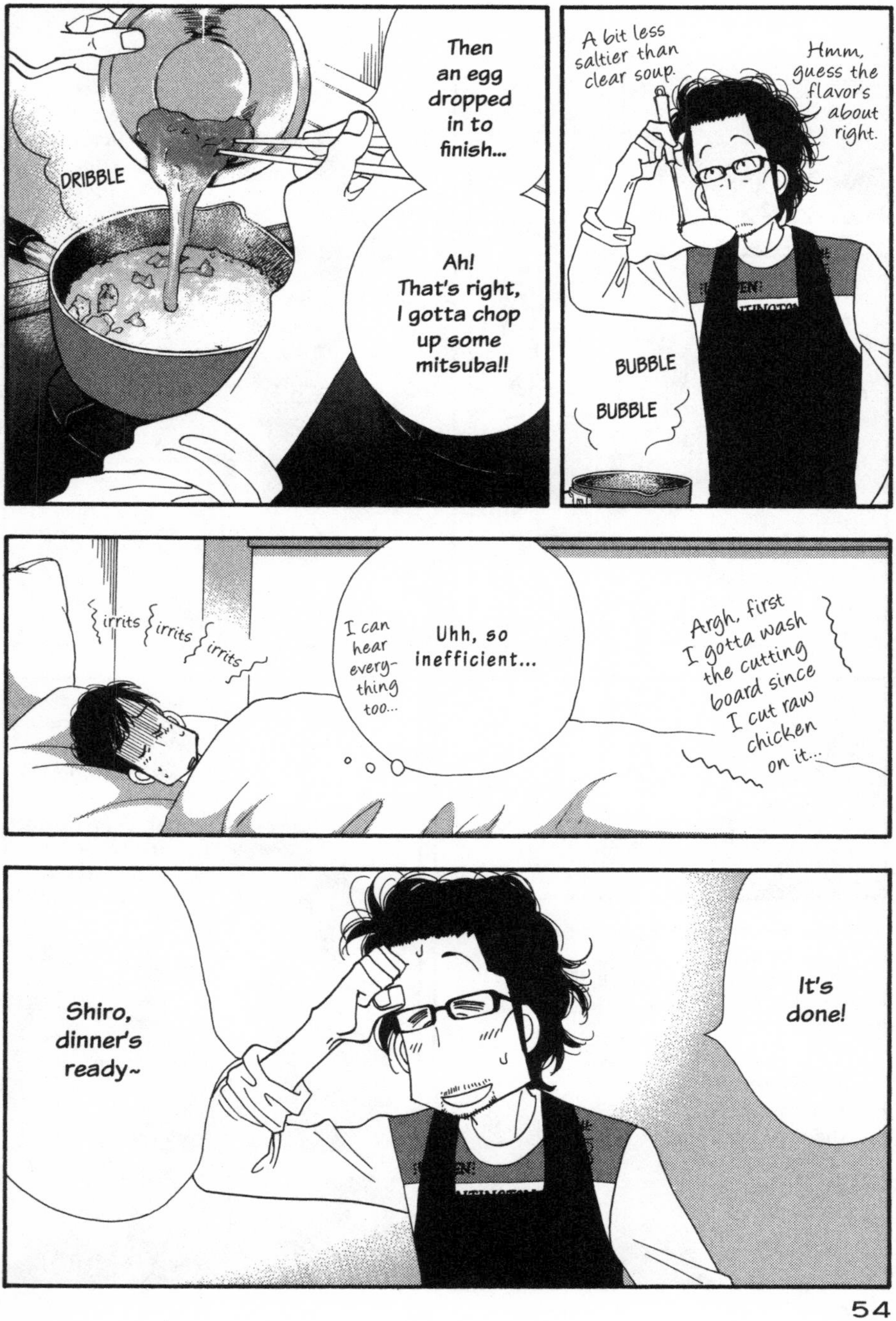
Hmm, guess the flavor's about right.
A bit less saltier than clear soup.
BUBBLE
BUBBLE
Then an egg dropped in to finish...
Ah! That's right, I gotta chop up some mitsuba!!
DRIBBLE
Argh, first I gotta wash the cutting board since I cut raw chicken on it...
Uhh, so inefficient...
I can hear every-thing too...
irrits irrits irrits
It's done!
Shiro, dinner's ready~

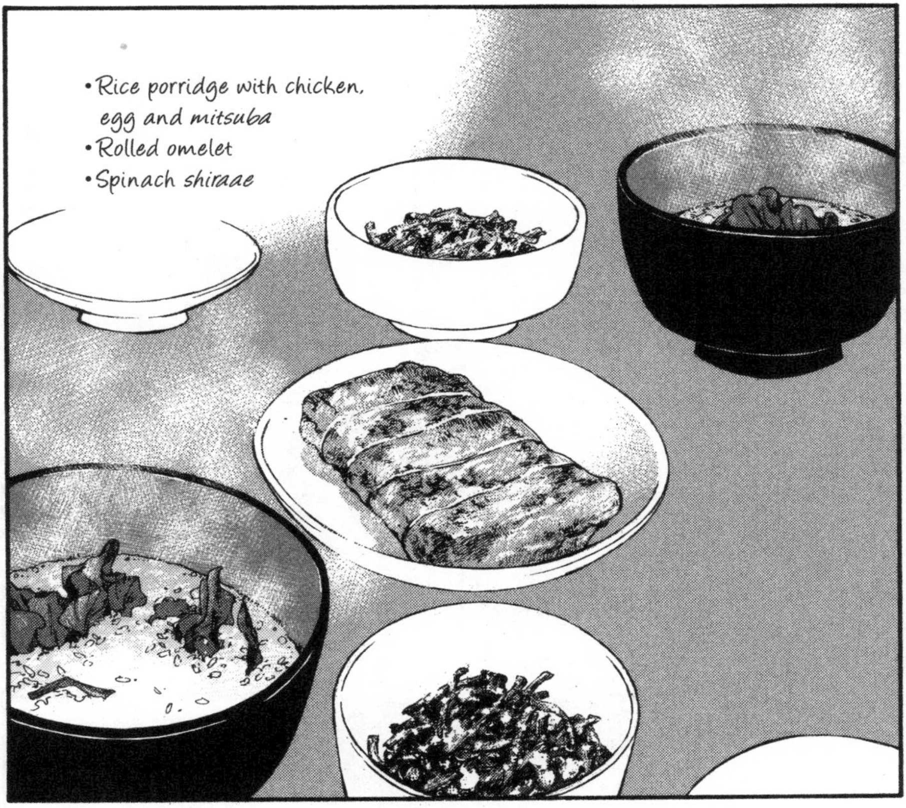
•Rice porridge with chicken, egg and mitsuba
•Rolled omelet
•Spinach shiraae

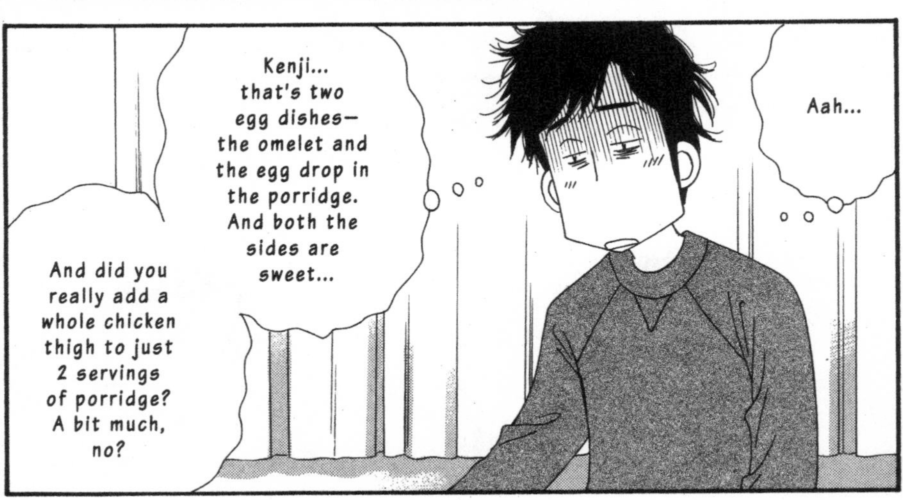
Aah...
Kenji... that's two egg dishes—the omelet and the egg drop in the porridge. And both the sides are sweet...
And did you really add a whole chicken thigh to just 2 servings of porridge? A bit much, no?

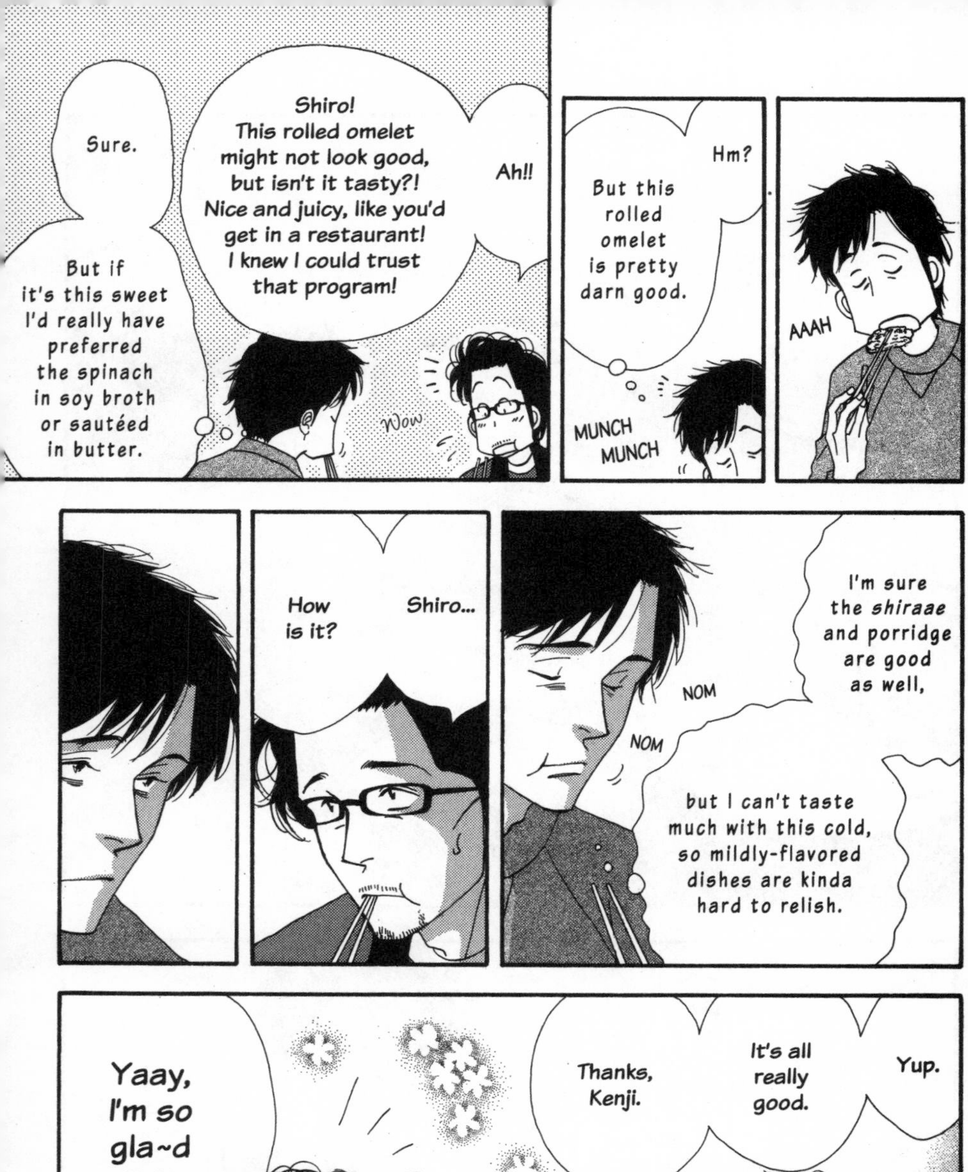
AAAH
Hm?
But this rolled omelet is pretty darn good.
MUNCH MUNCH
Ah!!
Shiro! This rolled omelet might not look good, but isn't it tasty?! Nice and juicy, like you'd get in a restaurant! I knew I could trust that program!
Wow
Sure.
But if it's this sweet I'd really have preferred the spinach in soy broth or sautéed in butter.
I'm sure the *shiraae* and porridge are good as well,
NOM
NOM
but I can't taste much with this cold, so mildly-flavored dishes are kinda hard to relish.
Shiro...
How is it?
Yup.
It's all really good.
Thanks, Kenji.
Yaay, I'm so gla~d ♡♡

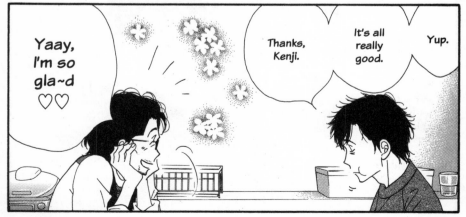

Even made without following the instructions to the letter, the **Public-Broadcasting (*Tameshite Gatten*) Rolled Omelet** tasted quite delicious.

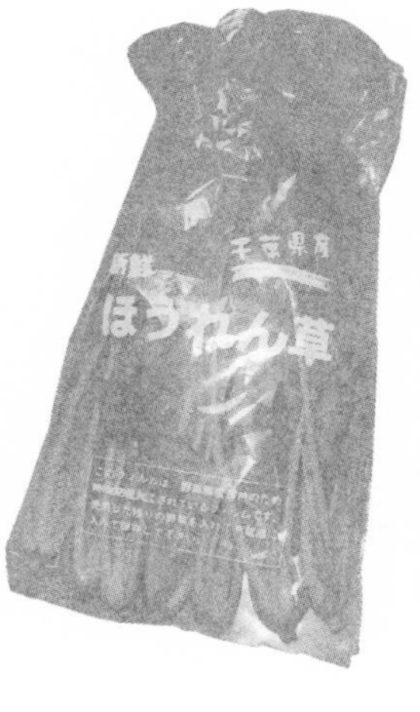
ほうれん草

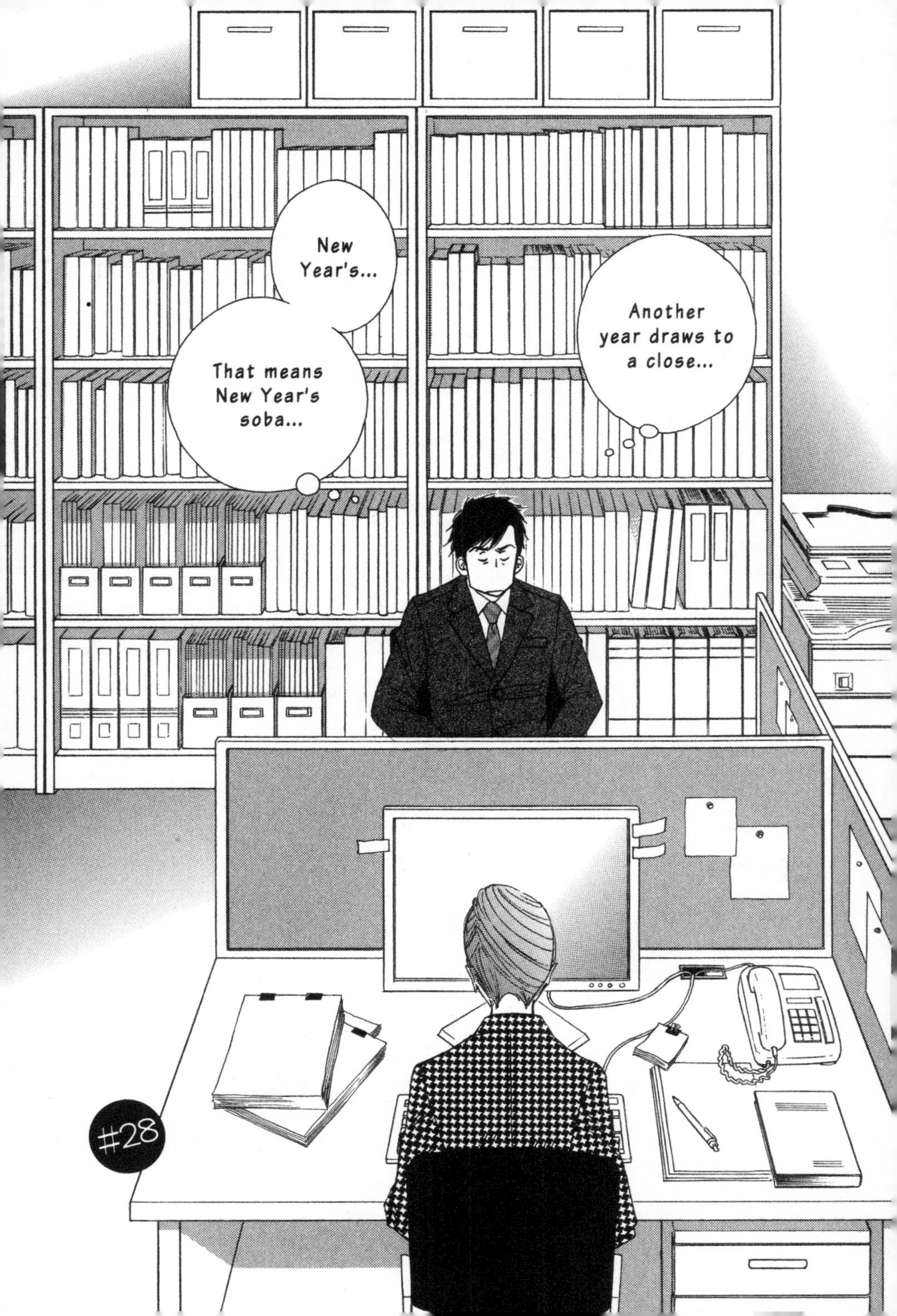
Another year draws to a close...
New Year's...
That means New Year's soba...
#28

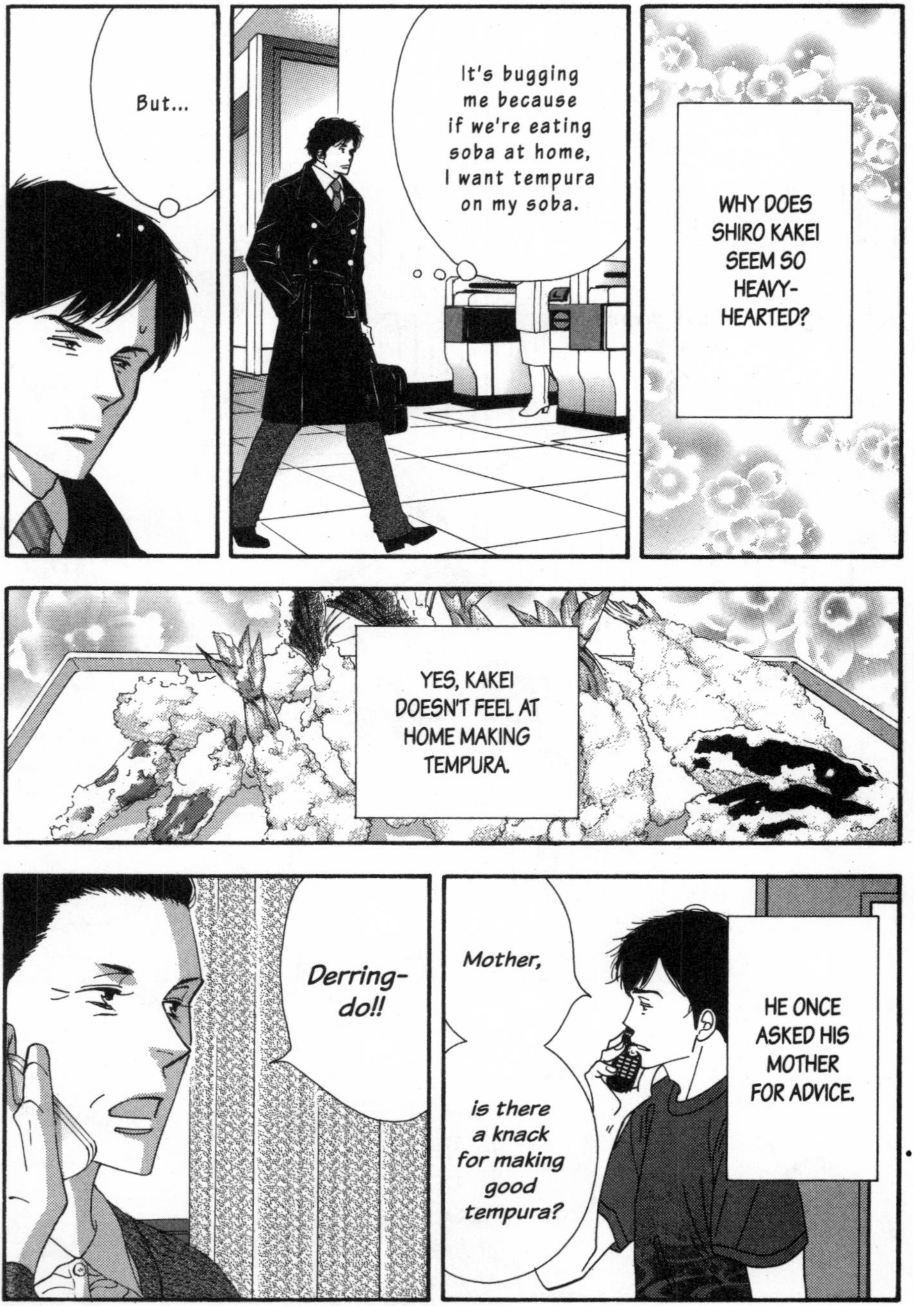
WHY DOES SHIRO KAKEI SEEM SO HEAVY-HEARTED?
It's bugging me because if we're eating soba at home, I want tempura on my soba.
But...
YES, KAKEI DOESN'T FEEL AT HOME MAKING TEMPURA.
HE ONCE ASKED HIS MOTHER FOR ADVICE.
Mother,
is there a knack for making good tempura?
Derring-do!!

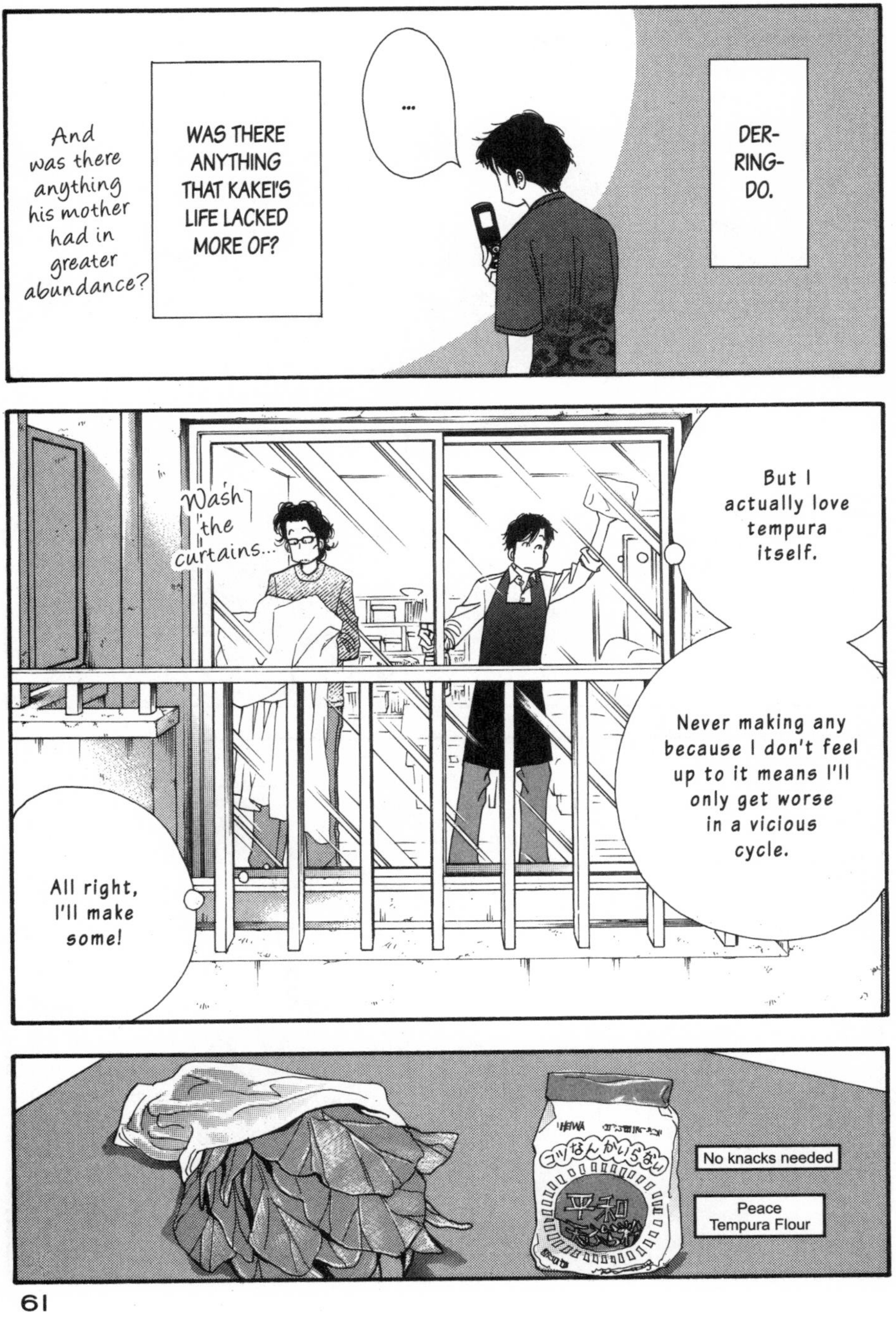
DER-RING-DO.
...
WAS THERE ANYTHING THAT KAKEI'S LIFE LACKED MORE OF?
And was there anything his mother had in greater abundance?
But I actually love tempura itself.
Never making any because I don't feel up to it means I'll only get worse in a vicious cycle.
Wash the curtains...
All right, I'll make some!
HEIWA
No knacks needed
Peace Tempura Flour

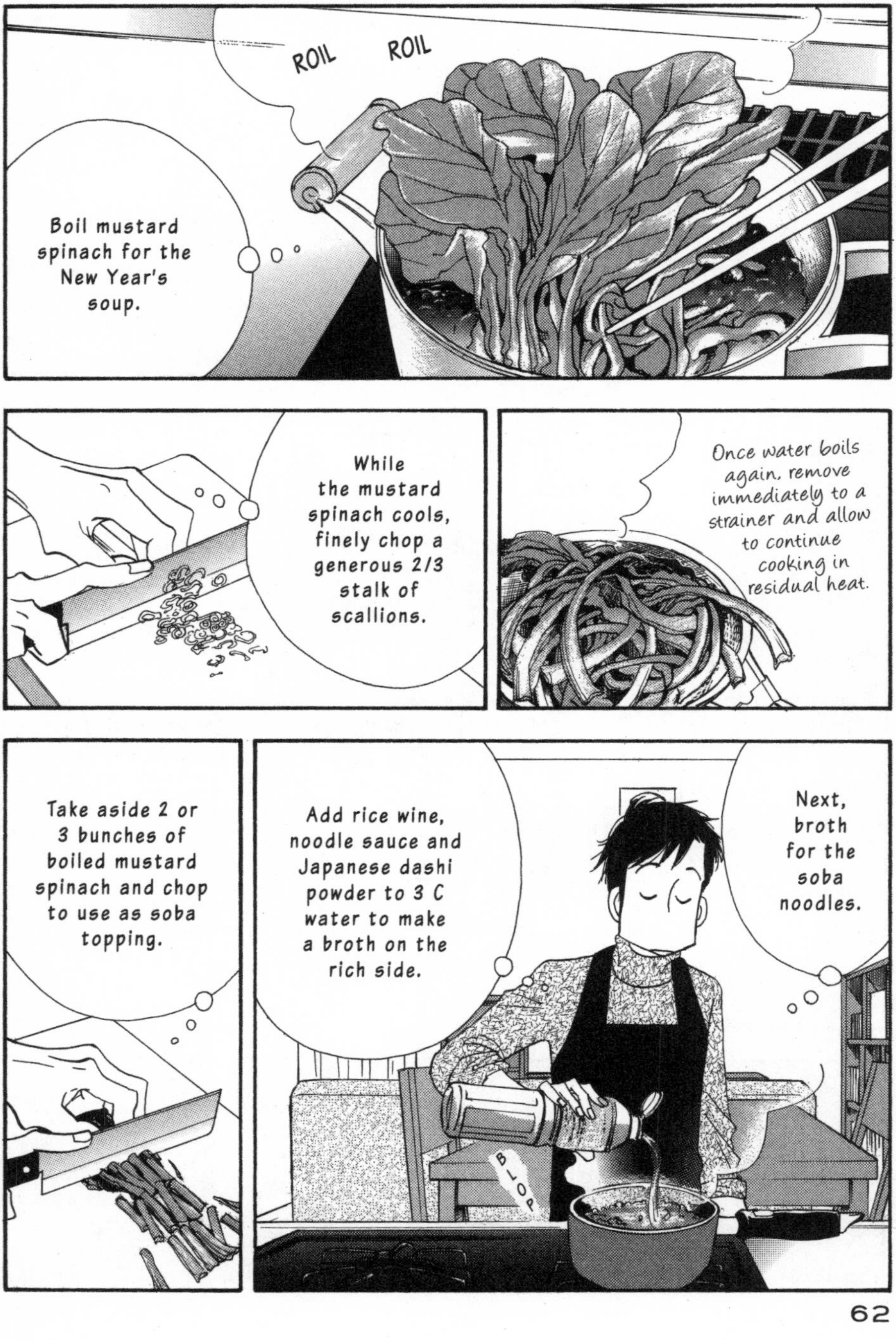
ROIL ROIL
Boil mustard spinach for the New Year's soup.
Once water boils again, remove immediately to a strainer and allow to continue cooking in residual heat.
While the mustard spinach cools, finely chop a generous 2/3 stalk of scallions.
Next, broth for the soba noodles.
Add rice wine, noodle sauce and Japanese dashi powder to 3 C water to make a broth on the rich side.
BLOP
Take aside 2 or 3 bunches of boiled mustard spinach and chop to use as soba topping.

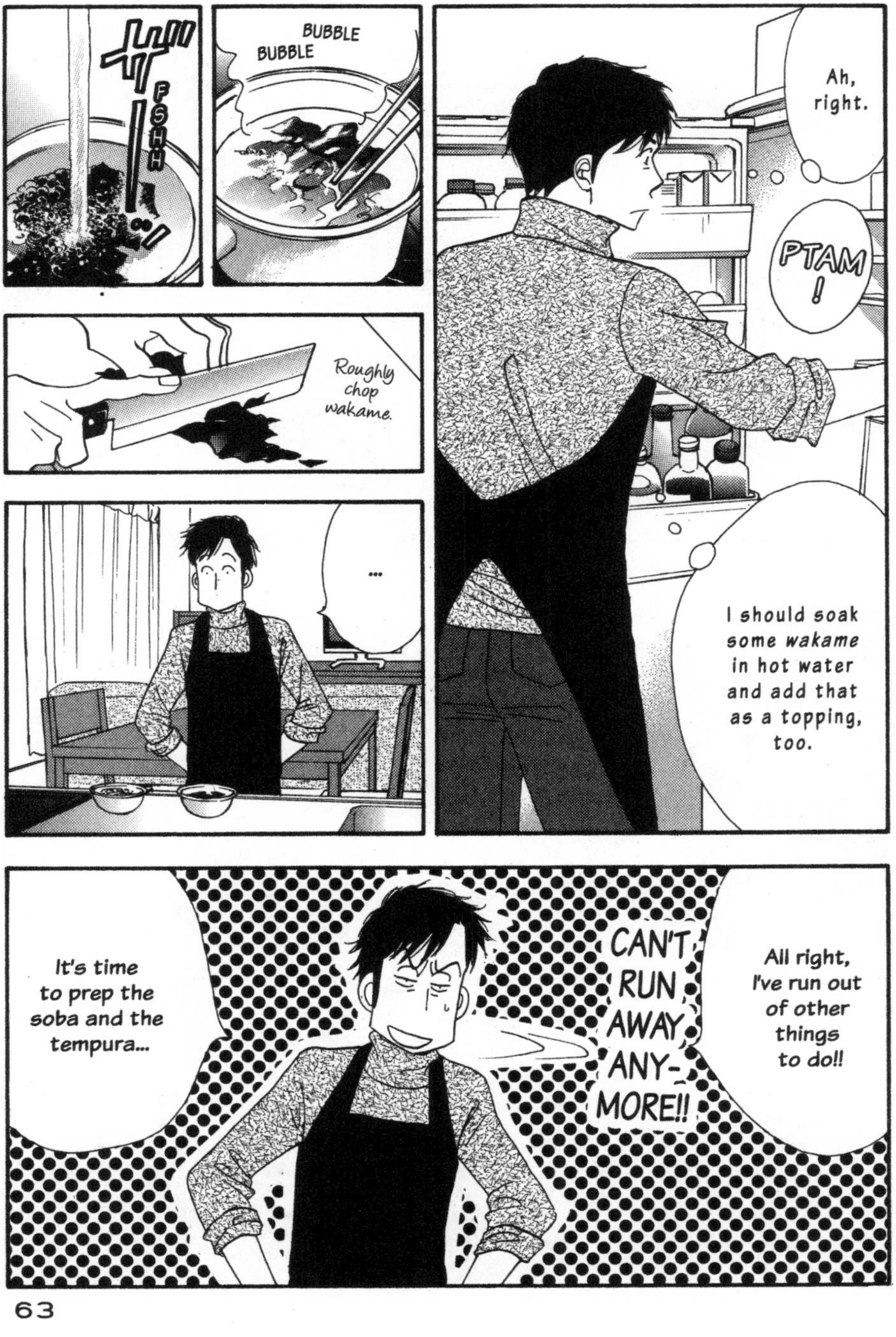
Ah, right.
PTAM!
I should soak some *wakame* in hot water and add that as a topping, too.
BUBBLE
BUBBLE
FSHH
Roughly chop wakame.
...
All right, I've run out of other things to do!!
CAN'T RUN AWAY ANY-MORE!!
It's time to prep the soba and the tempura...

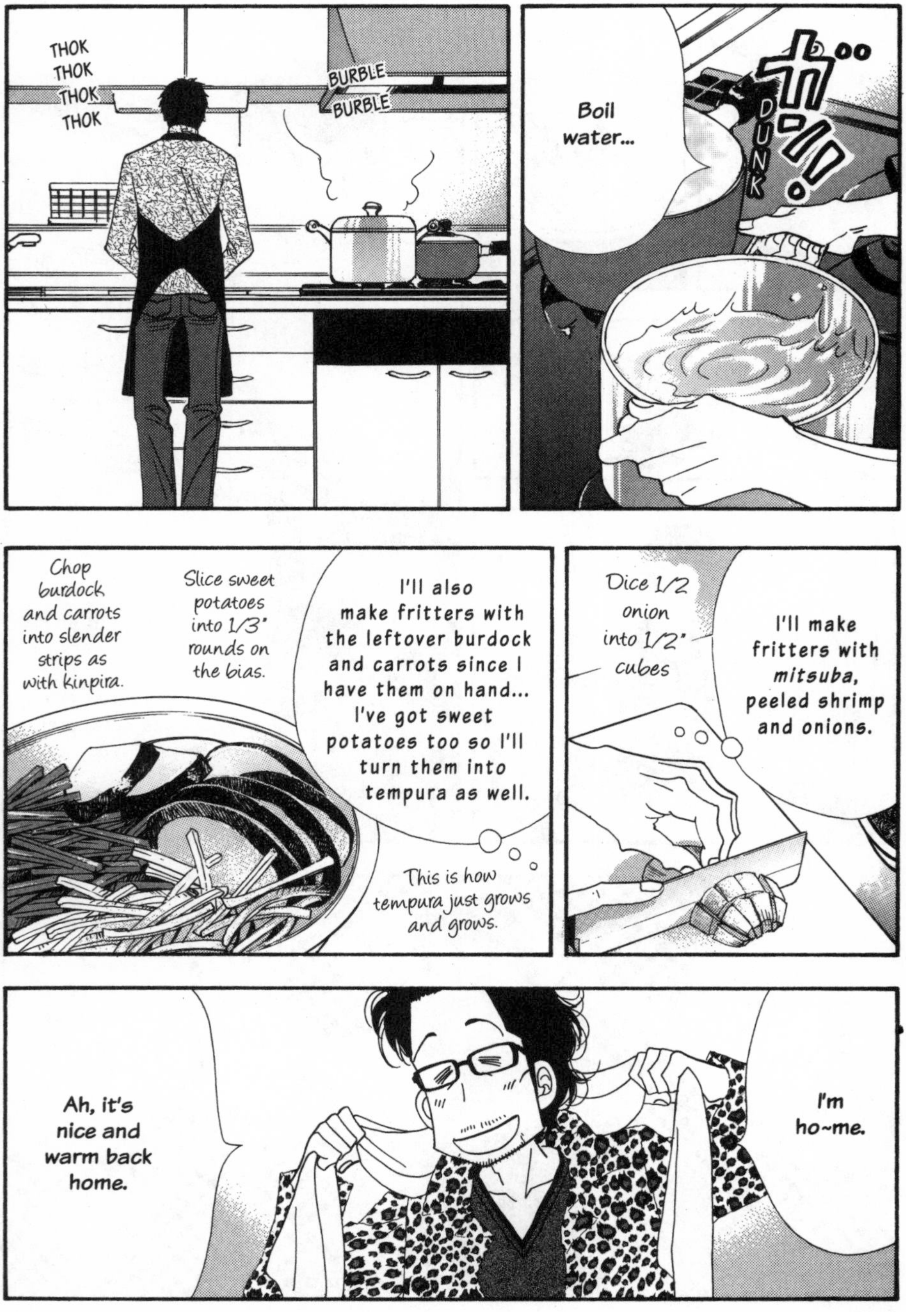
Boil water...
DUNK
THOK THOK THOK THOK
BURBLE BURBLE
Dice 1/2 onion into 1/2" cubes
I'll make fritters with mitsuba, peeled shrimp and onions.
I'll also make fritters with the leftover burdock and carrots since I have them on hand... I've got sweet potatoes too so I'll turn them into tempura as well.
Slice sweet potatoes into 1/3" rounds on the bias.
Chop burdock and carrots into slender strips as with kinpira.
This is how tempura just grows and grows.
I'm ho~me.
Ah, it's nice and warm back home.

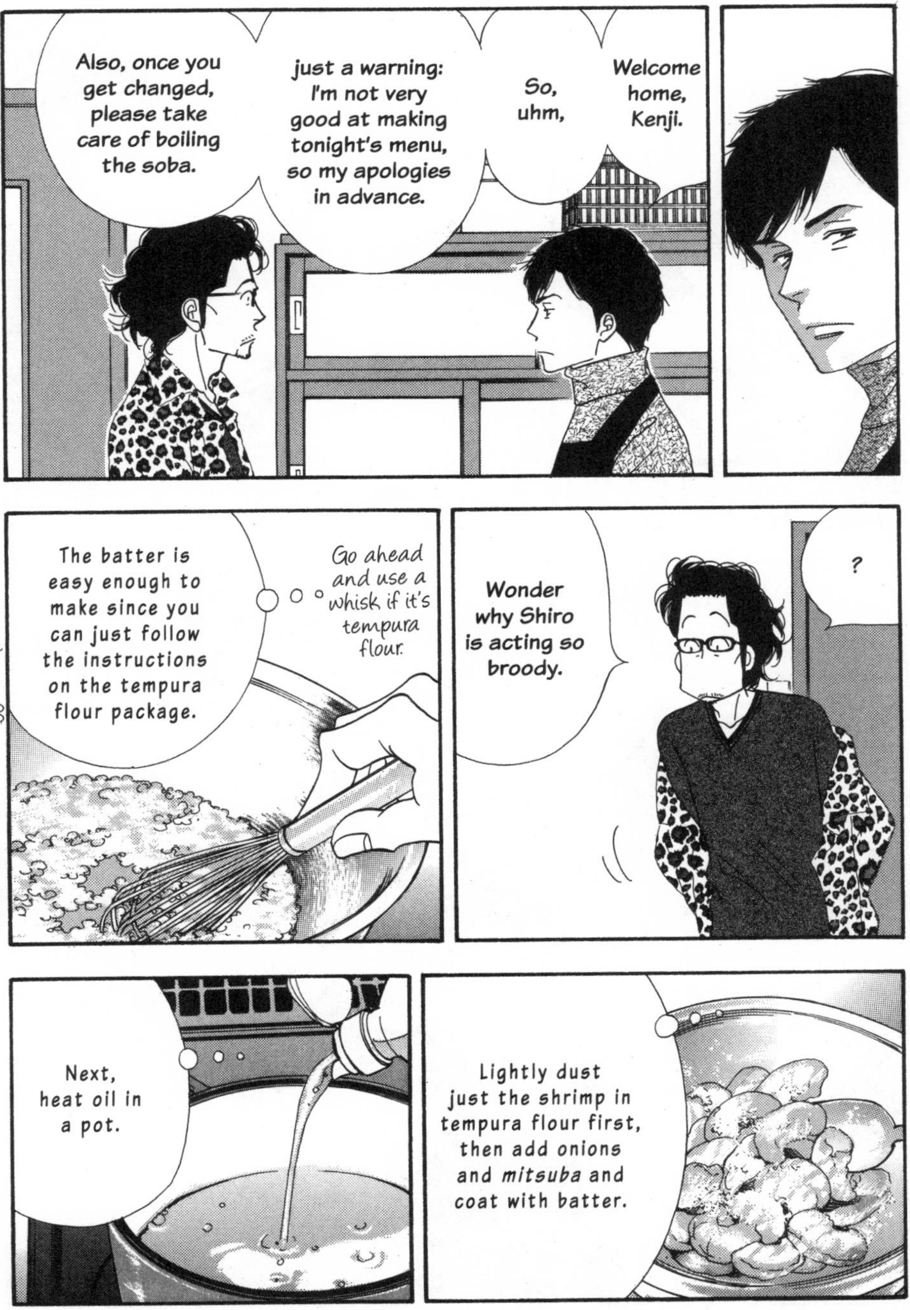

Welcome home, Kenji.
So, uhm,
just a warning: I'm not very good at making tonight's menu, so my apologies in advance.
Also, once you get changed, please take care of boiling the soba.
?
Wonder why Shiro is acting so broody.
Go ahead and use a whisk if it's tempura flour.
The batter is easy enough to make since you can just follow the instructions on the tempura flour package.
Lightly dust just the shrimp in tempura flour first, then add onions and *mitsuba* and coat with batter.
Next, heat oil in a pot.

Make batter thicker for veggie tempura or fritters.

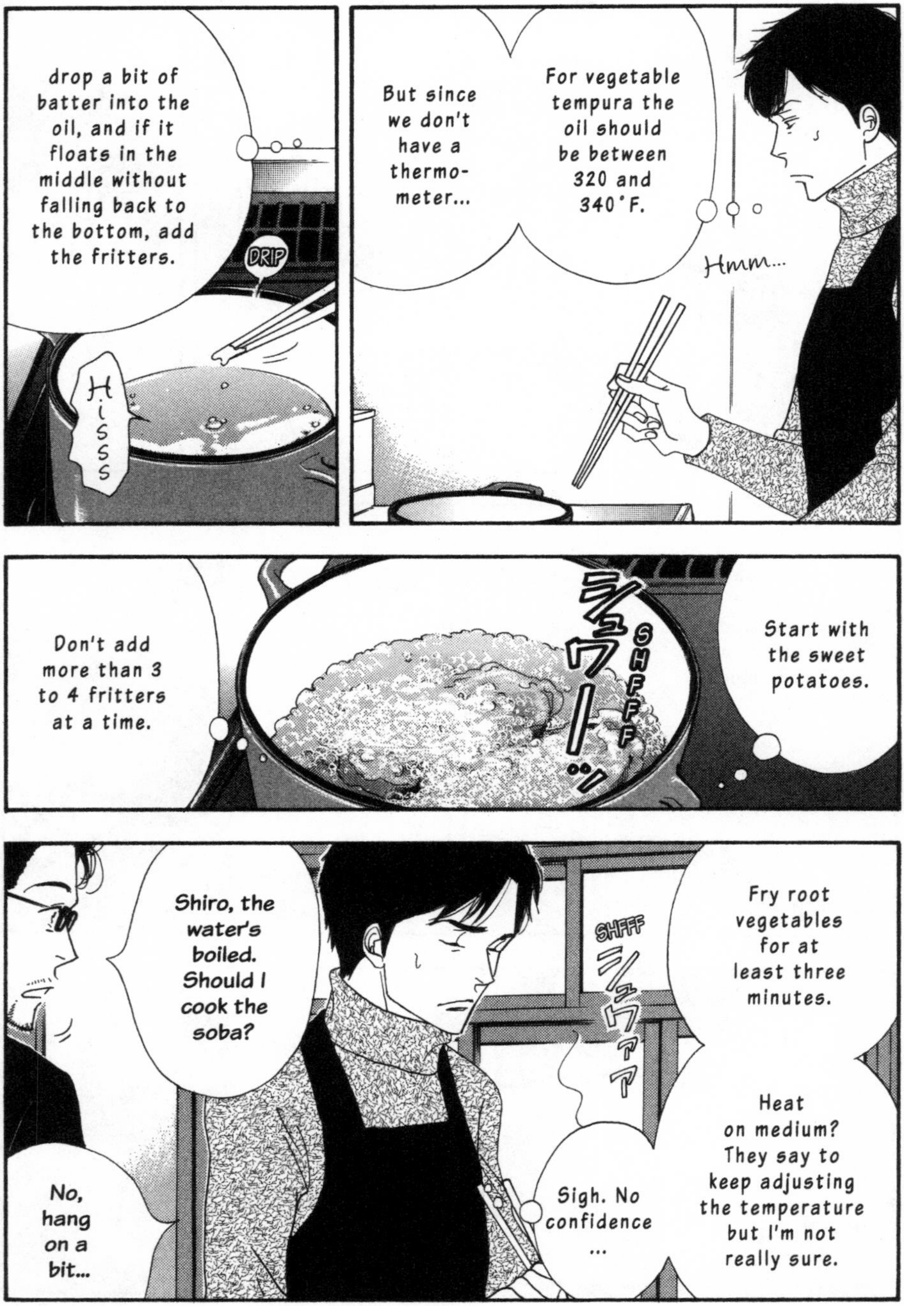
For vegetable tempura the oil should be between 320 and 340°F.
But since we don't have a thermo- meter...
Hmm...
drop a bit of batter into the oil, and if it floats in the middle without falling back to the bottom, add the fritters.
DRIP
Hisss
Start with the sweet potatoes.
シュウーーッ
SHFFF
Don't add more than 3 to 4 fritters at a time.
Fry root vegetables for at least three minutes.
Heat on medium? They say to keep adjusting the temperature but I'm not really sure.
SHFFF
シュワァァ
Sigh. No confidence ...
Shiro, the water's boiled. Should I cook the soba?
No, hang on a bit...

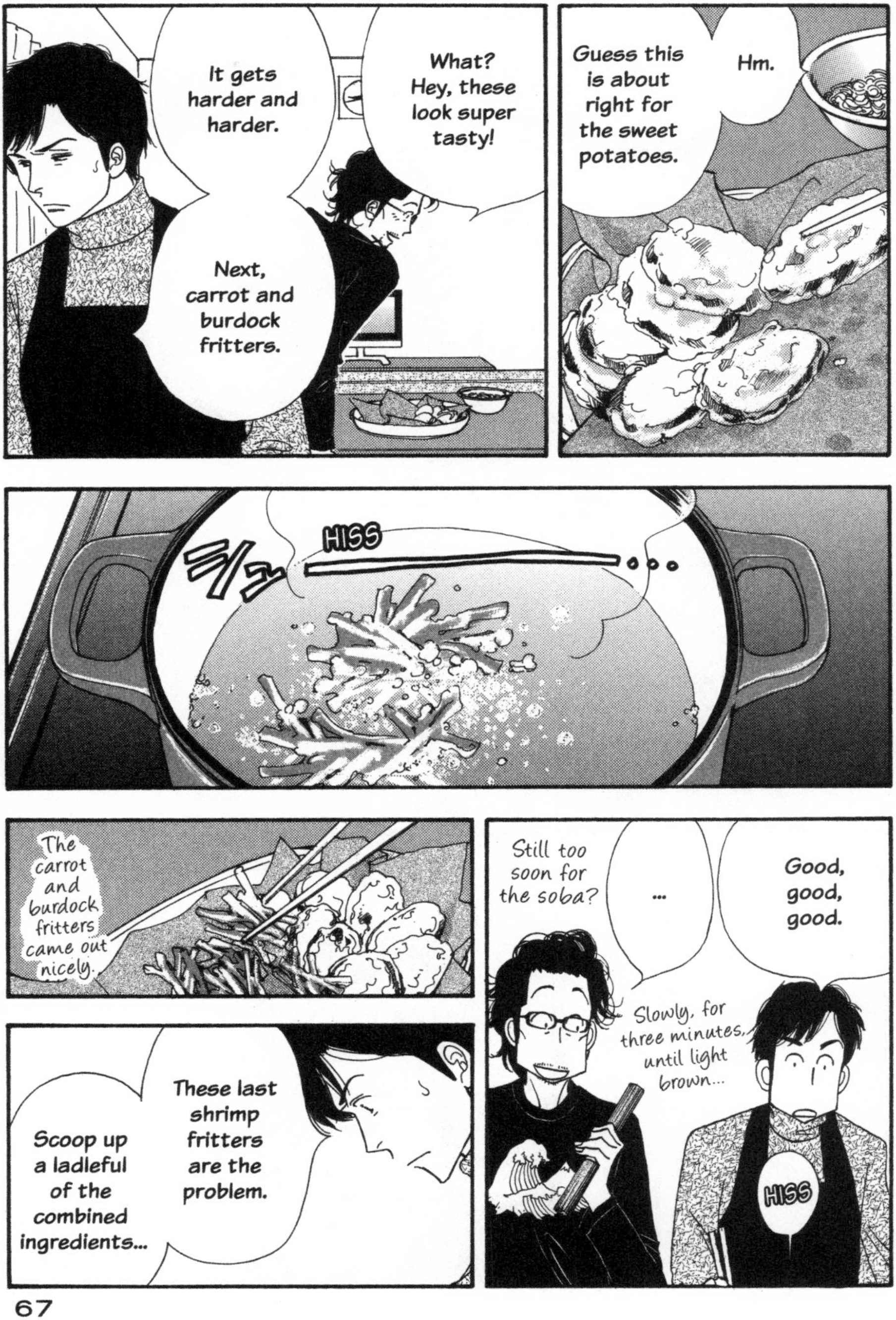
Hm.
Guess this is about right for the sweet potatoes.
What? Hey, these look super tasty!
It gets harder and harder.
Next, carrot and burdock fritters.
HISS
Good, good, good.
...
Still too soon for the soba?
Slowly, for three minutes, until light brown...
HISS
The carrot and burdock fritters came out nicely.
These last shrimp fritters are the problem.
Scoop up a ladleful of the combined ingredients...

CRUMBLE

SHFF

Argh
!!

Ignore me, just go ahead and boil the soba!

Huh?!

What, what?

Argh
!!

Argh
!!

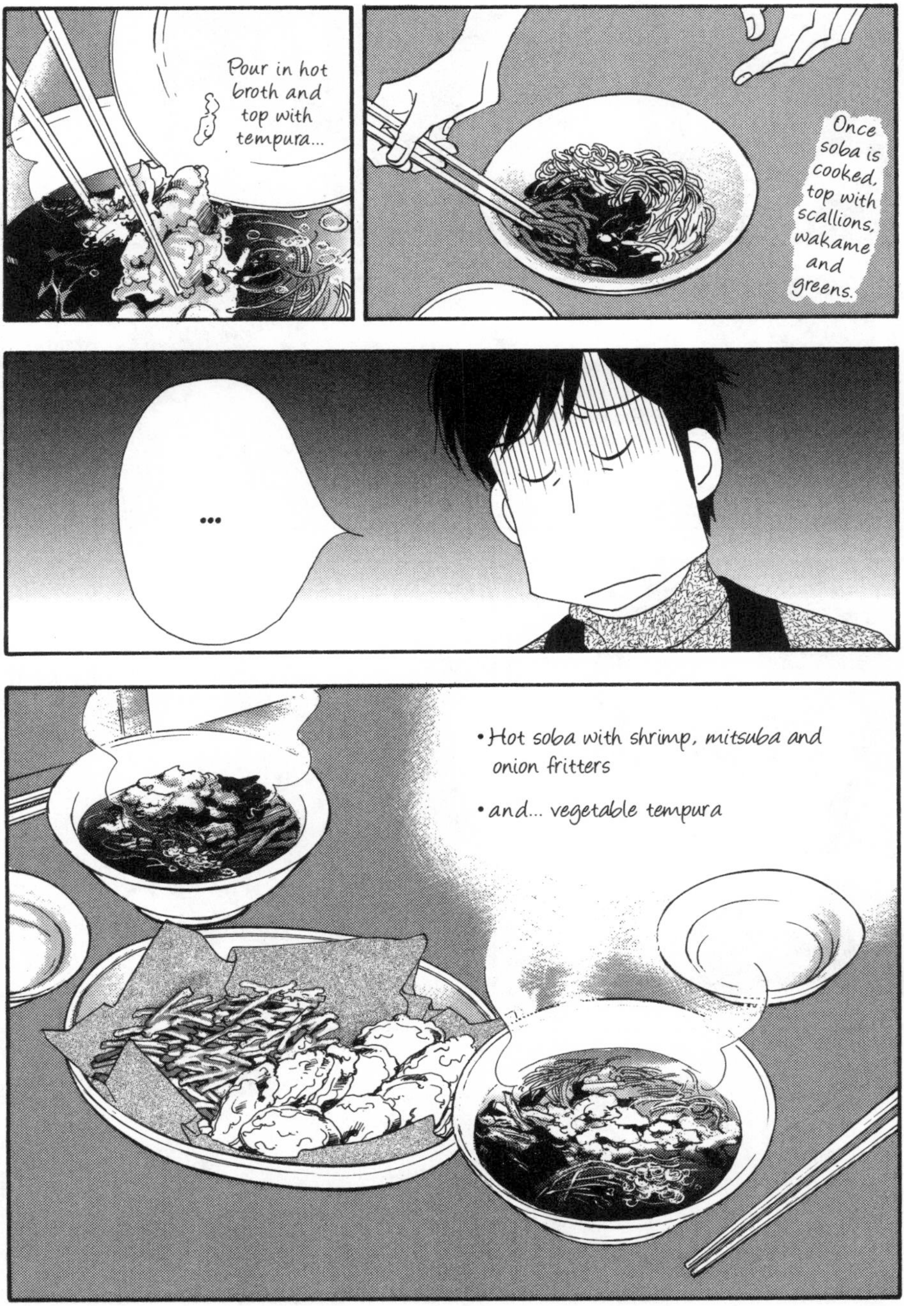
Once soba is cooked, top with scallions, wakame and greens.
Pour in hot broth and top with tempura...
...
•Hot soba with shrimp, mitsuba and onion fritters
•and... vegetable tempura

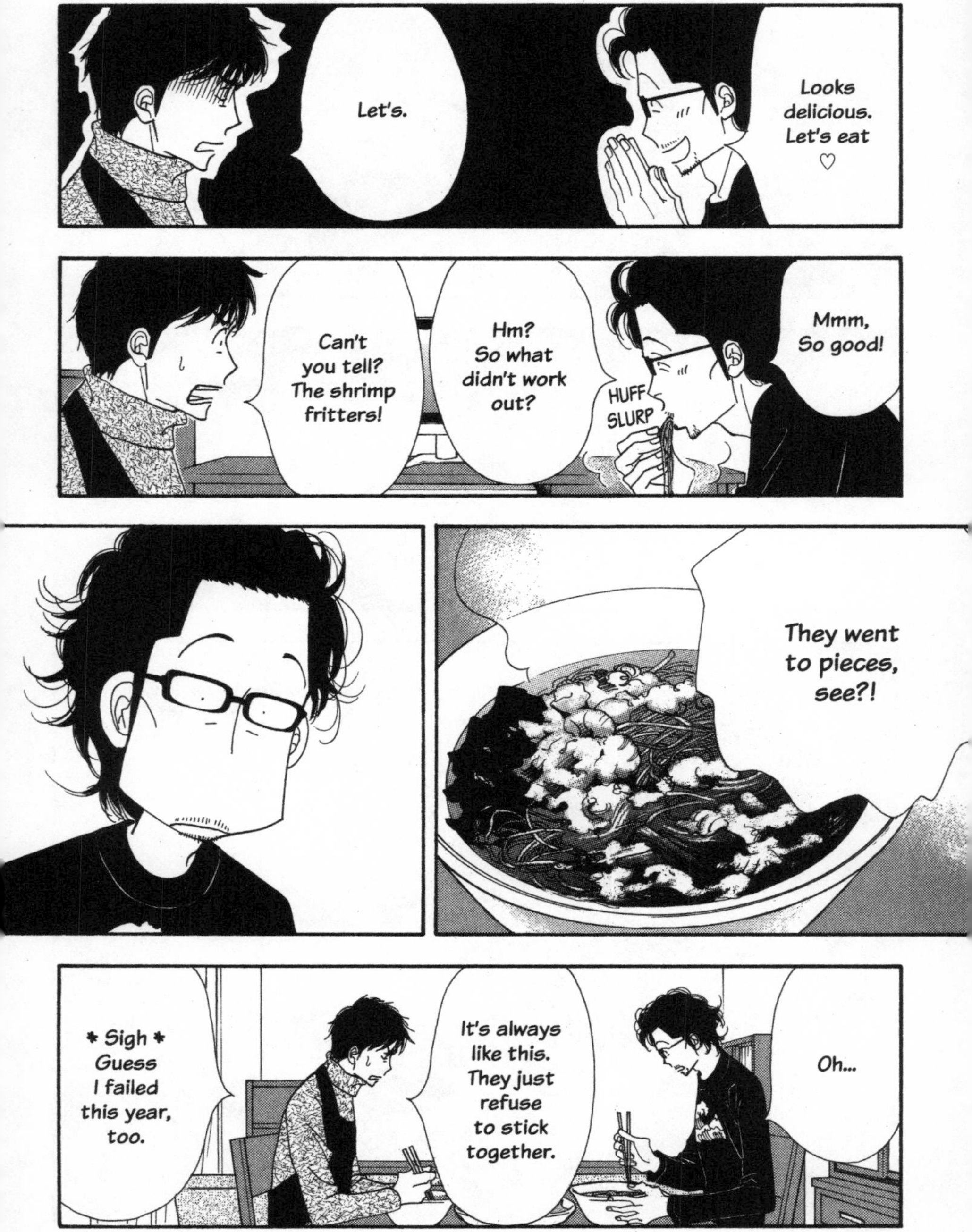
Looks delicious. Let's eat ♡
Let's.
Mmm, So good!
HUFF SLURP
Hm? So what didn't work out?
Can't you tell? The shrimp fritters!
They went to pieces, see?!
Oh...
It's always like this. They just refuse to stick together.
* Sigh * Guess I failed this year, too.

 if you don't mind my asking, what's the big deal? Even if they fall apart they taste the same.

It's delicious all the same.

Uhm,

 ...

 See? Delicious, I knew.

 Yup, yup.

Fair enough. What keeps a fritter together is just the coating of carbs and oil.

Haa...

 Yes, good!

Hmm.

 SLURP

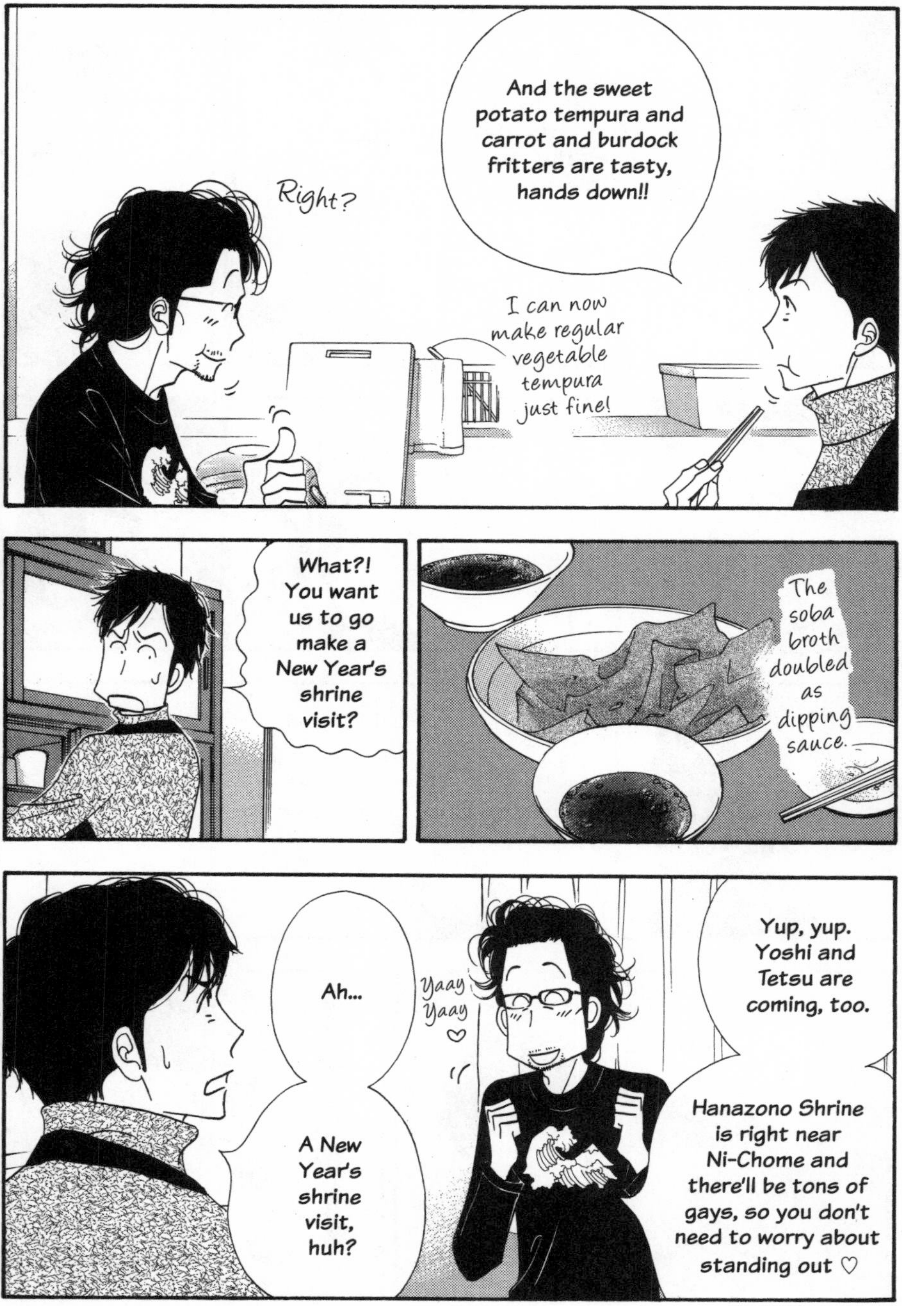
And the sweet potato tempura and carrot and burdock fritters are tasty, hands down!!
Right?
I can now make regular vegetable tempura just fine!
The soba broth doubled as dipping sauce.
What?! You want us to go make a New Year's shrine visit?
Yup, yup. Yoshi and Tetsu are coming, too.
Hanazono Shrine is right near Ni-Chome and there'll be tons of gays, so you don't need to worry about standing out ♡
Yaay Yaay ♡
Ah...
A New Year's shrine visit, huh?

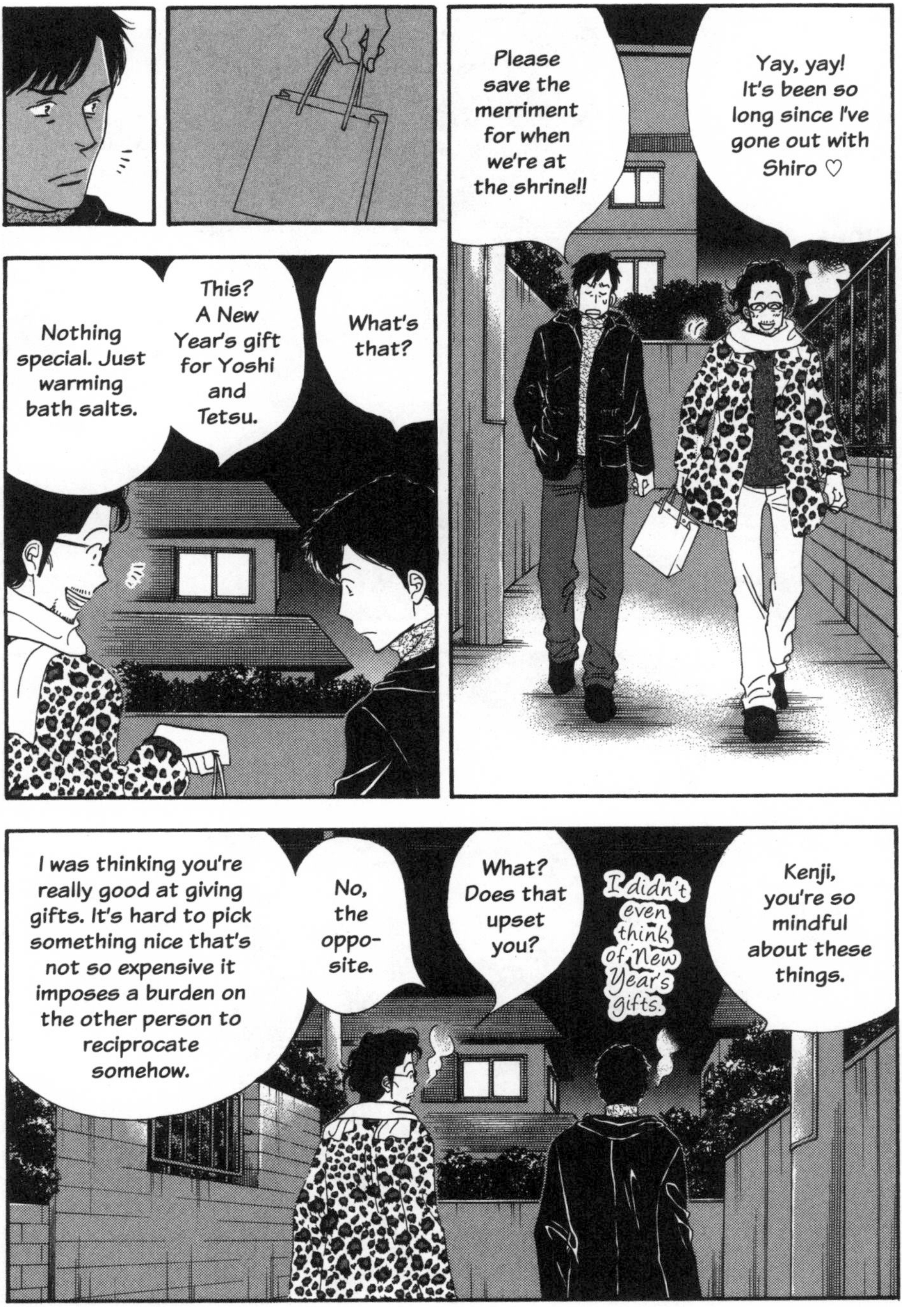
Yay, yay! It's been so long since I've gone out with Shiro ♡
Please save the merriment for when we're at the shrine!!
What's that?
This? A New Year's gift for Yoshi and Tetsu.
Nothing special. Just warming bath salts.
Kenji, you're so mindful about these things.
I didn't even think of New Year's gifts.
What? Does that upset you?
No, the oppo-site.
I was thinking you're really good at giving gifts. It's hard to pick something nice that's not so expensive it imposes a burden on the other person to reciprocate somehow.

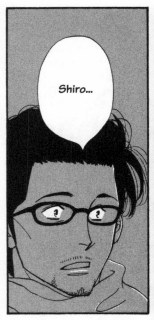

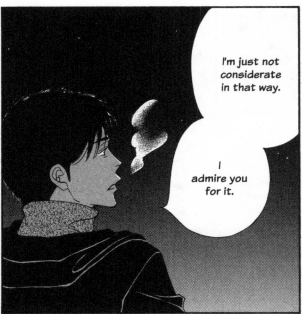

I'm just not considerate in that way.
I admire you for it.
Shiro...
Shiro!! Did you just praise me? You did, didn't you?!
Yaaay ~ ♡
No, don't get so close yet.
No, um, yeah, same here and all!!
I'm so happy! Let's make the next year a good one too ♡
You're so not capable of accepting a compliment graciously, though, are you...

#28 **END**

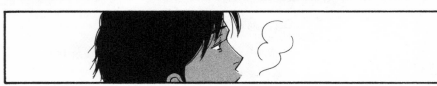

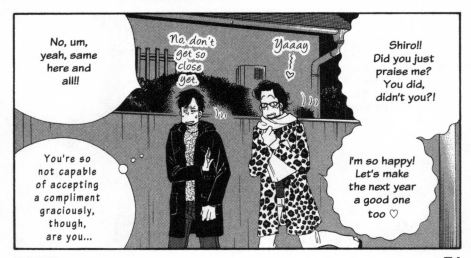

Kakei's mother had said the knack
was **"Derring-do!"**
but Kakei's impression seemed
to be **"actually patiently."**
This is especially true for root vegetables
like potatoes and pumpkin—
even if the outside looks done,
they might not be cooked through yet
so let them fry more **patiently** than not.

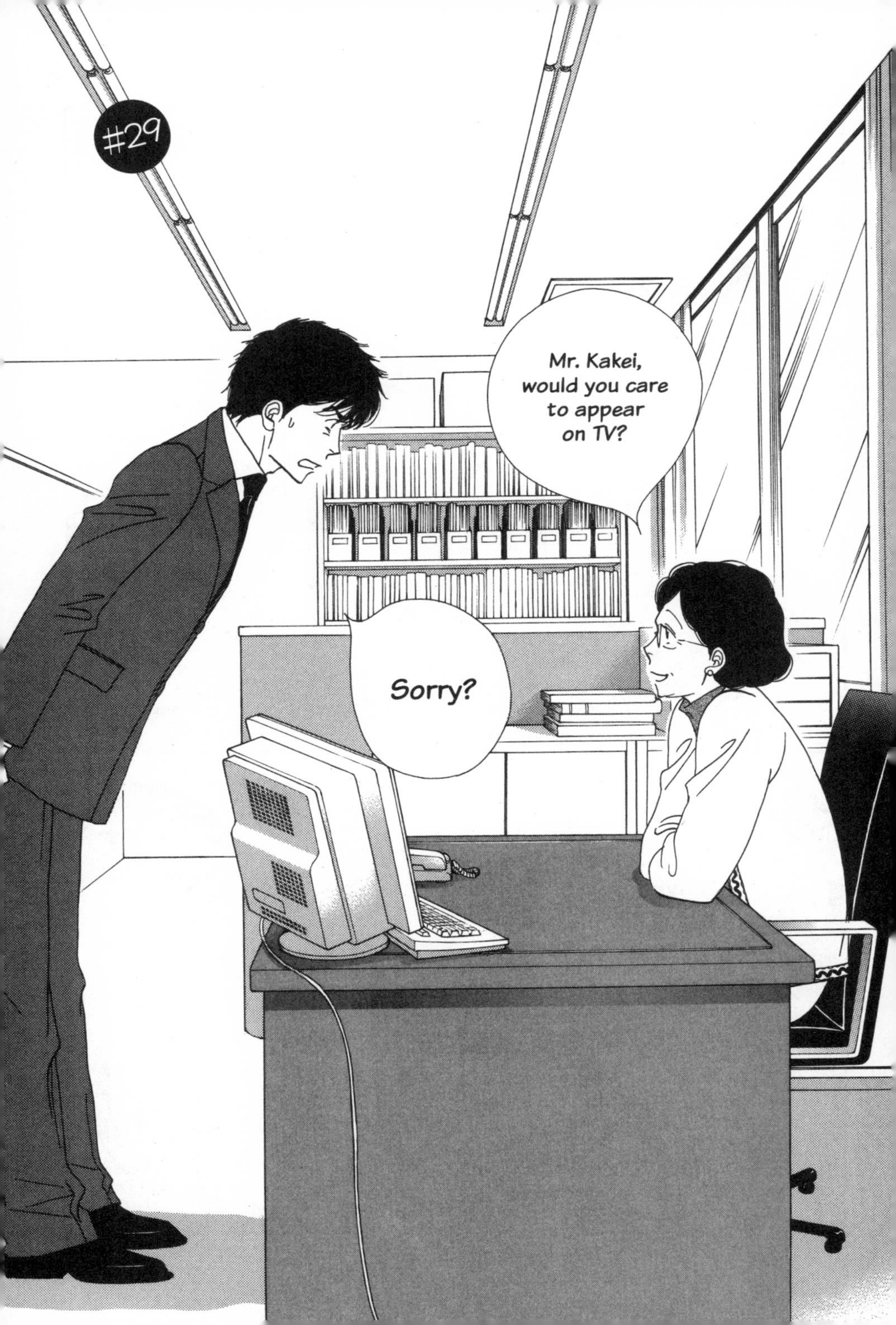
#29
Mr. Kakei, would you care to appear on TV?
Sorry?

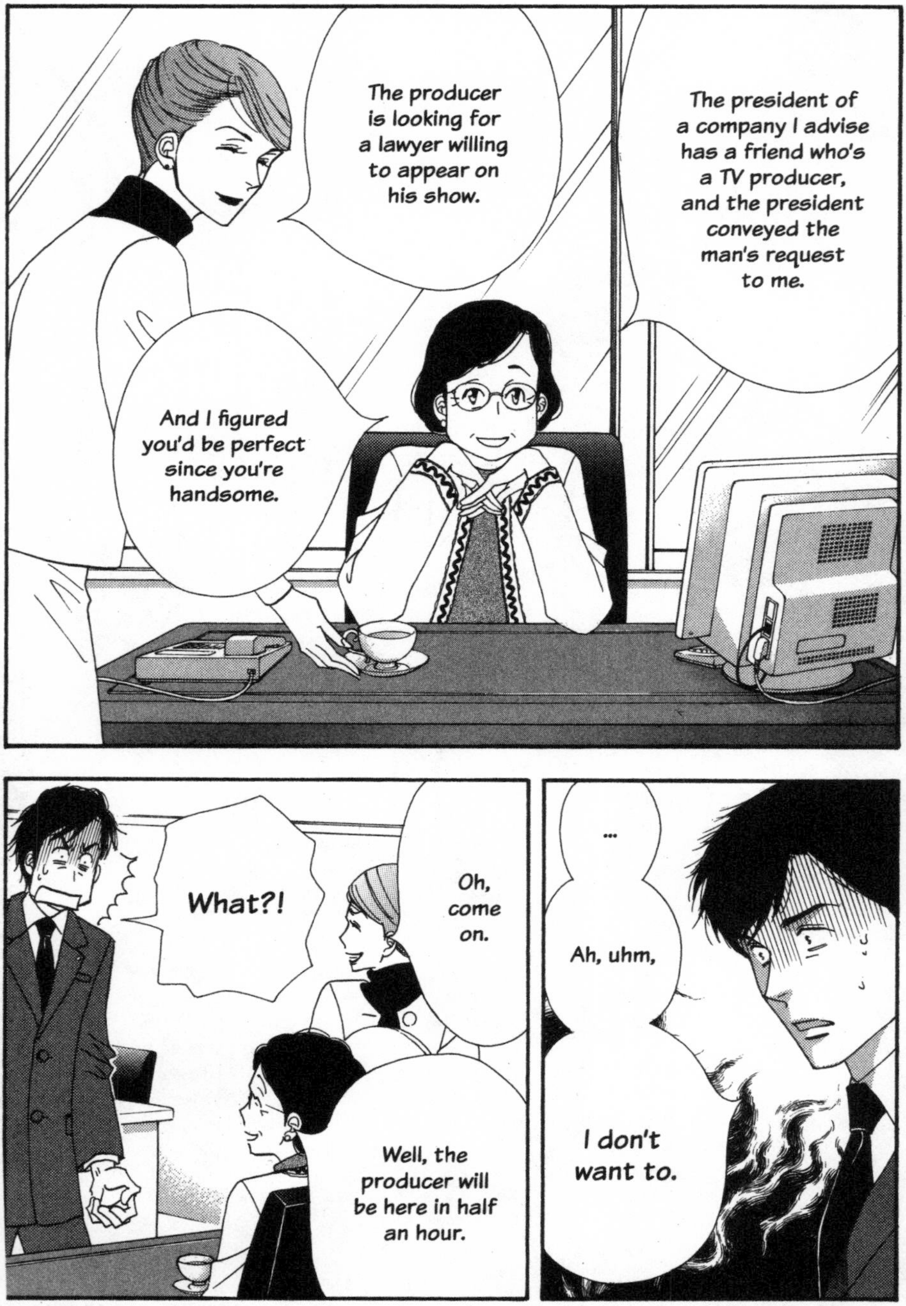
The president of a company I advise has a friend who's a TV producer, and the president conveyed the man's request to me.
The producer is looking for a lawyer willing to appear on his show.
And I figured you'd be perfect since you're handsome.
...
Ah, uhm,
I don't want to.
Oh, come on.
What?!
Well, the producer will be here in half an hour.

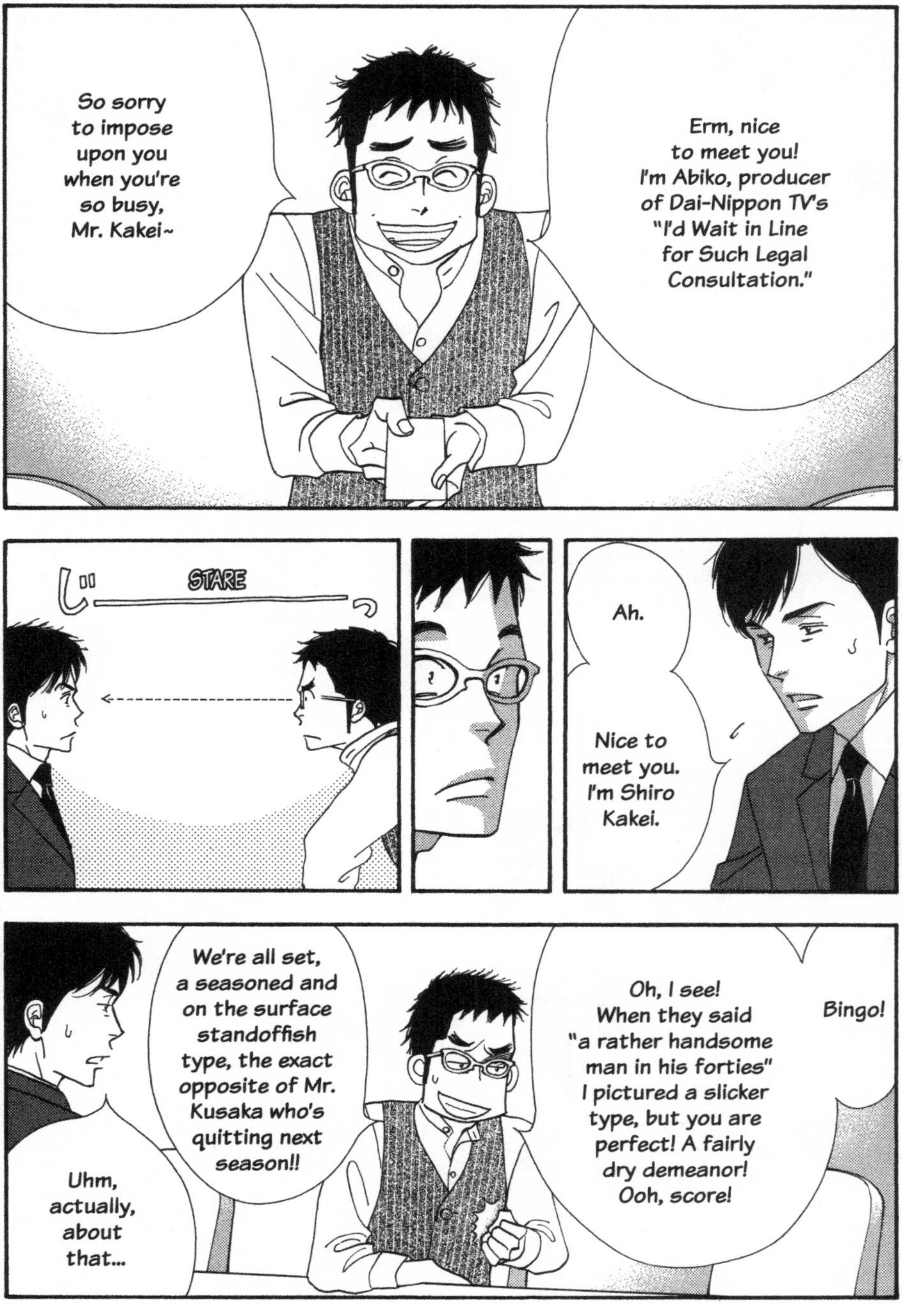
Erm, nice to meet you! I'm Abiko, producer of Dai-Nippon TV's "I'd Wait in Line for Such Legal Consultation."
So sorry to impose upon you when you're so busy, Mr. Kakei~
Ah.
Nice to meet you. I'm Shiro Kakei.
STARE
Bingo!
Oh, I see! When they said "a rather handsome man in his forties" I pictured a slicker type, but you are perfect! A fairly dry demeanor! Ooh, score!
We're all set, a seasoned and on the surface standoffish type, the exact opposite of Mr. Kusaka who's quitting next season!!
Uhm, actually, about that...

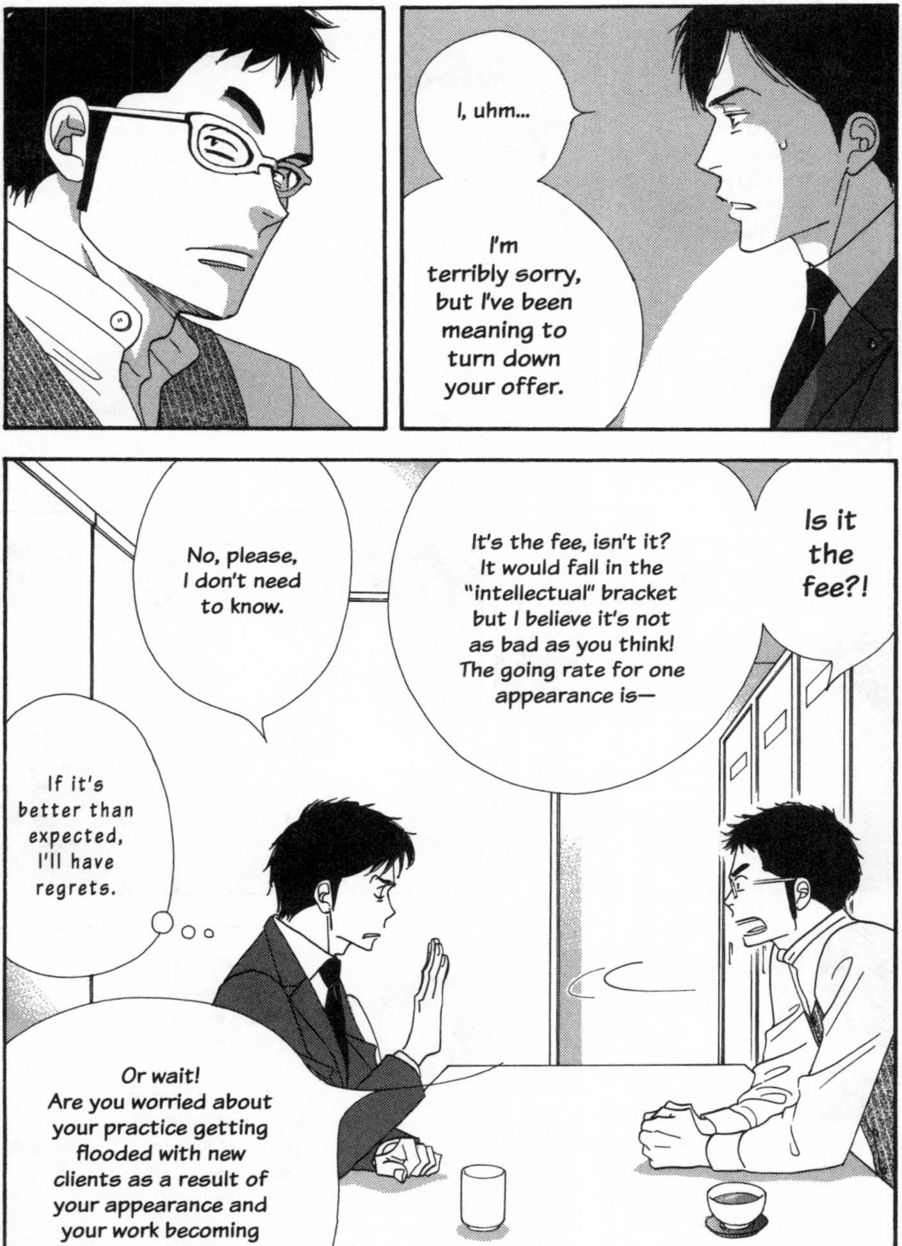
I, uhm...
I'm terribly sorry, but I've been meaning to turn down your offer.
Is it the fee?!
It's the fee, isn't it? It would fall in the "intellectual" bracket but I believe it's not as bad as you think! The going rate for one appearance is—
No, please, I don't need to know.
If it's better than expected, I'll have regrets.
Or wait! Are you worried about your practice getting flooded with new clients as a result of your appearance and your work becoming unmanageable?!

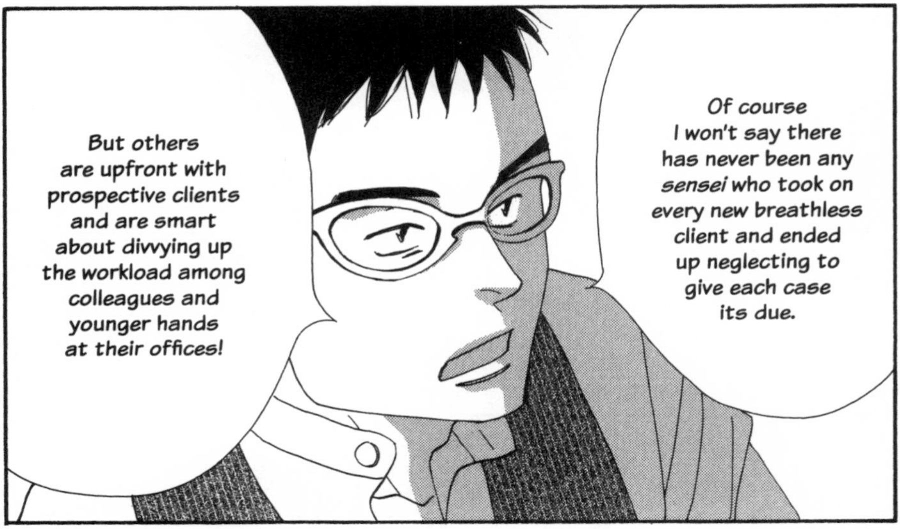
Of course I won't say there has never been any *sensei* who took on every new breathless client and ended up neglecting to give each case its due.
But others are upfront with prospective clients and are smart about divvying up the workload among colleagues and younger hands at their offices!

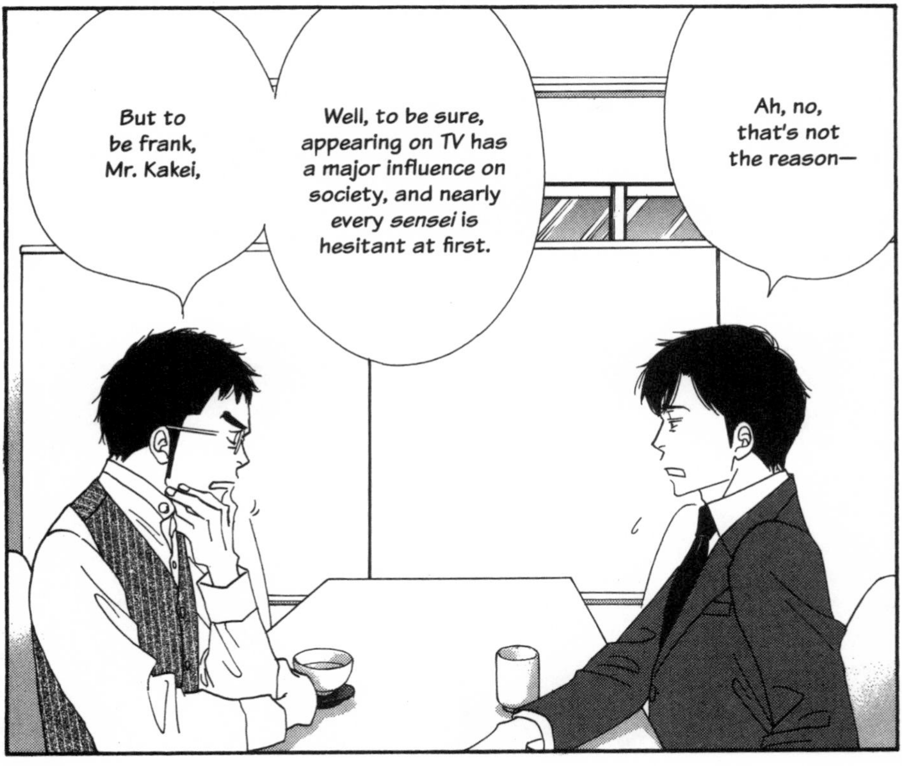
Ah, no, that's not the reason—
Well, to be sure, appearing on TV has a major influence on society, and nearly every *sensei* is hesitant at first.
But to be frank, Mr. Kakei,

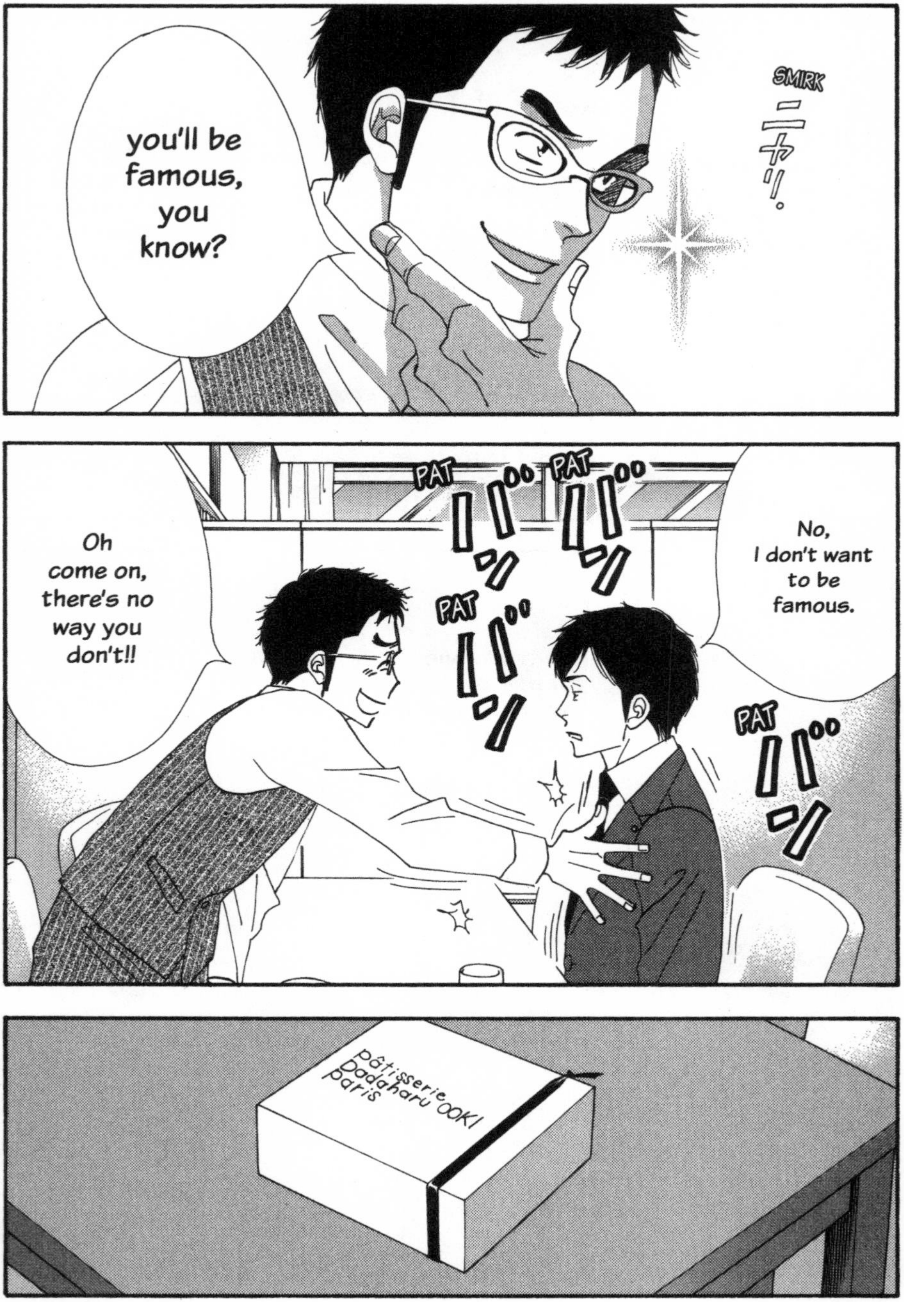
you'll be famous, you know?
SMIRK
ニヤリ。
No, I don't want to be famous.
PAT
PAT
PAT
PAT
Oh come on, there's no way you don't!!
pâtisserie Dadaharu OOKI paris

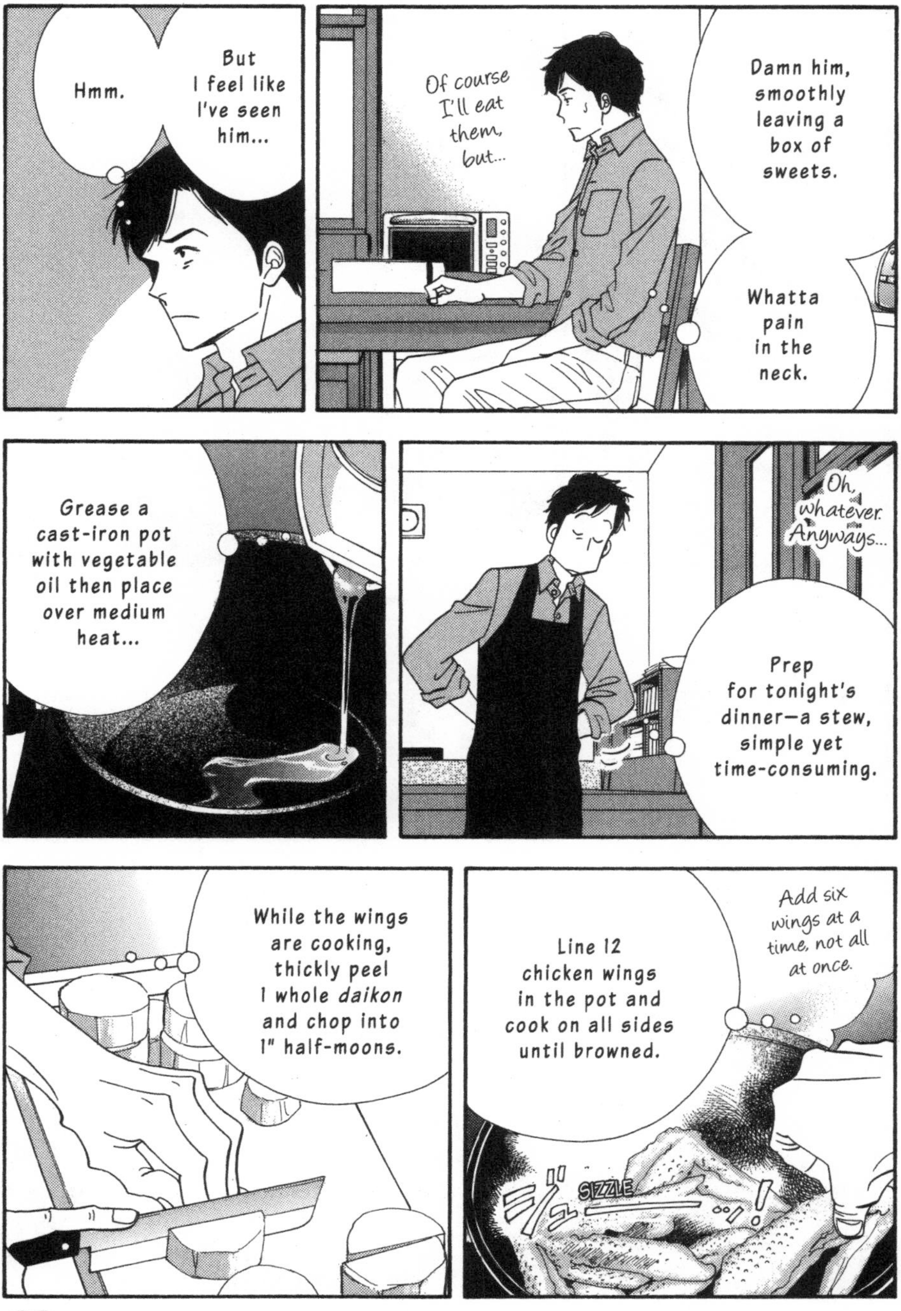
Damn him, smoothly leaving a box of sweets.
Whatta pain in the neck.
Of course I'll eat them, but...
But I feel like I've seen him...
Hmm.
Oh, whatever. Anyways...
Prep for tonight's dinner—a stew, simple yet time-consuming.
Grease a cast-iron pot with vegetable oil then place over medium heat...
Add six wings at a time, not all at once.
Line 12 chicken wings in the pot and cook on all sides until browned.
SIZZLE
While the wings are cooking, thickly peel 1 whole *daikon* and chop into 1" half-moons.

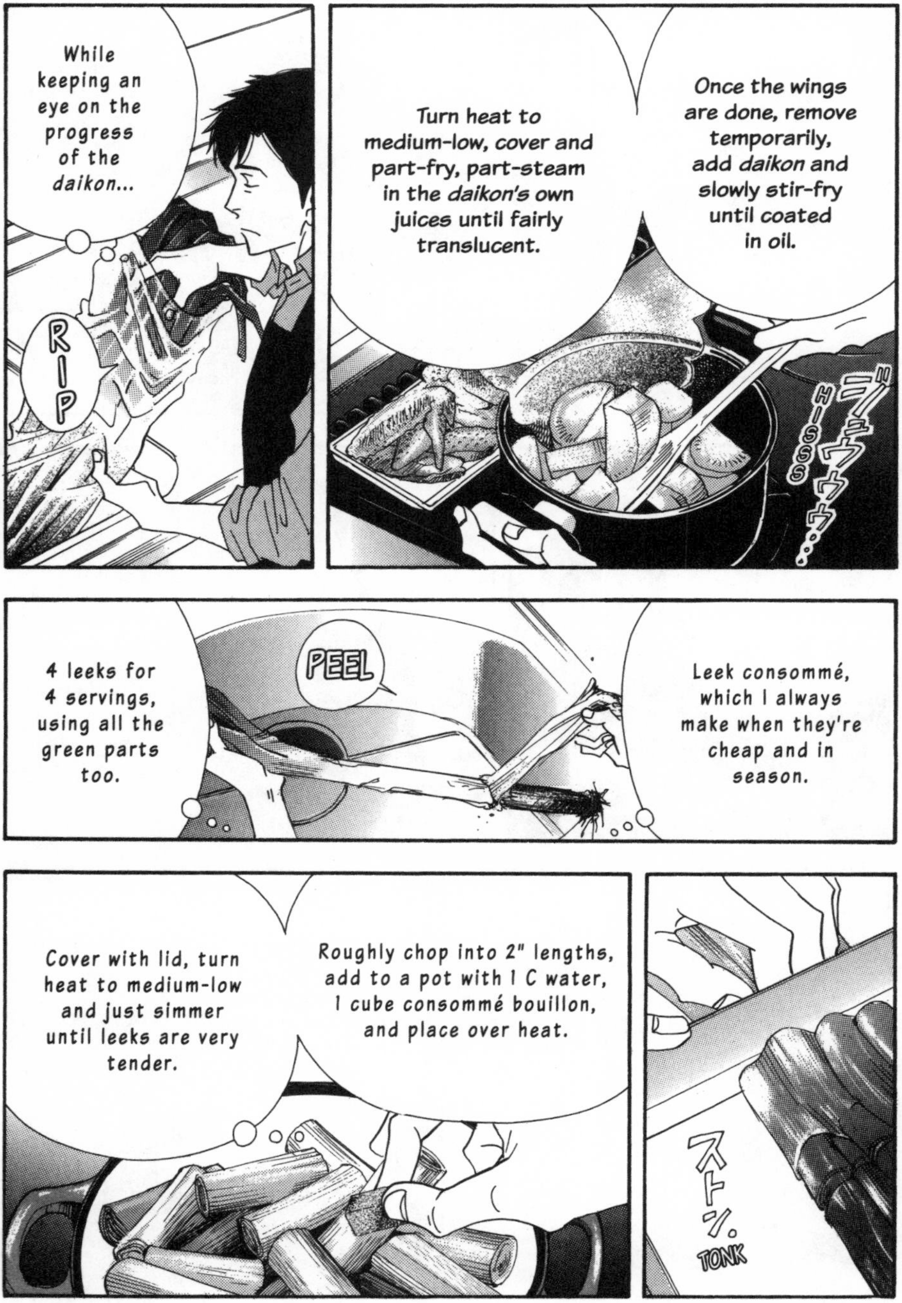
Once the wings are done, remove temporarily, add daikon and slowly stir-fry until coated in oil.
Turn heat to medium-low, cover and part-fry, part-steam in the daikon's own juices until fairly translucent.
ジュウウウウ…
HISSS
While keeping an eye on the progress of the daikon...
RIP
Leek consommé, which I always make when they're cheap and in season.
PEEL
4 leeks for 4 servings, using all the green parts too.
ストン。
TONK
Roughly chop into 2" lengths, add to a pot with 1 C water, 1 cube consommé bouillon, and place over heat.
Cover with lid, turn heat to medium-low and just simmer until leeks are very tender.

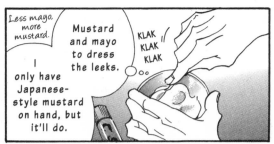

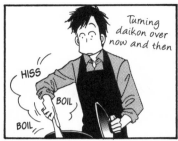

Turning daikon over now and then
HISS
BOIL
BOIL
KLAK
KLAK
KLAK
Mustard and mayo to dress the leeks.
Less mayo, more mustard.
I only have Japanese-style mustard on hand, but it'll do.
The *daikon* should be translucent by now. Return the chicken wings and add 2 C water and, if available, a piece of *kombu* kelp.
Bring to a boil over high heat and skim off any white foam that floats to the surface.
ROIL
ROIL
ROIL
ROIL
BUBBLE
Once you skim the surface, reduce heat to medium and season.
BUBBLE
BUBBLE
Pour in plenty of rice wine, 1 Tbsp sugar, 4 Tbsp soy sauce and 3 or 4 Tbsp mirin. Now simply simmer until the liquid boils off.
ROIL
ROIL

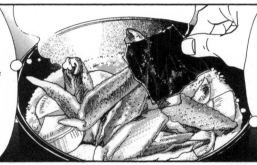

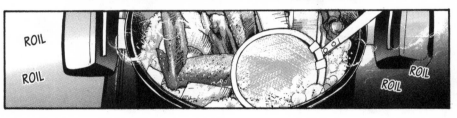

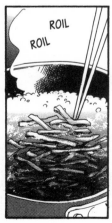

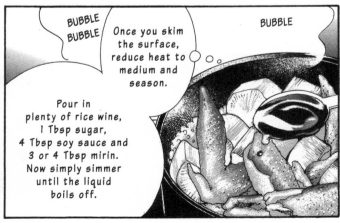

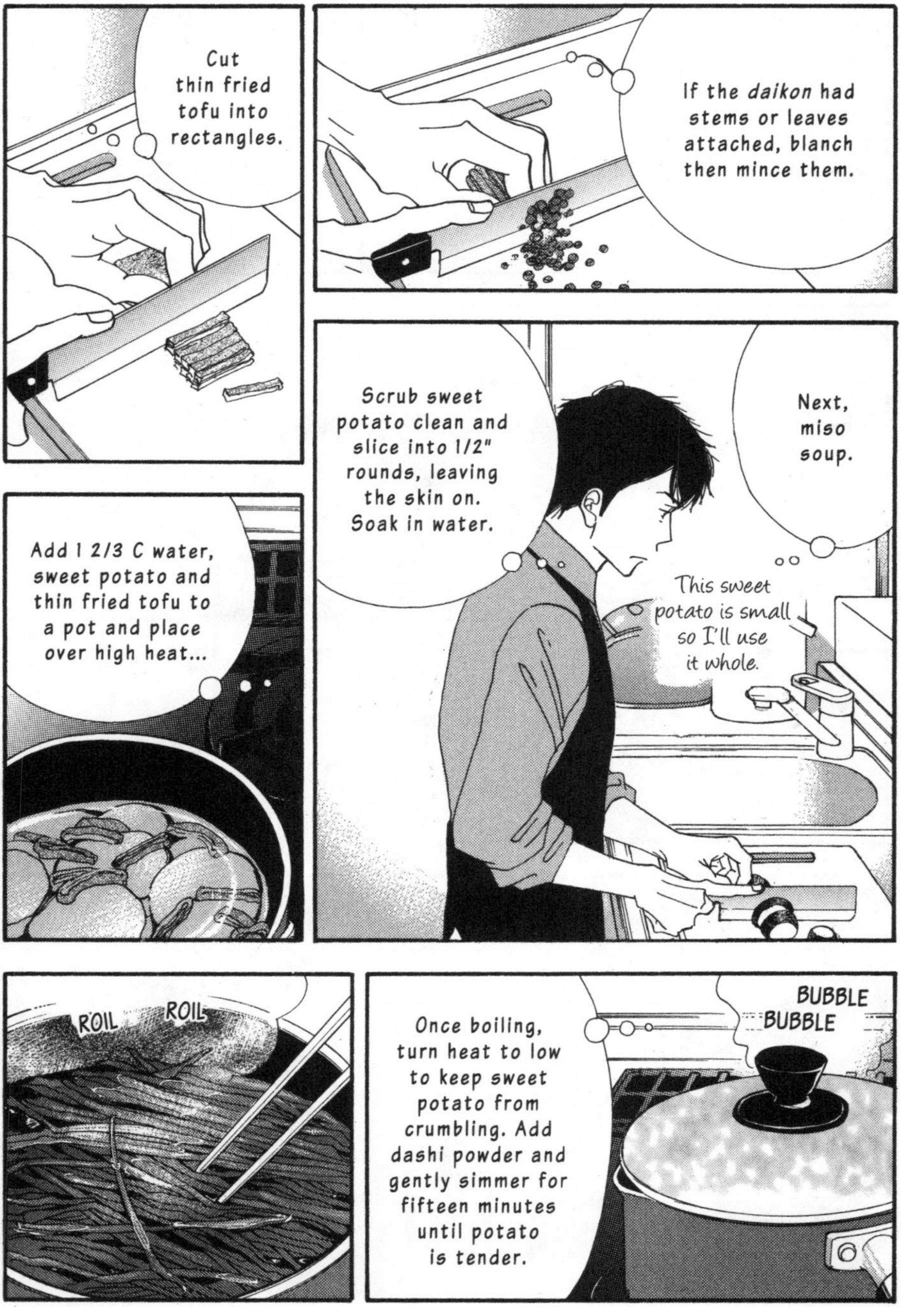
If the *daikon* had stems or leaves attached, blanch then mince them.
Cut thin fried tofu into rectangles.
Next, miso soup.
Scrub sweet potato clean and slice into 1/2" rounds, leaving the skin on. Soak in water.
This sweet potato is small so I'll use it whole.
Add 1 2/3 C water, sweet potato and thin fried tofu to a pot and place over high heat...
BUBBLE BUBBLE
Once boiling, turn heat to low to keep sweet potato from crumbling. Add dashi powder and gently simmer for fifteen minutes until potato is tender.
ROIL ROIL

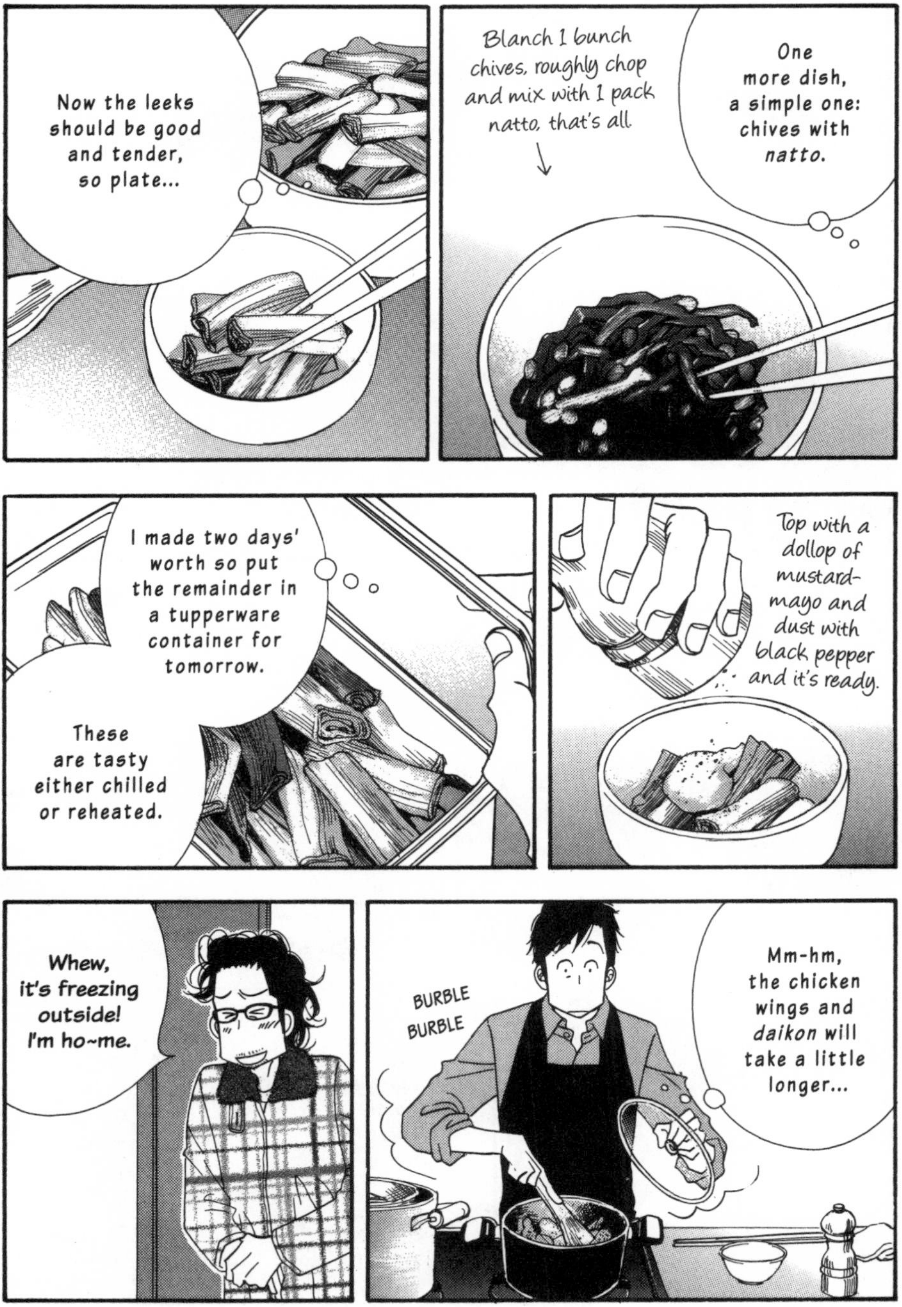
One more dish, a simple one: chives with *natto*.
Blanch 1 bunch chives, roughly chop and mix with 1 pack natto, that's all.
Now the leeks should be good and tender, so plate...
Top with a dollop of mustard-mayo and dust with black pepper and it's ready.
I made two days' worth so put the remainder in a tupperware container for tomorrow.
These are tasty either chilled or reheated.
Mm-hm, the chicken wings and *daikon* will take a little longer...
BURBLE
BURBLE
Whew, it's freezing outside! I'm ho~me.

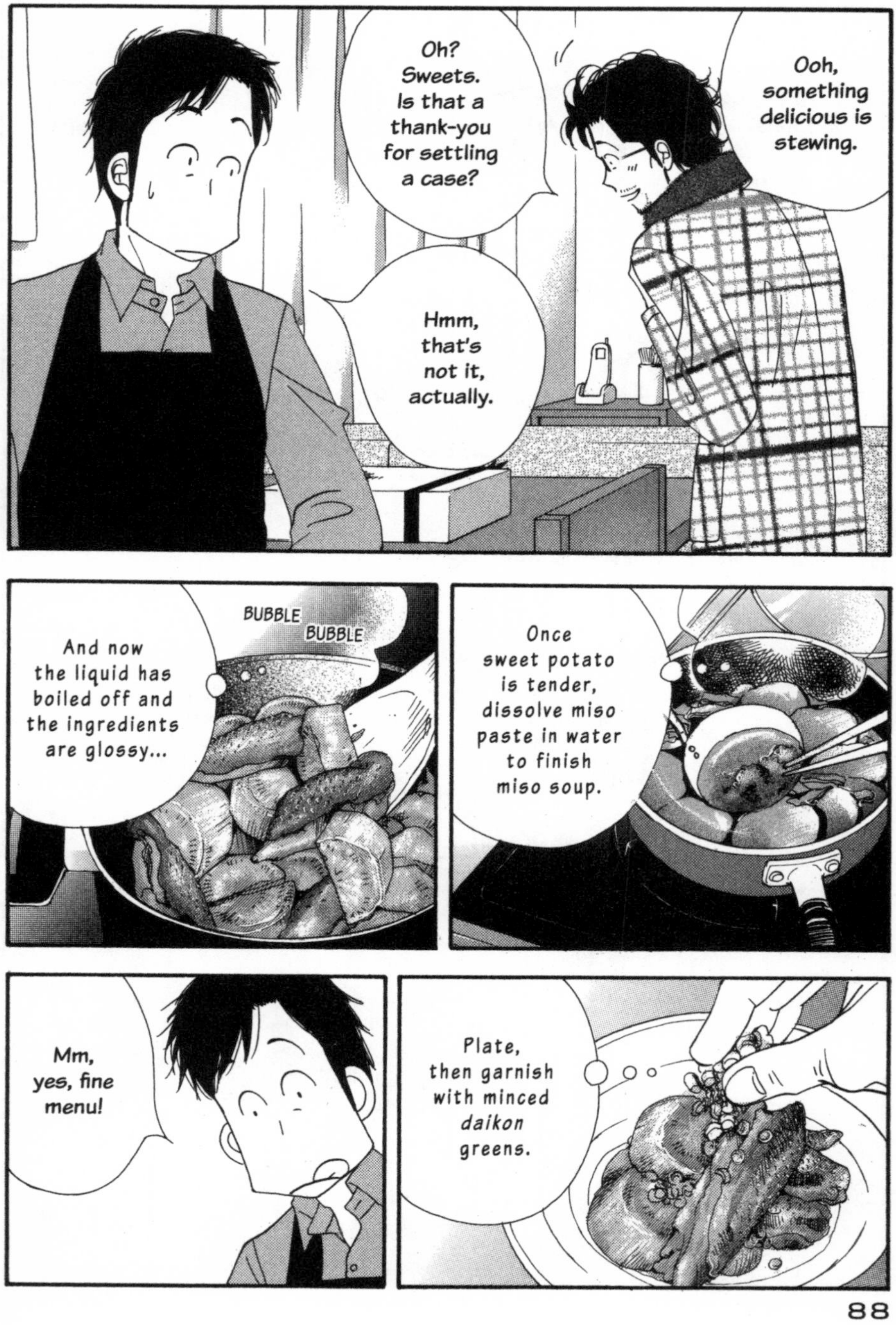
Ooh, something delicious is stewing.
Oh? Sweets. Is that a thank-you for settling a case?
Hmm, that's not it, actually.
Once sweet potato is tender, dissolve miso paste in water to finish miso soup.
BUBBLE BUBBLE
And now the liquid has boiled off and the ingredients are glossy...
Plate, then garnish with minced *daikon* greens.
Mm, yes, fine menu!

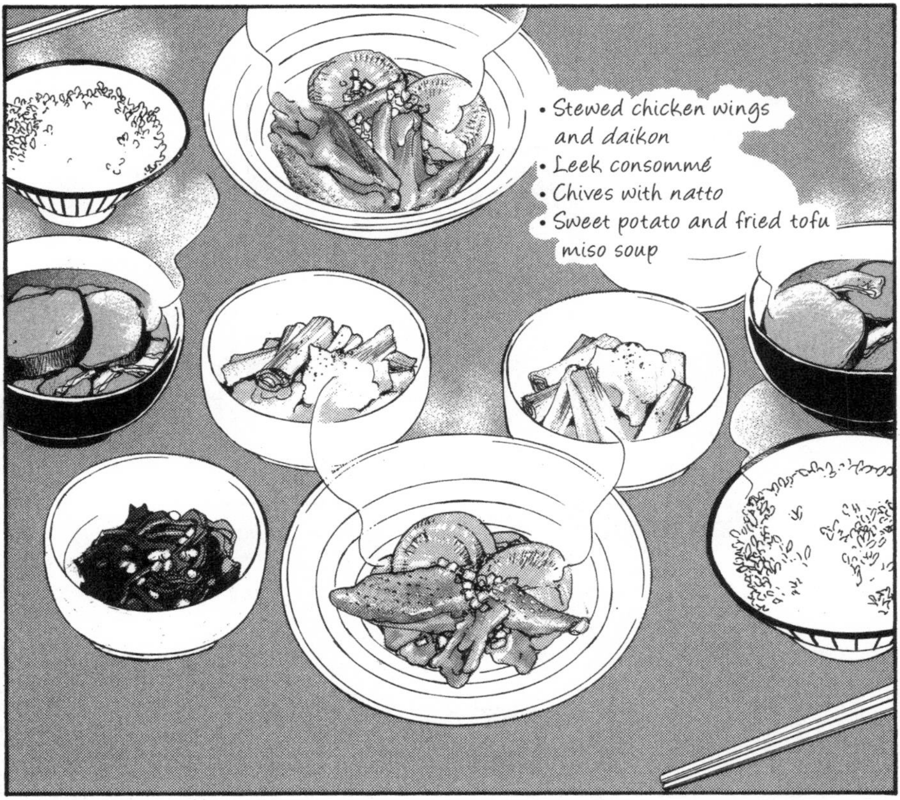
• Stewed chicken wings and daikon
• Leek consommé
• Chives with natto
• Sweet potato and fried tofu miso soup

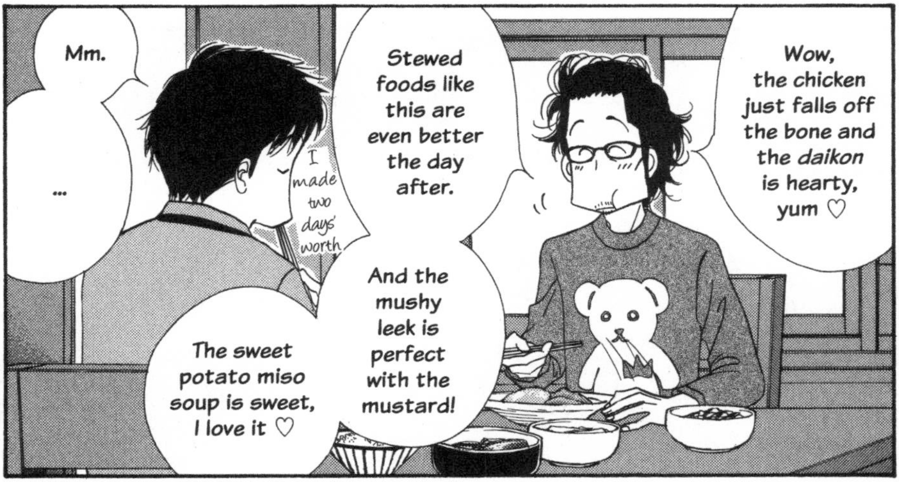
Wow, the chicken just falls off the bone and the *daikon* is hearty, yum ♡
Stewed foods like this are even better the day after.
I made two days' worth
Mm.
...
And the mushy leek is perfect with the mustard!
The sweet potato miso soup is sweet, I love it ♡

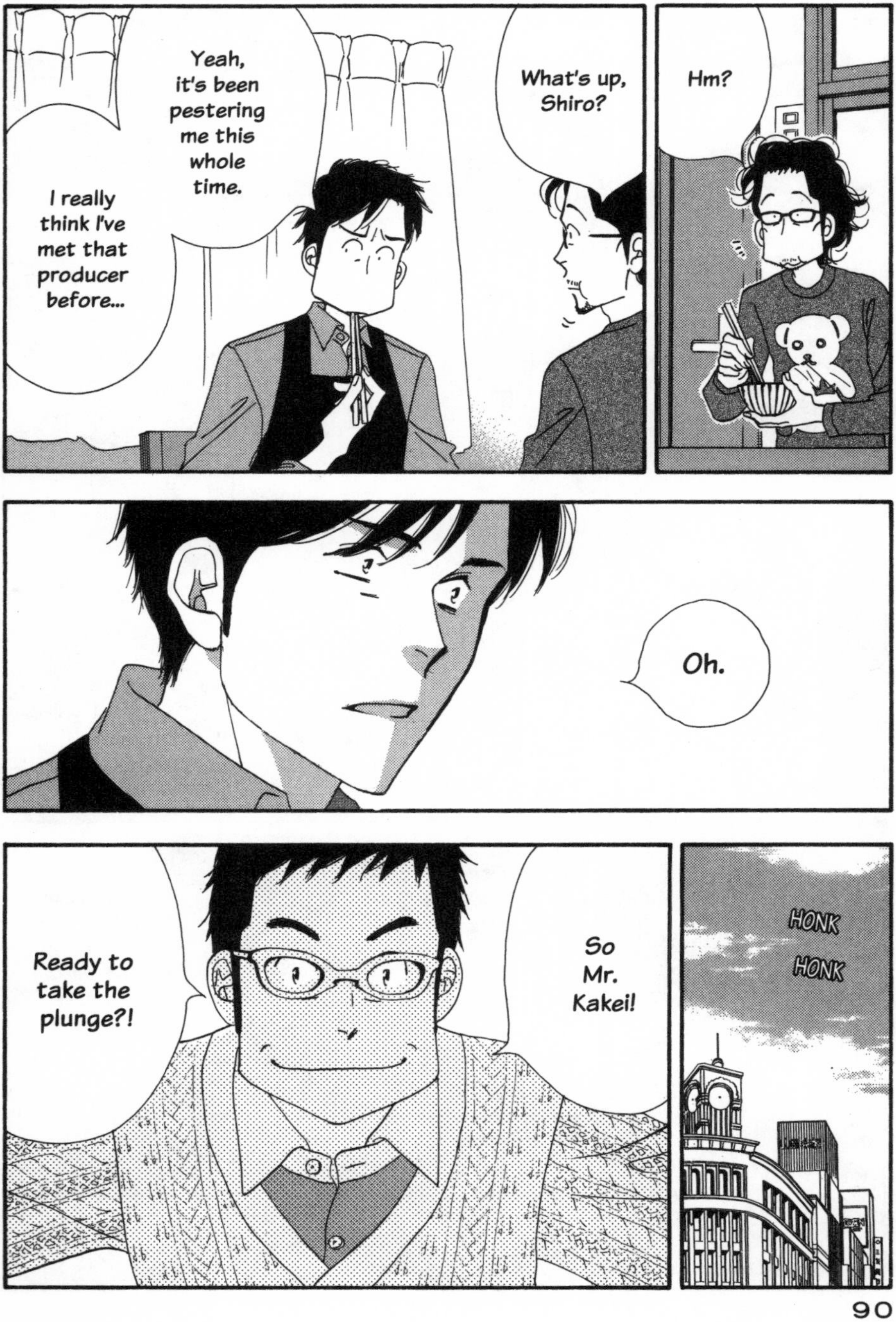
Hm?
What's up, Shiro?
Yeah, it's been pestering me this whole time.
I really think I've met that producer before...
Oh.
HONK
HONK
So Mr. Kakei!
Ready to take the plunge?!

Hey, hey, hey, c'mon...

I won't go on TV.

Mr. Abiko, you and I met several years ago...

in Ni-Chome.

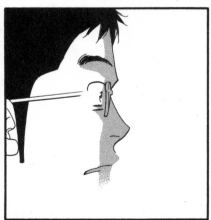

You're one of us, aren't you.

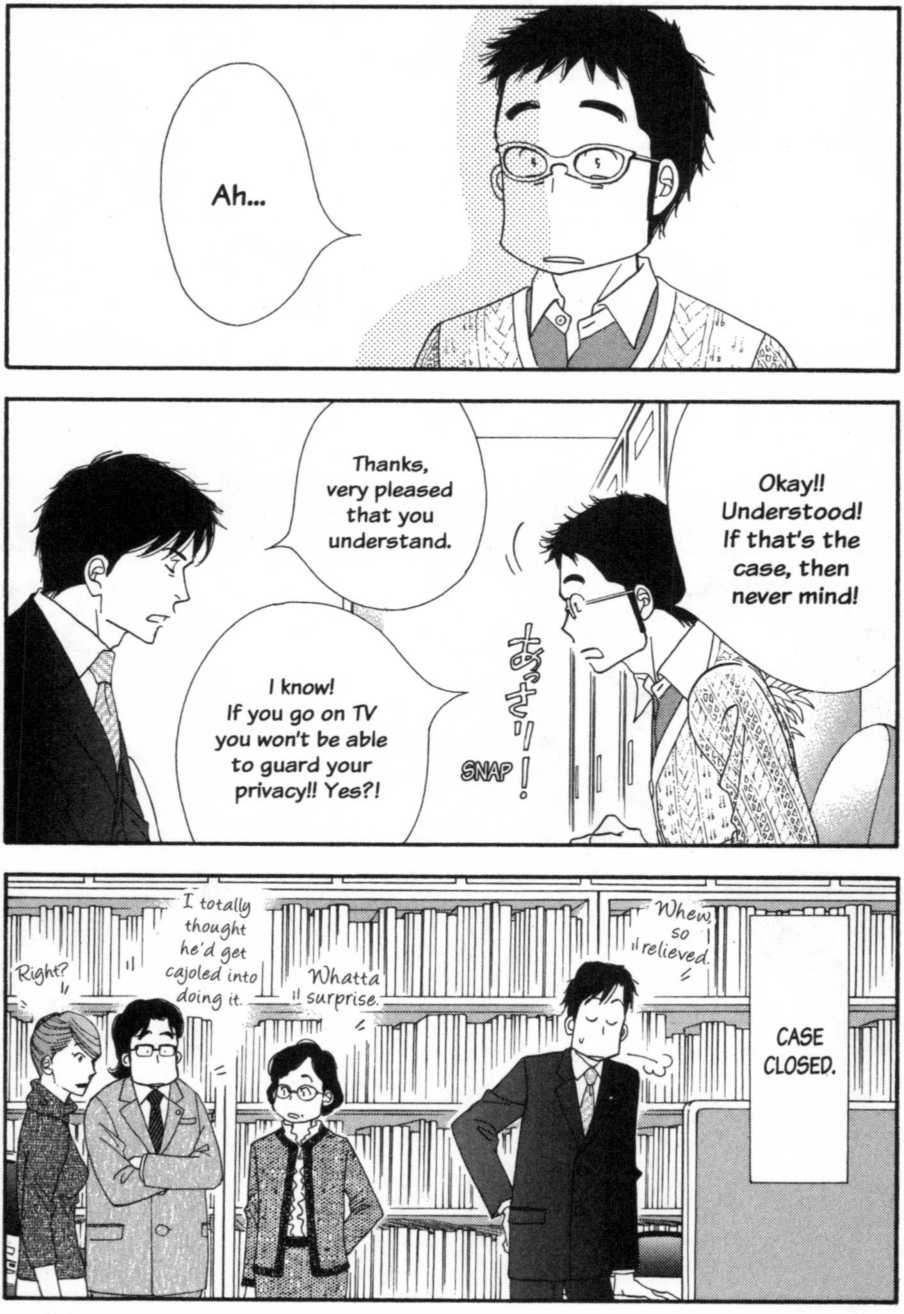
Ah...
Okay!! Understood! If that's the case, then never mind!
あっさり!
SNAP
Thanks, very pleased that you understand.
I know! If you go on TV you won't be able to guard your privacy!! Yes?!
CASE CLOSED.
Whew, so relieved.
Whatta surprise.
I totally thought he'd get cajoled into doing it.
Right?

#29 END

It was omitted since the menu included leek consommé, but you can top the stewed chicken wings and *daikon* with finely sliced pieces of **white leek**.
Also try garnishing with **julienned citrus peel**.

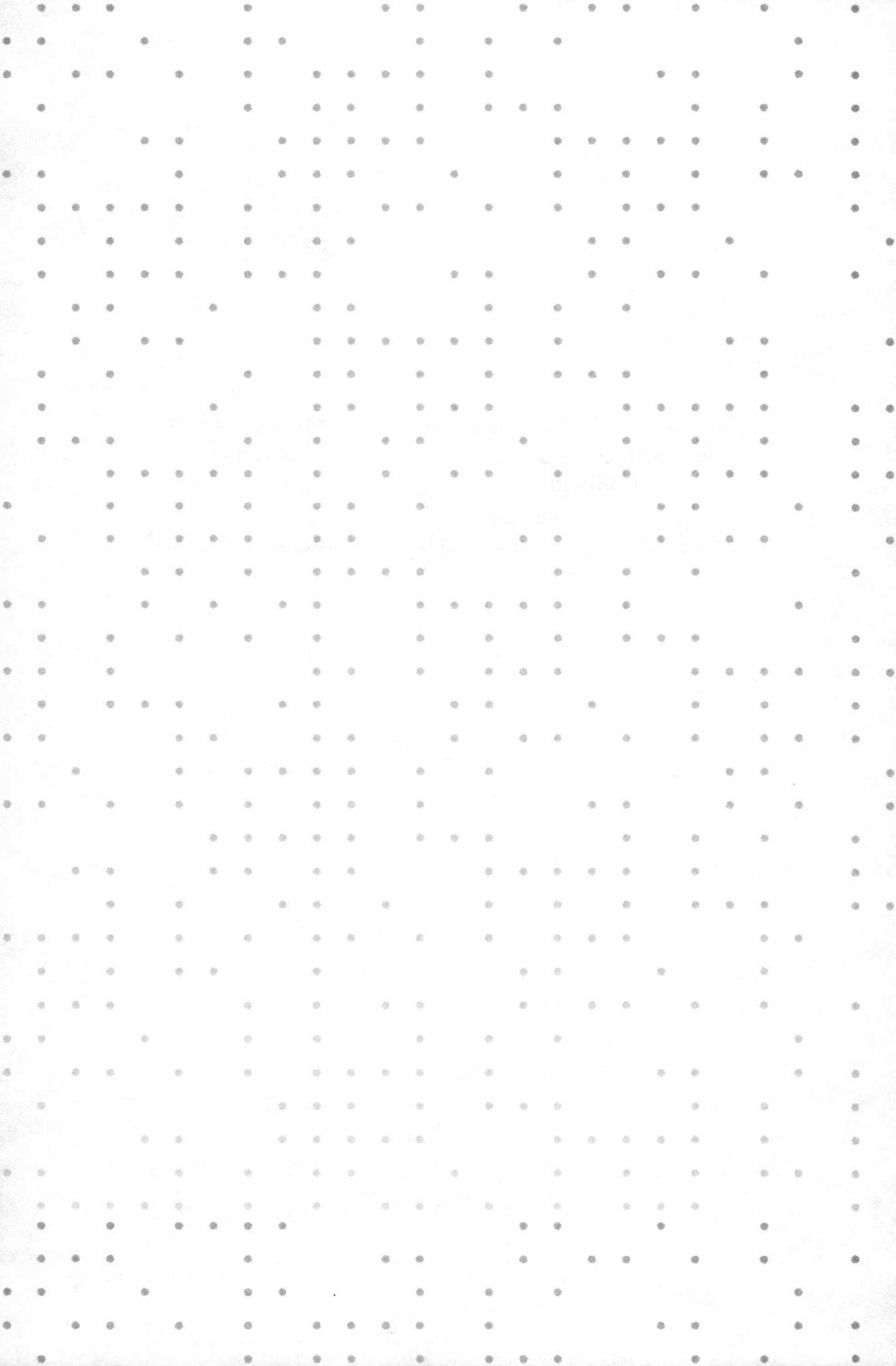

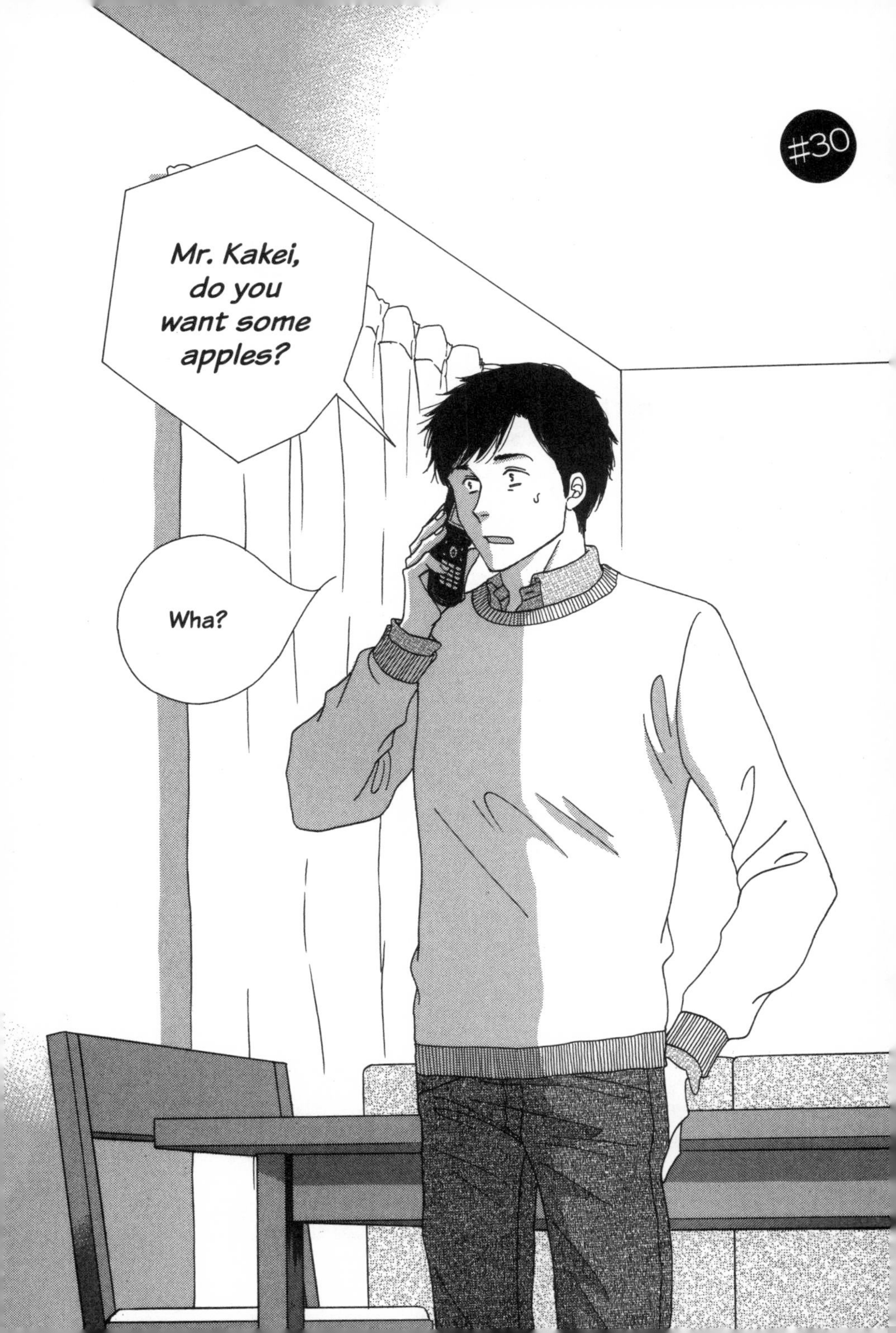
#30
Mr. Kakei, do you want some apples?
Wha?

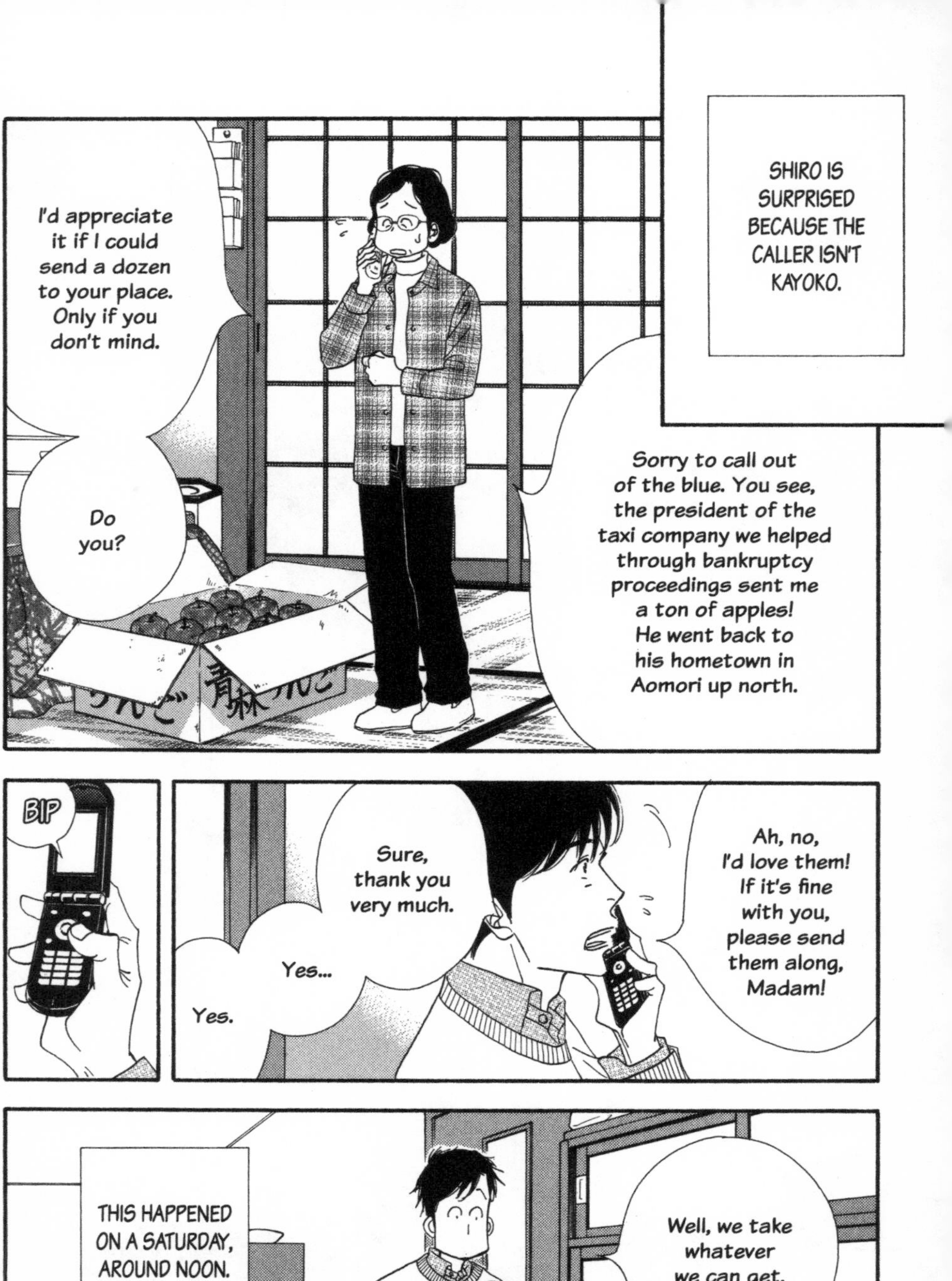
SHIRO IS SURPRISED BECAUSE THE CALLER ISN'T KAYOKO.
Sorry to call out of the blue. You see, the president of the taxi company we helped through bankruptcy proceedings sent me a ton of apples! He went back to his hometown in Aomori up north.
I'd appreciate it if I could send a dozen to your place. Only if you don't mind.
Do you?
Ah, no, I'd love them! If it's fine with you, please send them along, Madam!
Sure, thank you very much.
Yes...
Yes.
BIP
Well, we take whatever we can get.
THIS HAPPENED ON A SATURDAY, AROUND NOON.

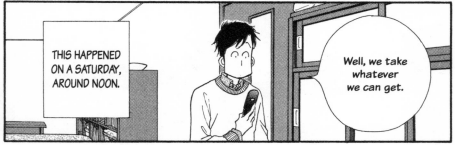

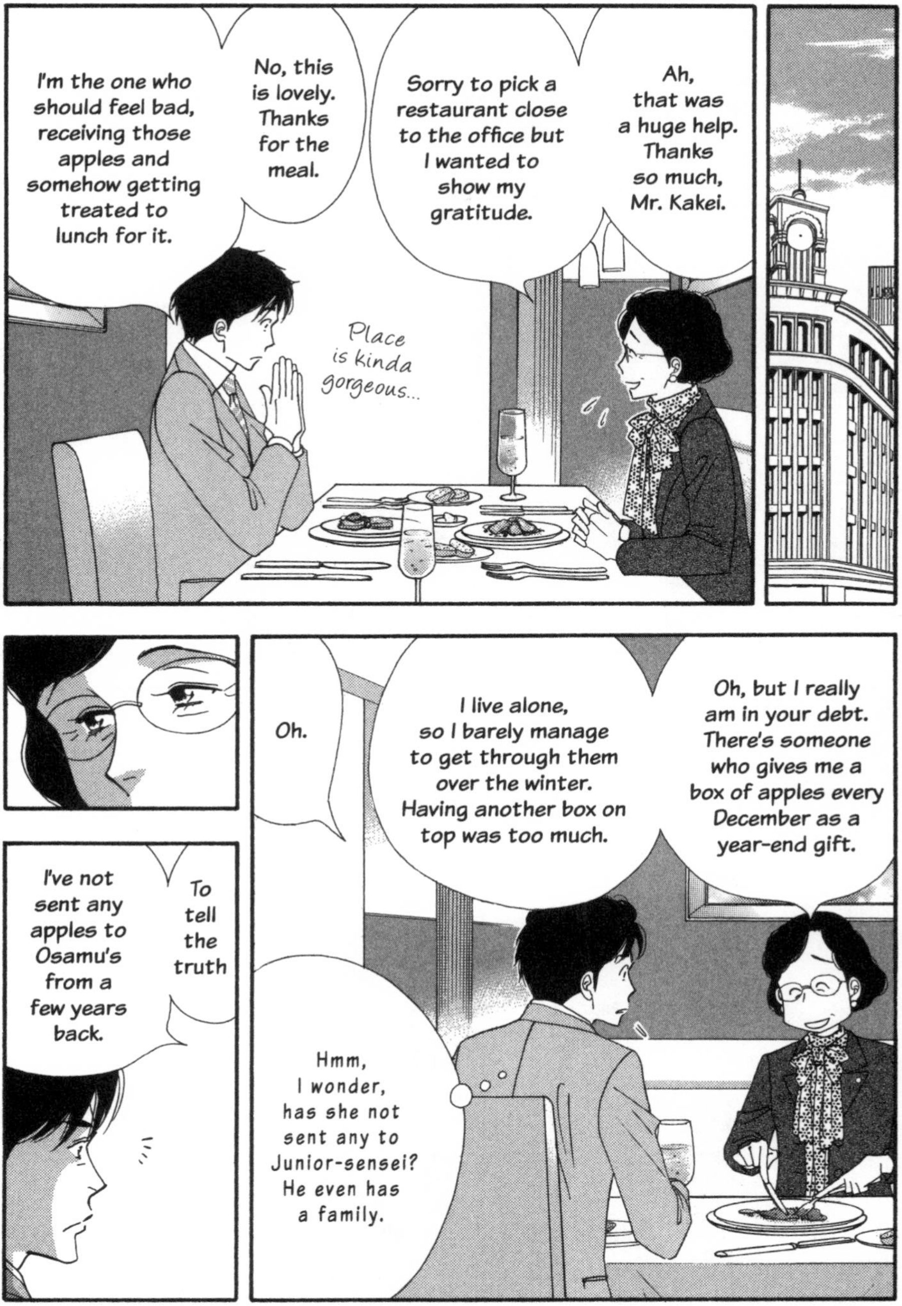
Ah, that was a huge help. Thanks so much, Mr. Kakei.
Sorry to pick a restaurant close to the office but I wanted to show my gratitude.
No, this is lovely. Thanks for the meal.
I'm the one who should feel bad, receiving those apples and somehow getting treated to lunch for it.
Place is kinda gorgeous...
Oh, but I really am in your debt. There's someone who gives me a box of apples every December as a year-end gift.
I live alone, so I barely manage to get through them over the winter. Having another box on top was too much.
Oh.
Hmm, I wonder, has she not sent any to Junior-sensei? He even has a family.
To tell the truth
I've not sent any apples to Osamu's from a few years back.

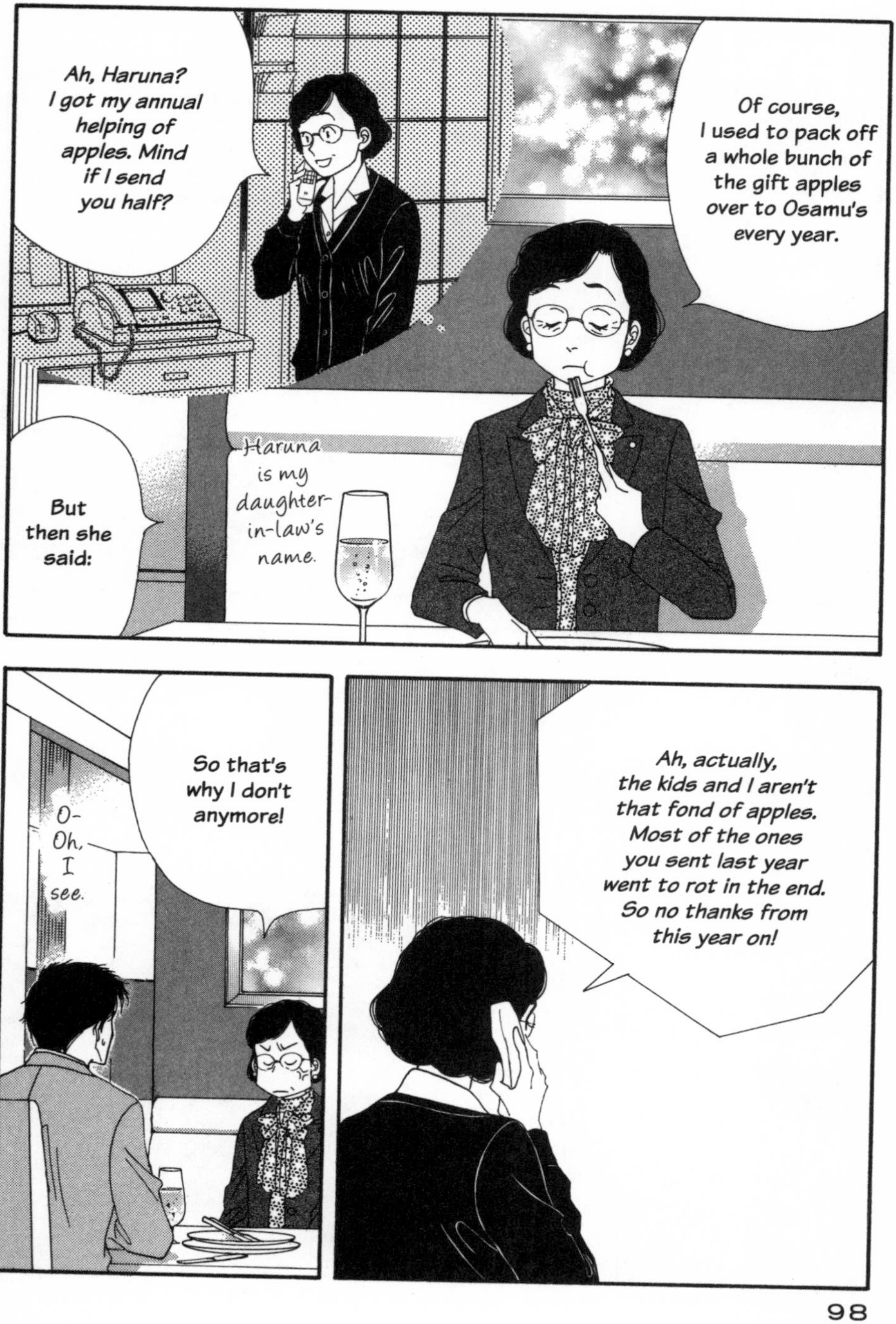

Of course, I used to pack off a whole bunch of the gift apples over to Osamu's every year.
Ah, Haruna? I got my annual helping of apples. Mind if I send you half?
Haruna is my daughter-in-law's name.
But then she said:
Ah, actually, the kids and I aren't that fond of apples. Most of the ones you sent last year went to rot in the end. So no thanks from this year on!
So that's why I don't anymore!
O-Oh, I see.

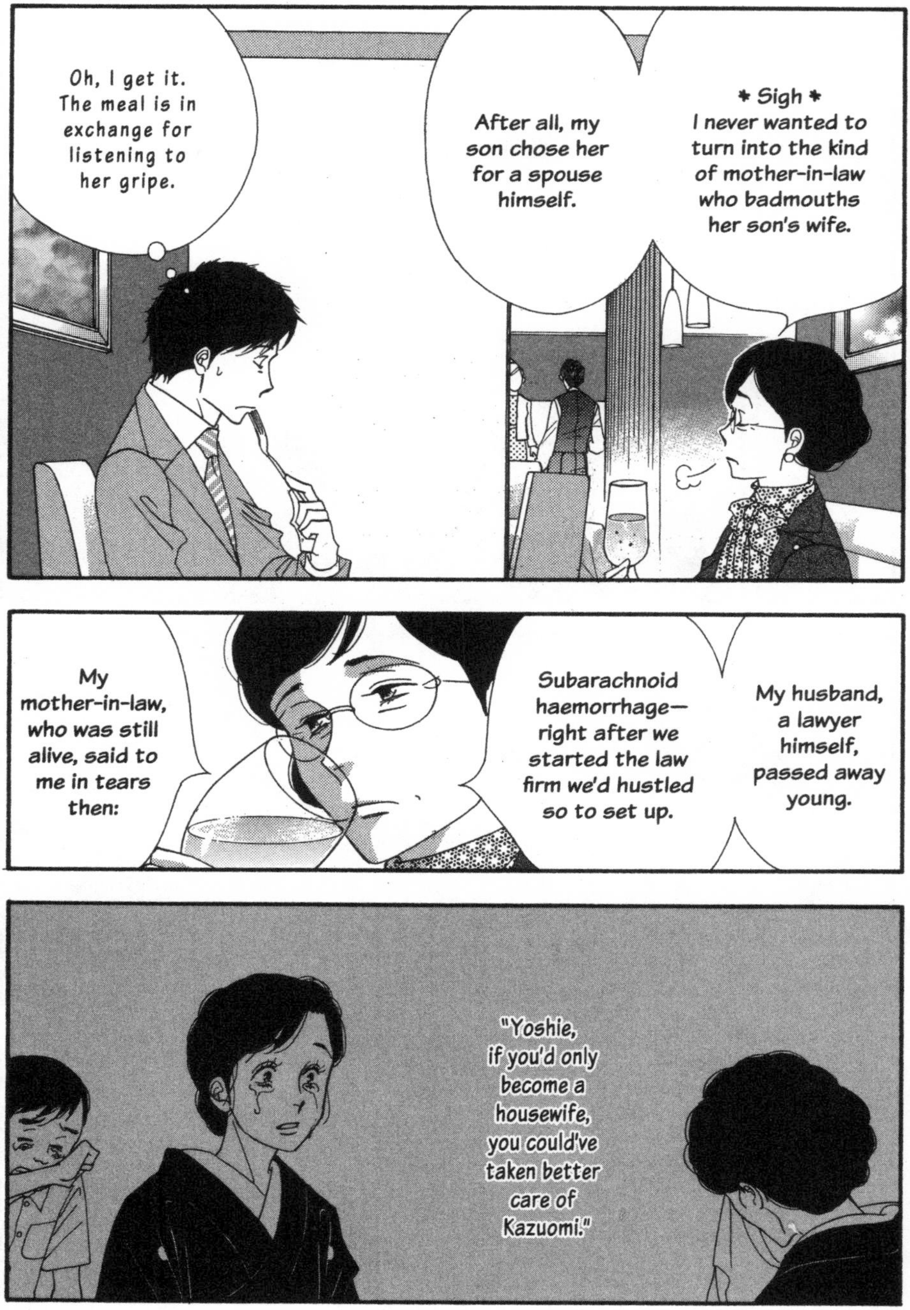
* Sigh * I never wanted to turn into the kind of mother-in-law who badmouths her son's wife.
After all, my son chose her for a spouse himself.
Oh, I get it. The meal is in exchange for listening to her gripe.
My husband, a lawyer himself, passed away young.
Subarachnoid haemorrhage—right after we started the law firm we'd hustled so to set up.
My mother-in-law, who was still alive, said to me in tears then:
"Yoshie, if you'd only become a housewife, you could've taken better care of Kazuomi."

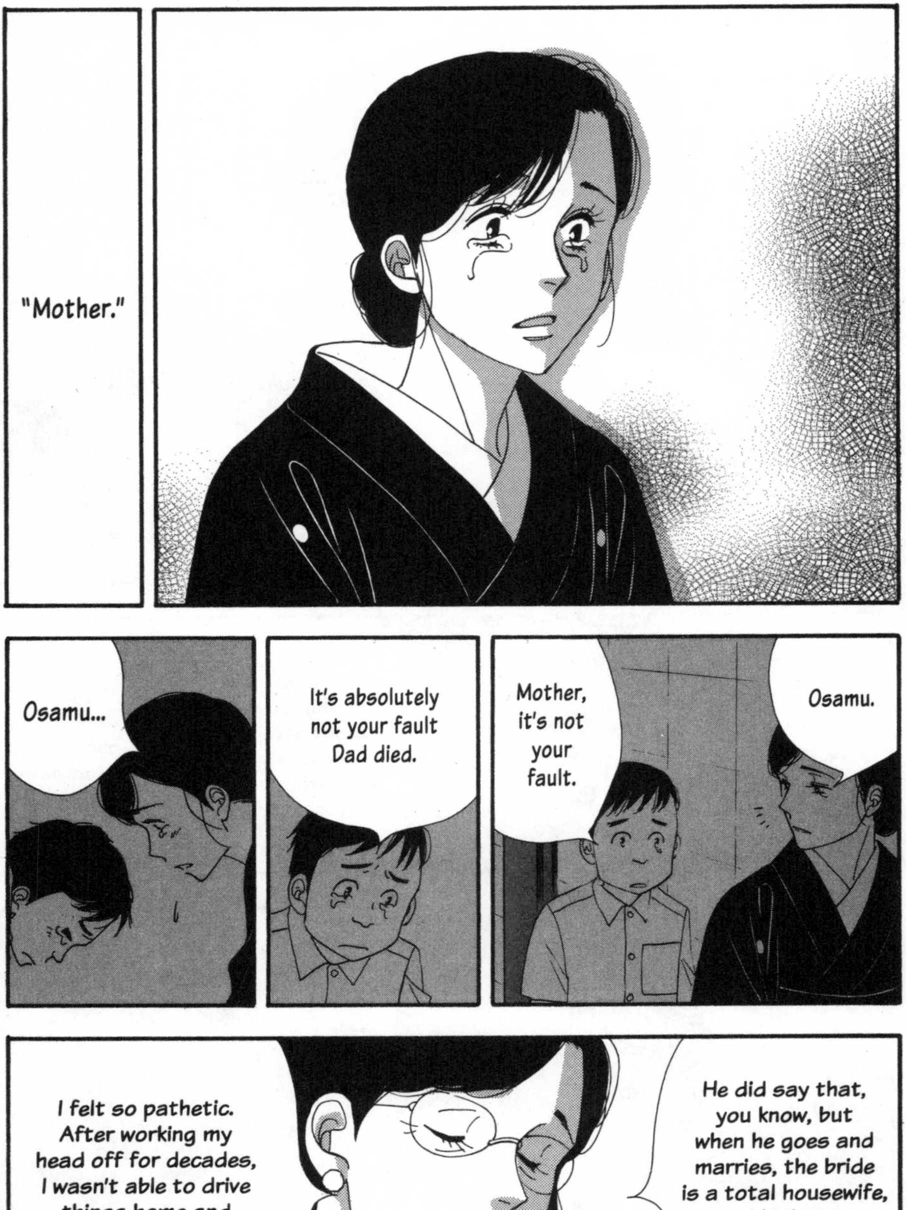
"Mother."
Osamu.
Mother, it's not your fault.
It's absolutely not your fault Dad died.
Osamu...
He did say that, you know, but when he goes and marries, the bride is a total housewife, and he leaves everything to her.
I felt so pathetic. After working my head off for decades, I wasn't able to drive things home and he's my own son.

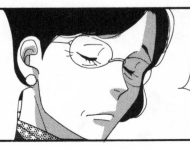

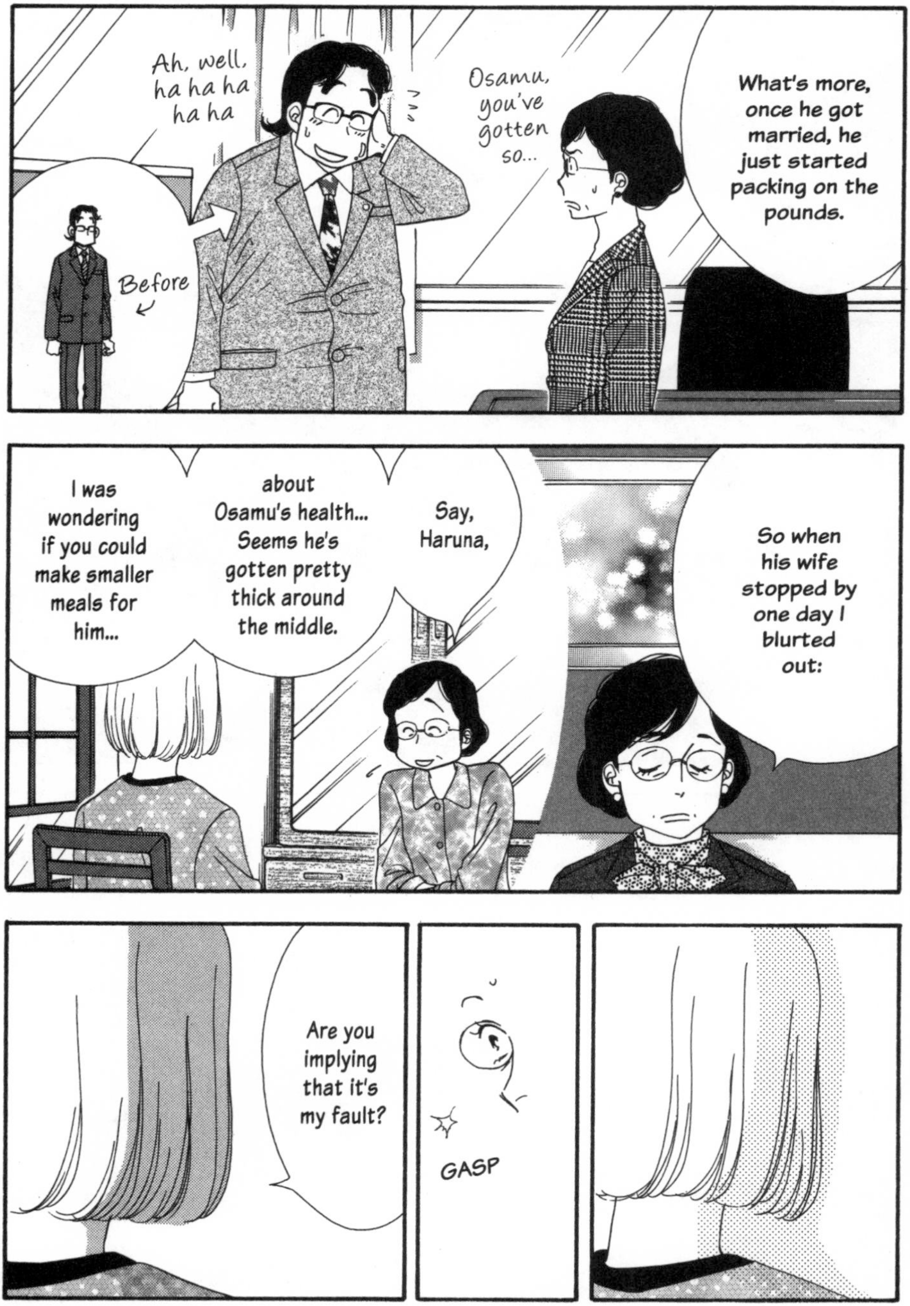
What's more, once he got married, he just started packing on the pounds.
Osamu, you've gotten so...
Ah, well, ha ha ha ha ha
Before
So when his wife stopped by one day I blurted out:
Say, Haruna,
about Osamu's health... Seems he's gotten pretty thick around the middle.
I was wondering if you could make smaller meals for him...
GASP
Are you implying that it's my fault?

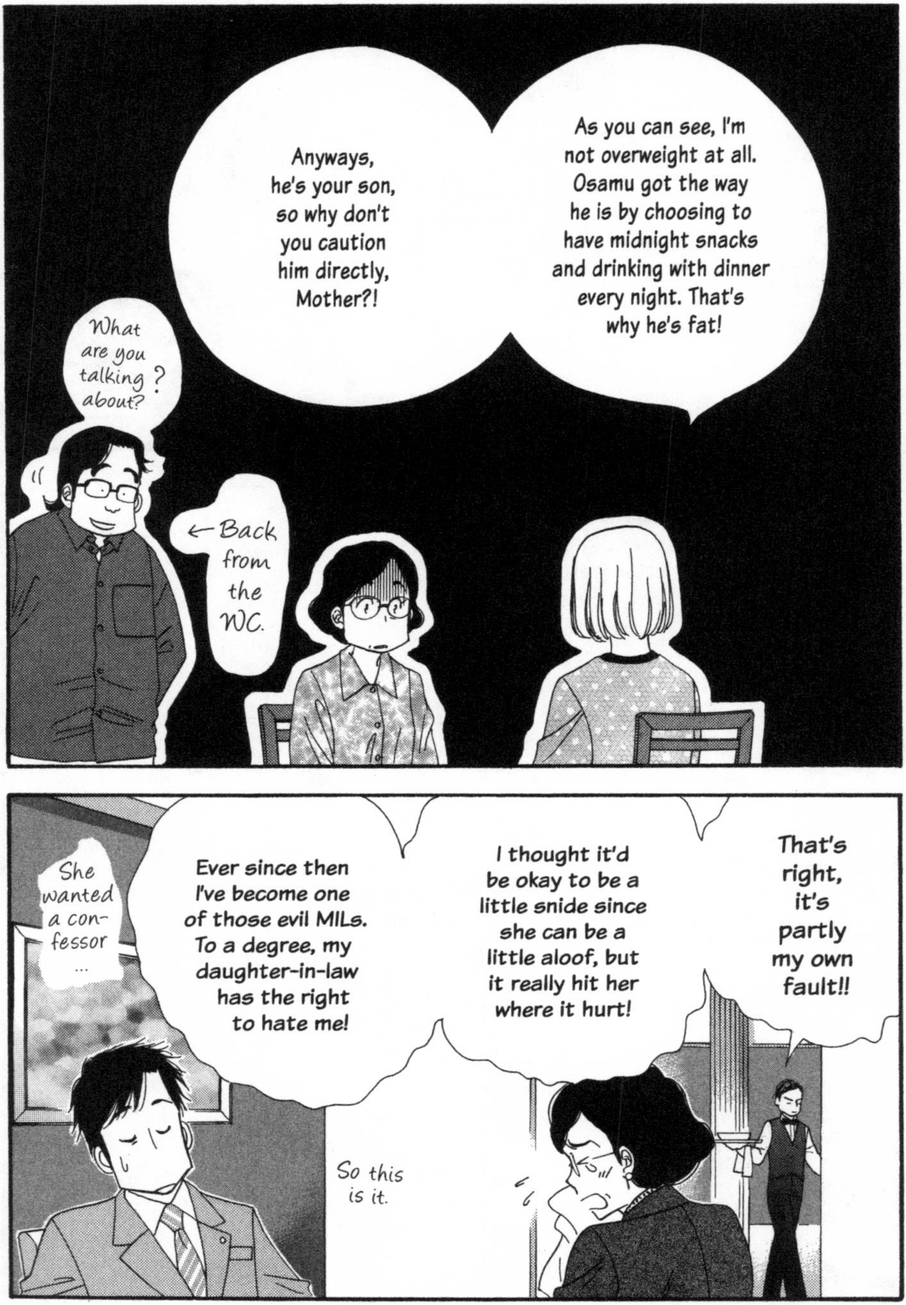
As you can see, I'm not overweight at all. Osamu got the way he is by choosing to have midnight snacks and drinking with dinner every night. That's why he's fat!
Anyways, he's your son, so why don't you caution him directly, Mother?!
What are you talking about? ?
←Back from the WC.
That's right, it's partly my own fault!!
I thought it'd be okay to be a little snide since she can be a little aloof, but it really hit her where it hurt!
Ever since then I've become one of those evil MILs. To a degree, my daughter-in-law has the right to hate me!
She wanted a confessor ...
So this is it.

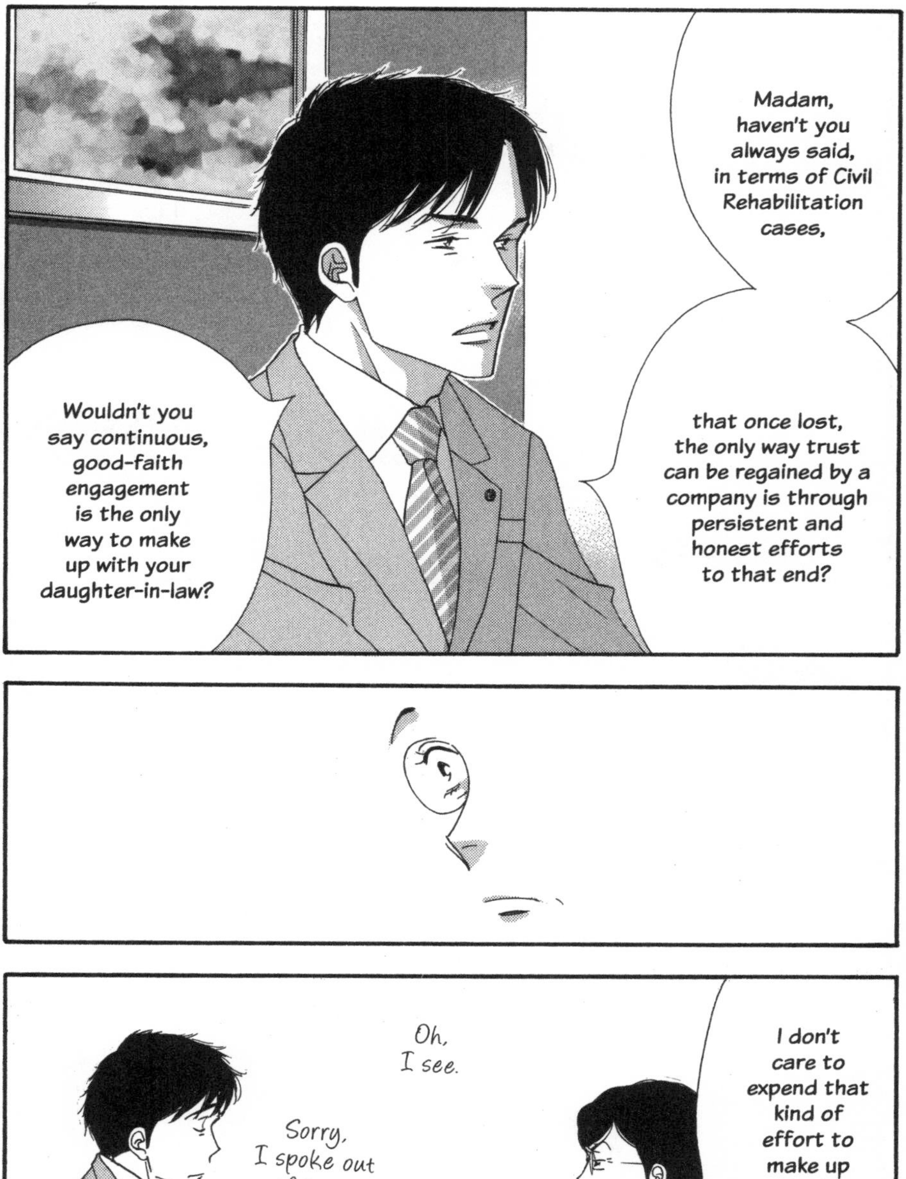
Madam, haven't you always said, in terms of Civil Rehabilitation cases,
that once lost, the only way trust can be regained by a company is through persistent and honest efforts to that end?
Wouldn't you say continuous, good-faith engagement is the only way to make up with your daughter-in-law?
I don't care to expend that kind of effort to make up with that woman!
Oh, I see.
Sorry, I spoke out of turn. Very sorry.

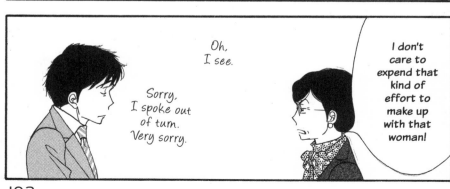

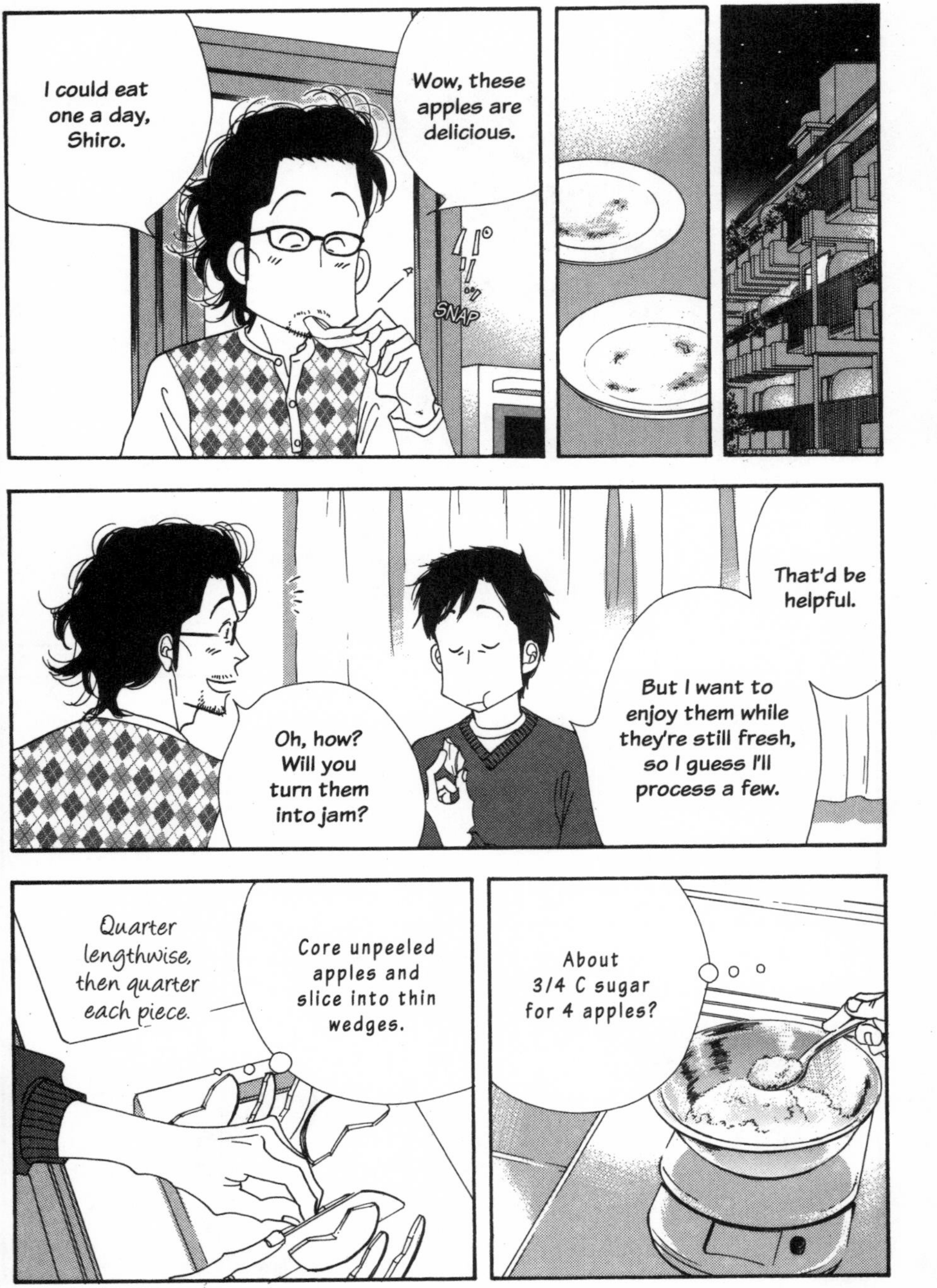
Wow, these apples are delicious.
SNAP
I could eat one a day, Shiro.
That'd be helpful.
But I want to enjoy them while they're still fresh, so I guess I'll process a few.
Oh, how? Will you turn them into jam?
About 3/4 C sugar for 4 apples?
Core unpeeled apples and slice into thin wedges.
Quarter lengthwise, then quarter each piece.

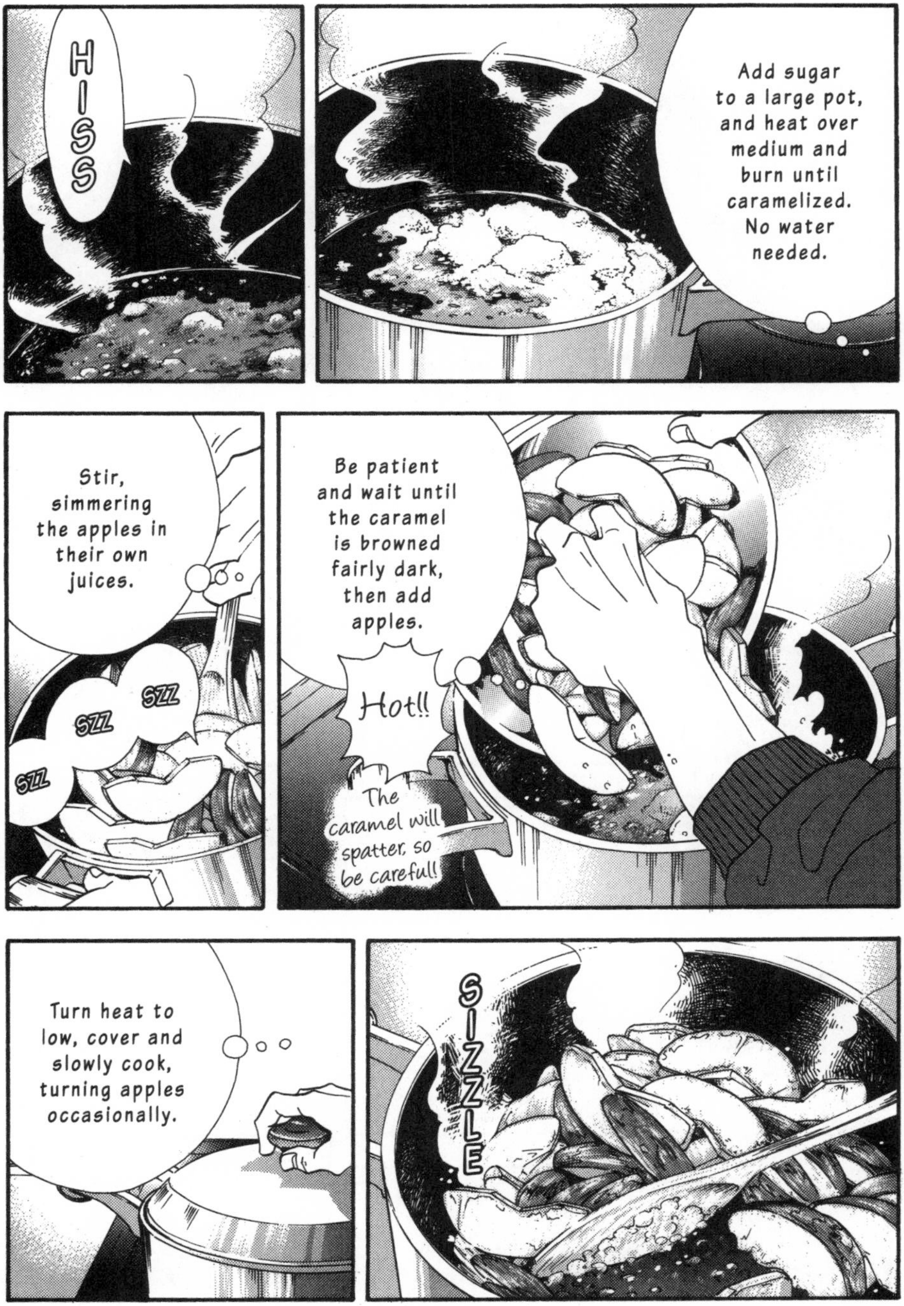
Add sugar to a large pot, and heat over medium and burn until caramelized. No water needed.
HISS
Be patient and wait until the caramel is browned fairly dark, then add apples.
Hot!!
The caramel will spatter, so be careful!
Stir, simmering the apples in their own juices.
SZZ
SZZ
SZZ
SIZZLE
Turn heat to low, cover and slowly cook, turning apples occasionally.

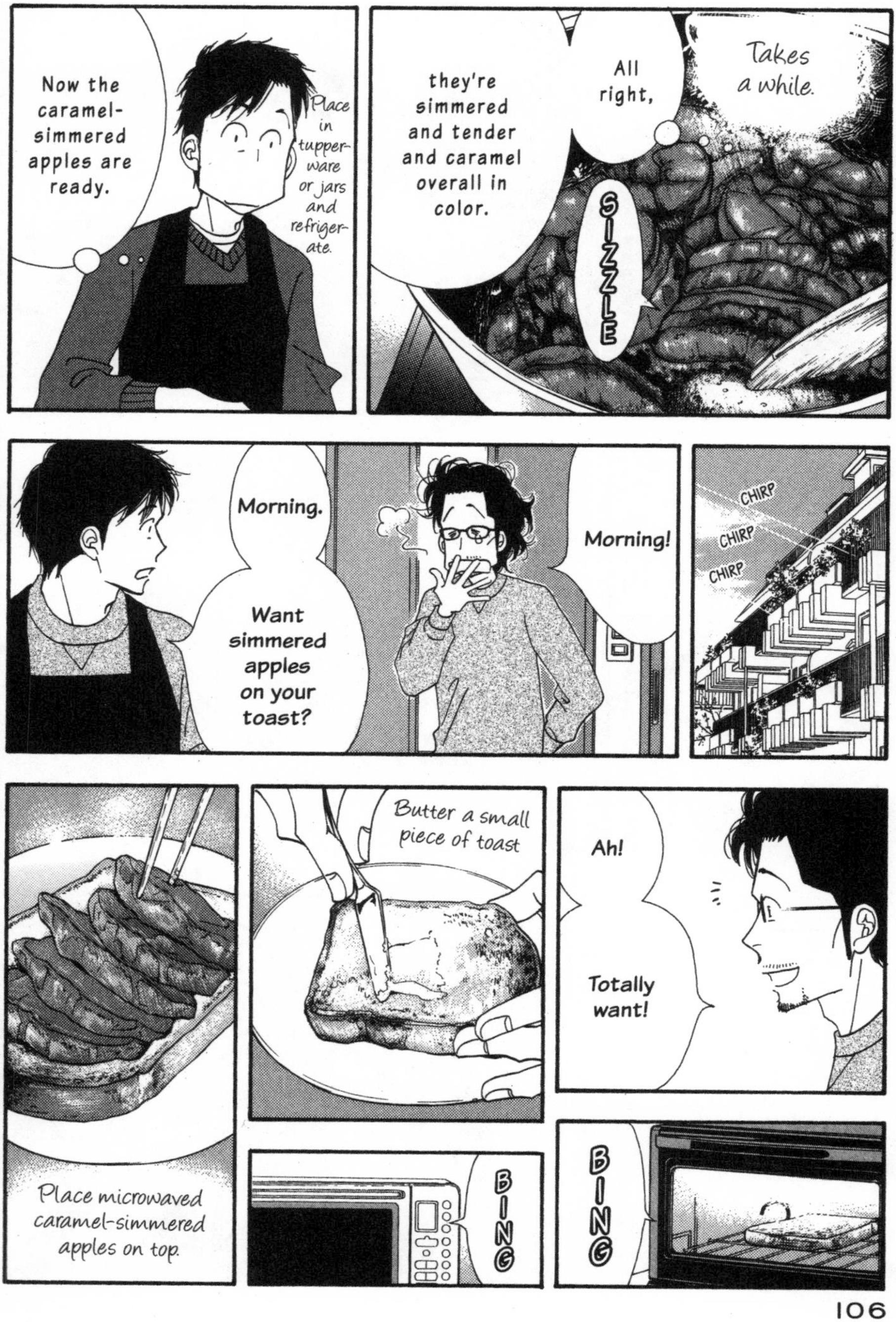
Takes a while.
All right,
they're simmered and tender and caramel overall in color.
SIZZLE
Place in tupperware or jars and refrigerate.
Now the caramel-simmered apples are ready.
CHIRP
CHIRP
CHIRP
Morning!
Morning.
Want simmered apples on your toast?
Ah!
Totally want!
BING
Butter a small piece of toast
BING
Place microwaved caramel-simmered apples on top.

Yaay!!

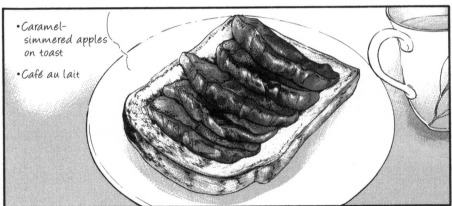

- Caramel-simmered apples on toast
- Café au lait

CRUNCH

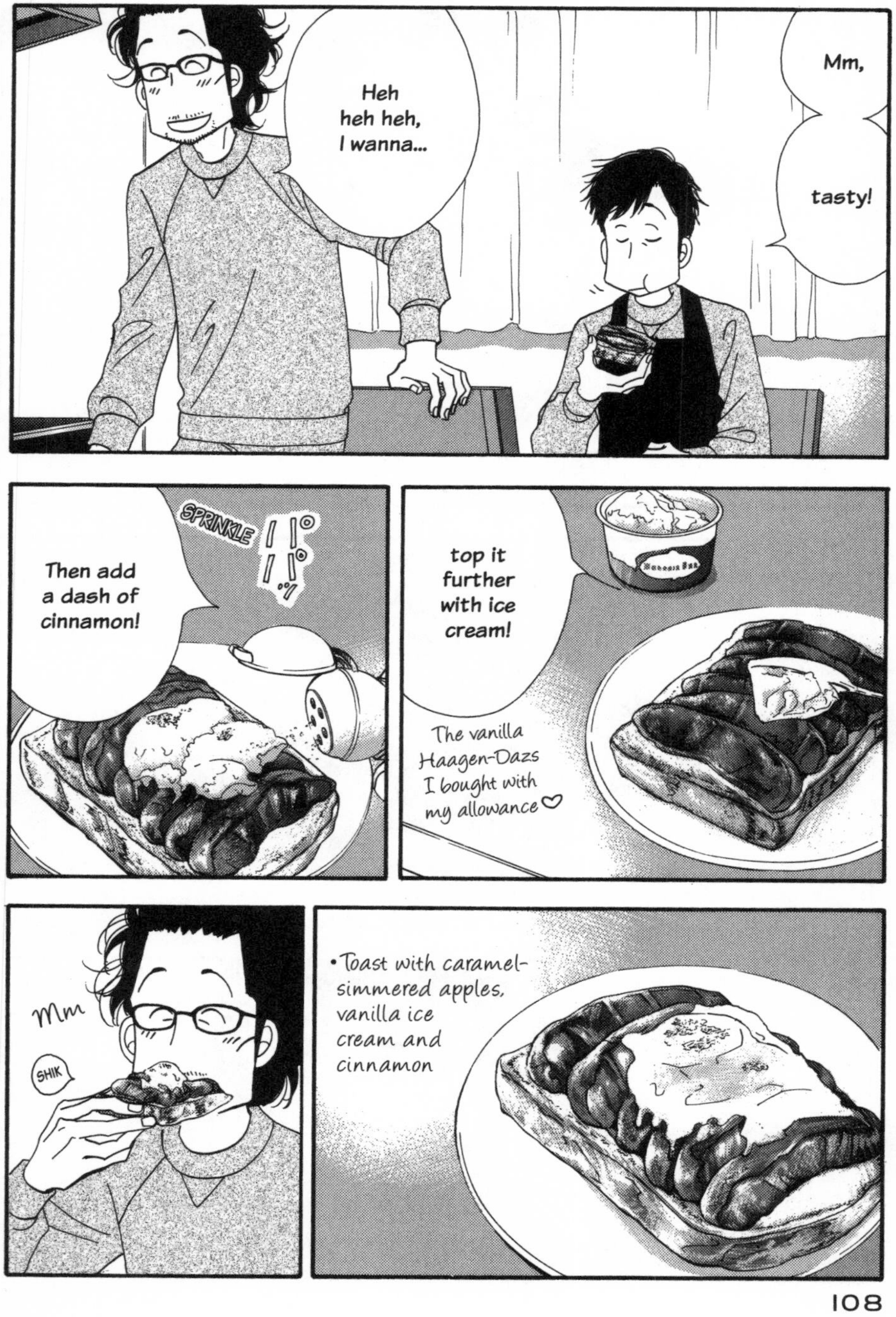
Mm, tasty!
Heh heh heh, I wanna...
top it further with ice cream!
The vanilla Haagen-Dazs I bought with my allowance ♡
SPRINKLE
Then add a dash of cinnamon!
•Toast with caramel-simmered apples, vanilla ice cream and cinnamon
Mm
SHIK

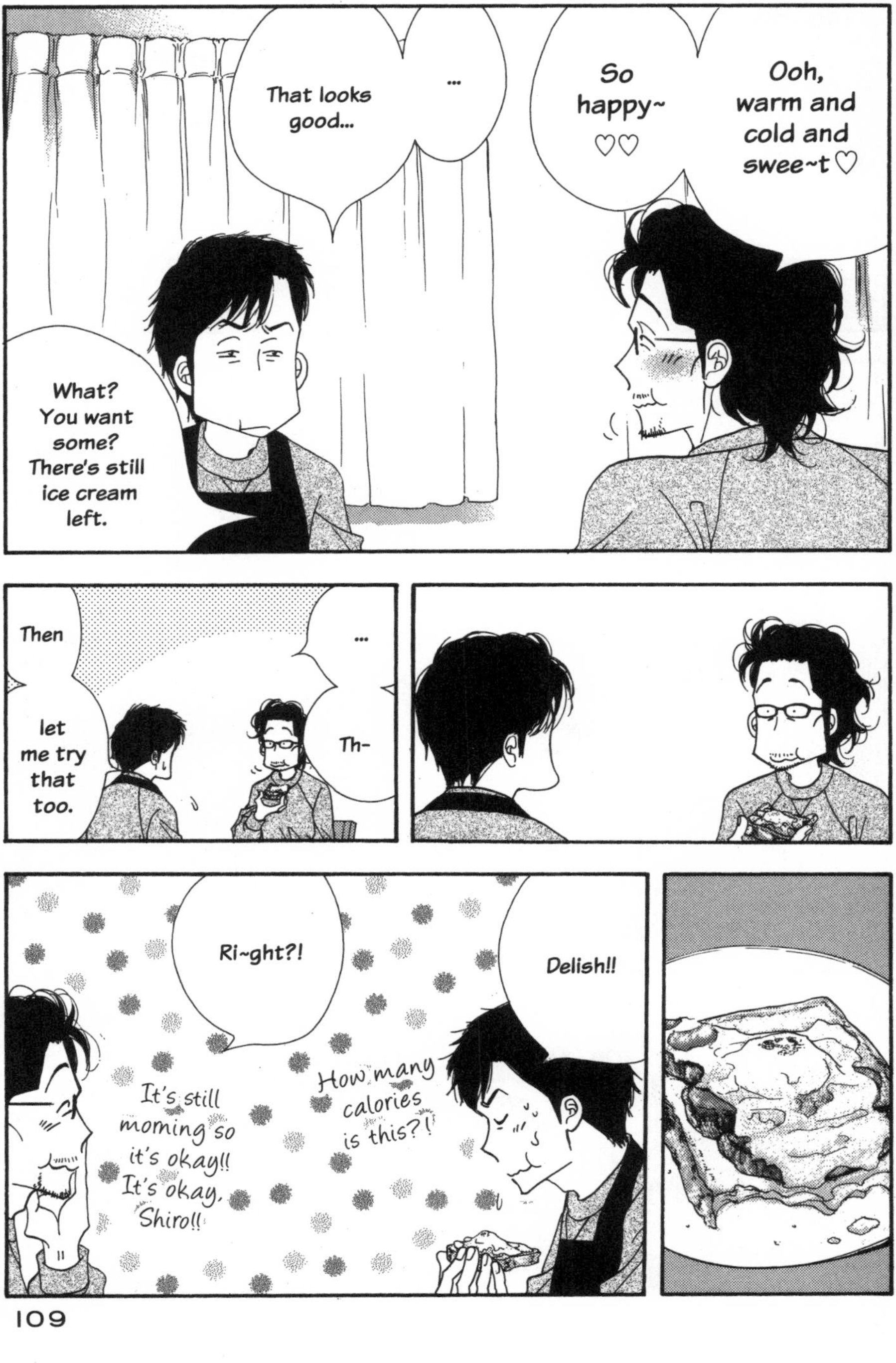
Ooh, warm and cold and swee~t♡
So happy~ ♡♡
...
That looks good...
What? You want some? There's still ice cream left.
...
Th-
Then
let me try that too.
Delish!!
How many calories is this?!
Ri~ght?!
It's still morning so it's okay!! It's okay, Shiro!!

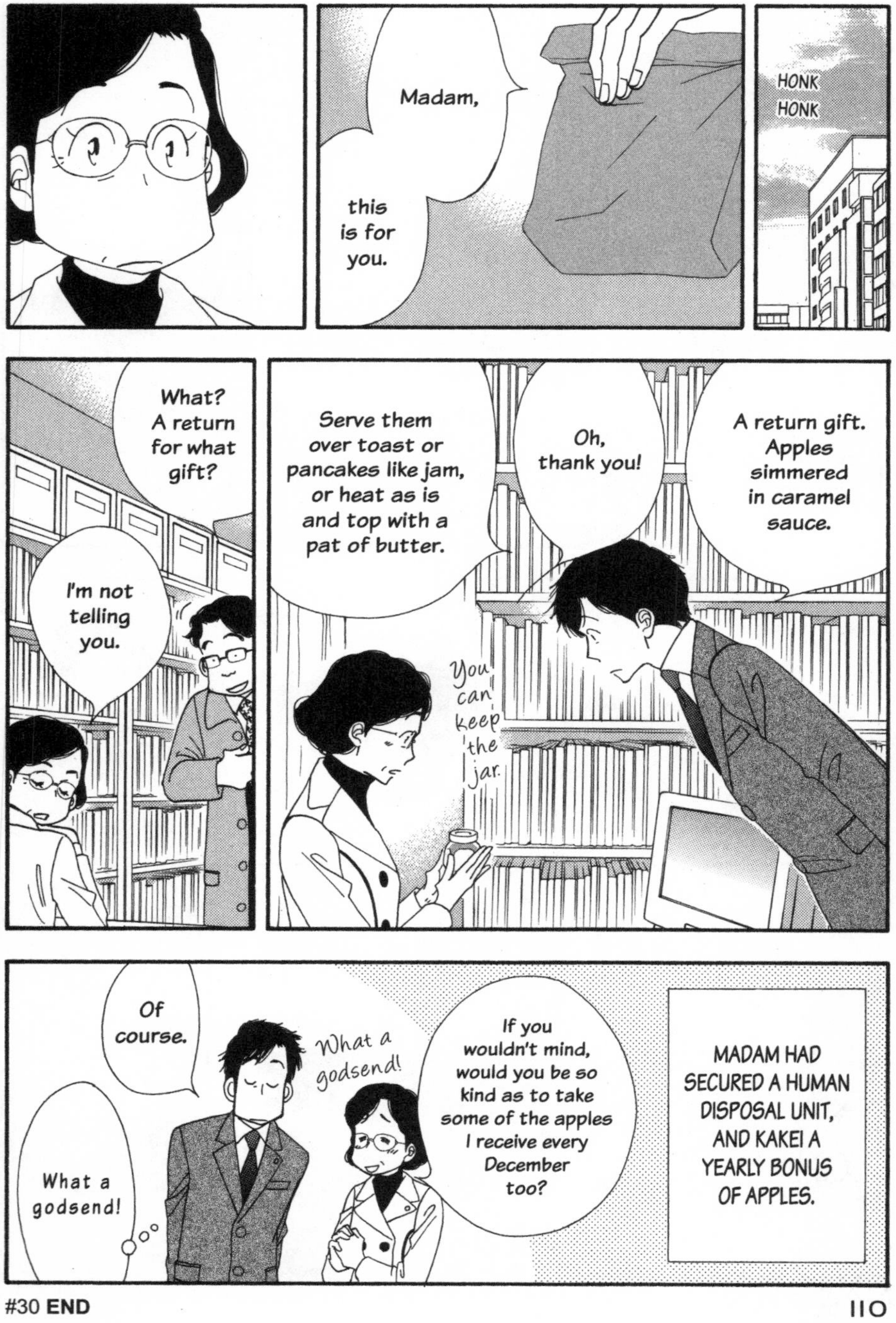
HONK
HONK
Madam,
this is for you.
A return gift. Apples simmered in caramel sauce.
Oh, thank you!
Serve them over toast or pancakes like jam, or heat as is and top with a pat of butter.
You can keep the jar.
What? A return for what gift?
I'm not telling you.
MADAM HAD SECURED A HUMAN DISPOSAL UNIT, AND KAKEI A YEARLY BONUS OF APPLES.
If you wouldn't mind, would you be so kind as to take some of the apples I receive every December too?
What a godsend!
Of course.
What a godsend!

You can reduce the amount of sugar down to **1/2 C per 4 apples,** although they won't last as long. Heating the sugar until dark brown will bring out the most caramel-like flavor.

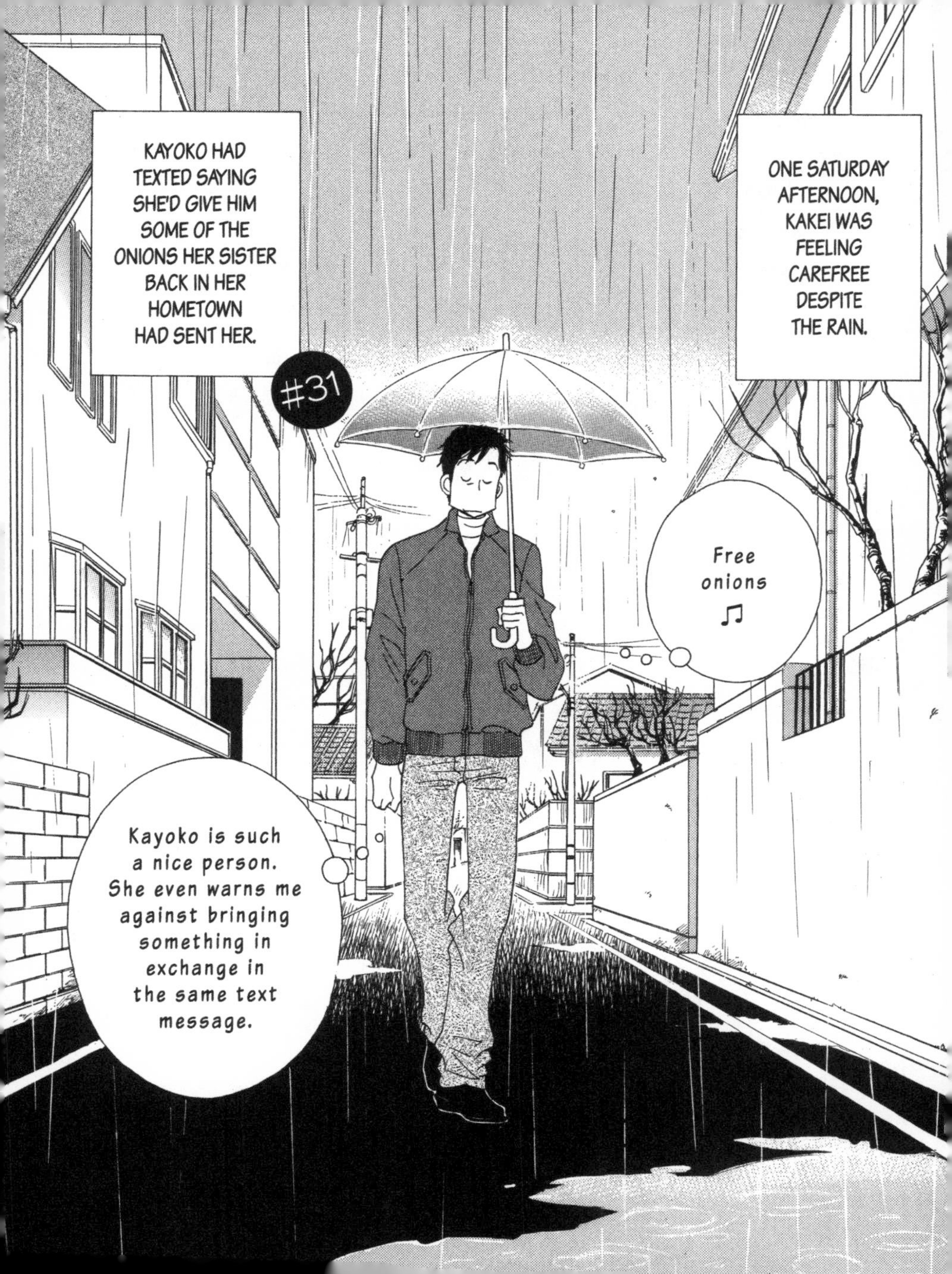
ONE SATURDAY AFTERNOON, KAKEI WAS FEELING CAREFREE DESPITE THE RAIN.
KAYOKO HAD TEXTED SAYING SHE'D GIVE HIM SOME OF THE ONIONS HER SISTER BACK IN HER HOMETOWN HAD SENT HER.
#31
Free onions ♫
Kayoko is such a nice person. She even warns me against bringing something in exchange in the same text message.

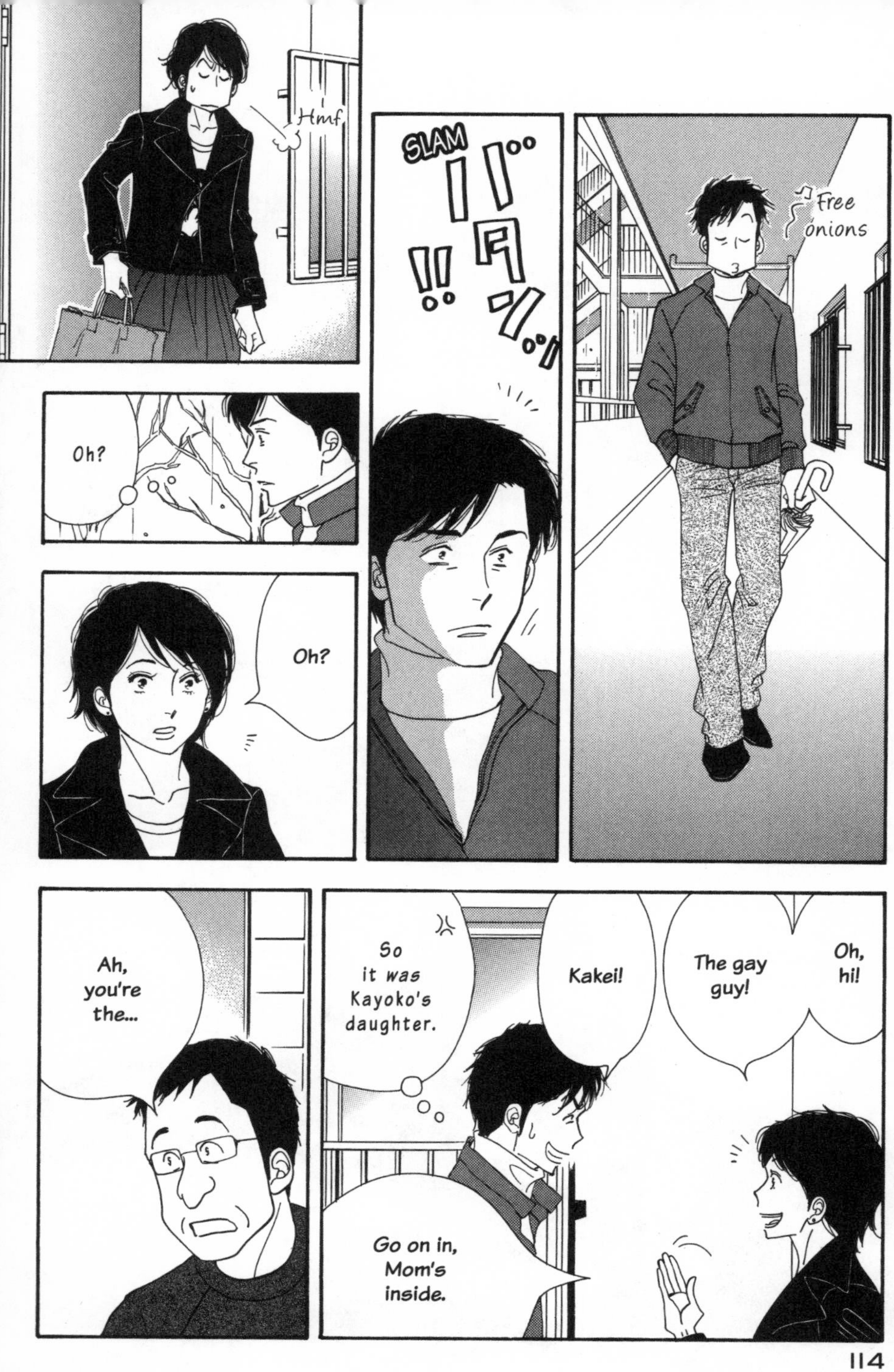
Hmf
Free onions
SLAM
Oh?
Oh?
Oh, hi!
The gay guy!
Kakei!
So it was Kayoko's daughter.
Go on in, Mom's inside.
Ah, you're the...

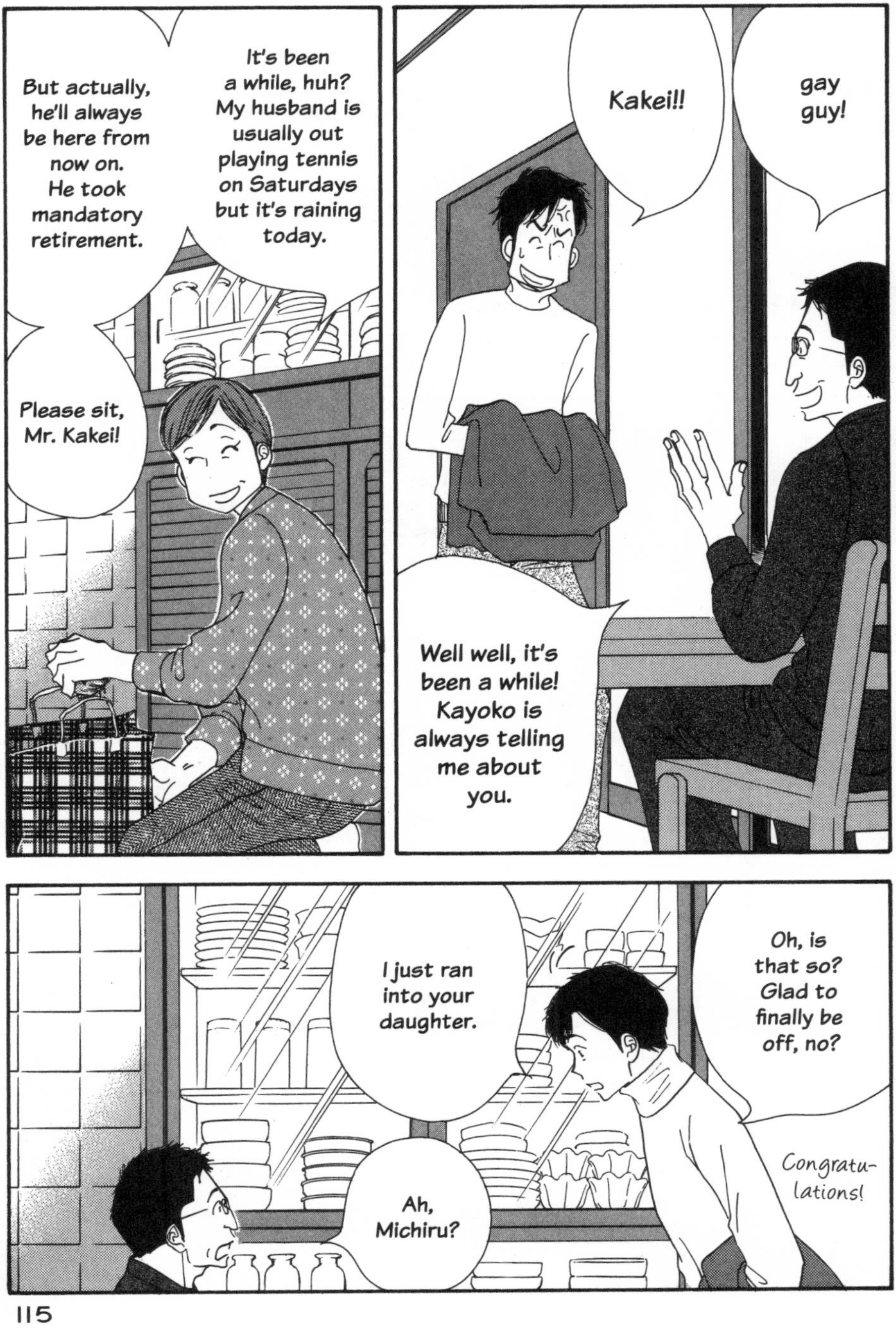
gay guy!
Kakei!!
Well well, it's been a while! Kayoko is always telling me about you.
It's been a while, huh? My husband is usually out playing tennis on Saturdays but it's raining today.
But actually, he'll always be here from now on. He took mandatory retirement.
Please sit, Mr. Kakei!
Oh, is that so? Glad to finally be off, no?
Congratu-lations!
I just ran into your daughter.
Ah, Michiru?

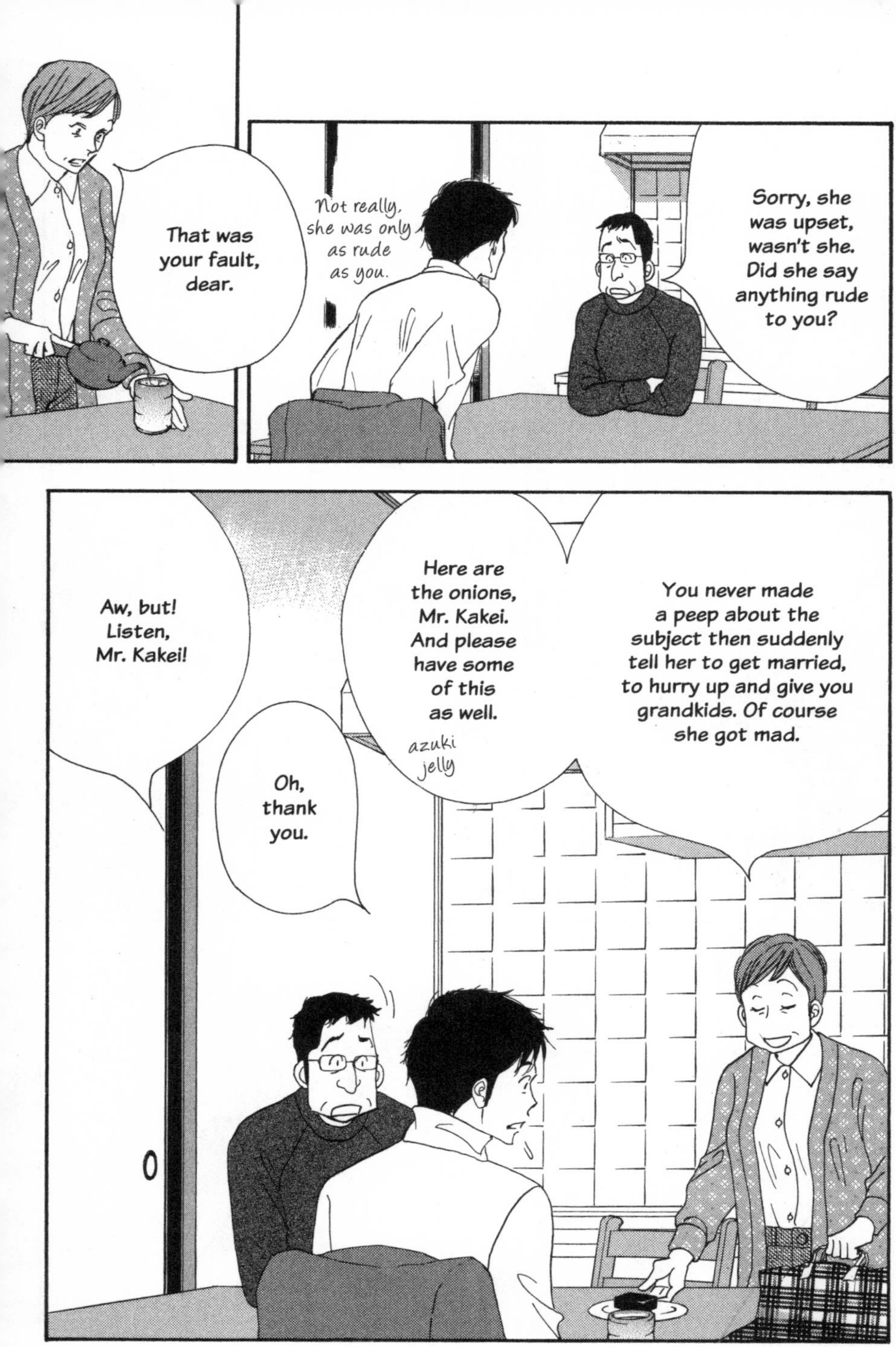
Sorry, she was upset, wasn't she. Did she say anything rude to you?
Not really, she was only as rude as you.
That was your fault, dear.
You never made a peep about the subject then suddenly tell her to get married, to hurry up and give you grandkids. Of course she got mad.
Here are the onions, Mr. Kakei. And please have some of this as well.
azuki jelly
Aw, but! Listen, Mr. Kakei!
Oh, thank you.

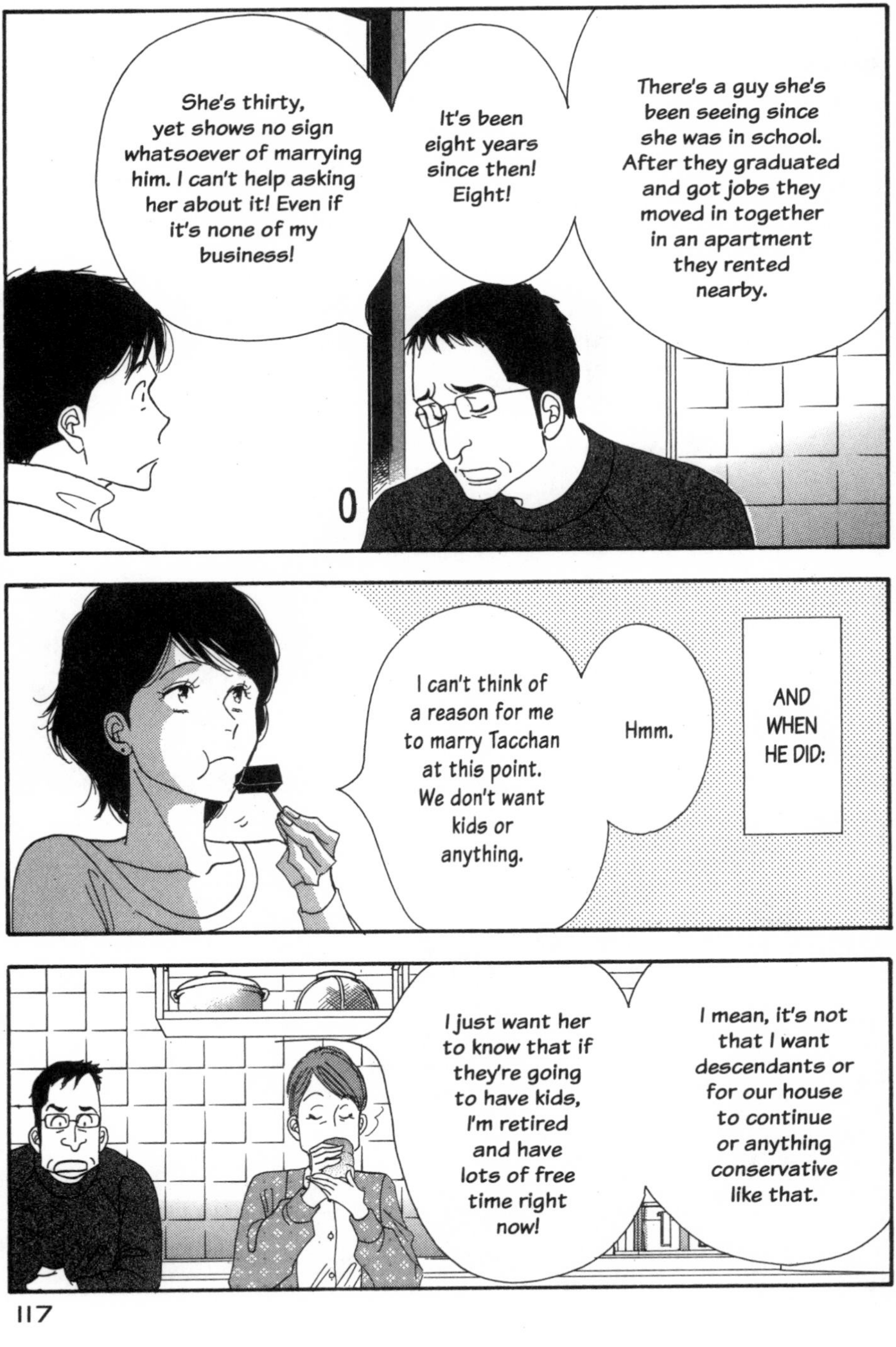
There's a guy she's been seeing since she was in school. After they graduated and got jobs they moved in together in an apartment they rented nearby.
It's been eight years since then! Eight!
She's thirty, yet shows no sign whatsoever of marrying him. I can't help asking her about it! Even if it's none of my business!
AND WHEN HE DID:
Hmm.
I can't think of a reason for me to marry Tacchan at this point. We don't want kids or anything.
I mean, it's not that I want descendants or for our house to continue or anything conservative like that.
I just want her to know that if they're going to have kids, I'm retired and have lots of free time right now!

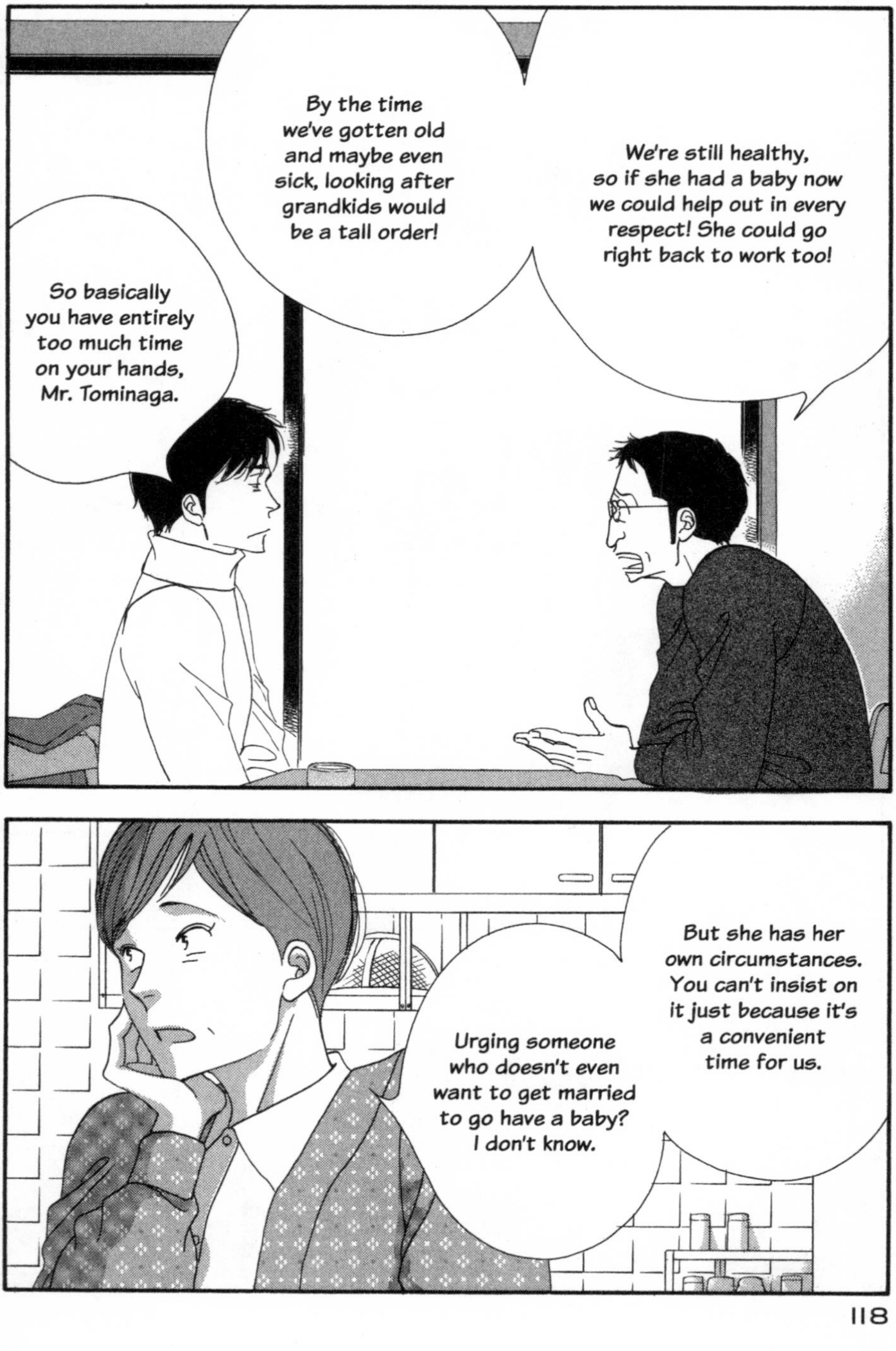
We're still healthy, so if she had a baby now we could help out in every respect! She could go right back to work too!
By the time we've gotten old and maybe even sick, looking after grandkids would be a tall order!
So basically you have entirely too much time on your hands, Mr. Tominaga.
But she has her own circumstances. You can't insist on it just because it's a convenient time for us.
Urging someone who doesn't even want to get married to go have a baby? I don't know.

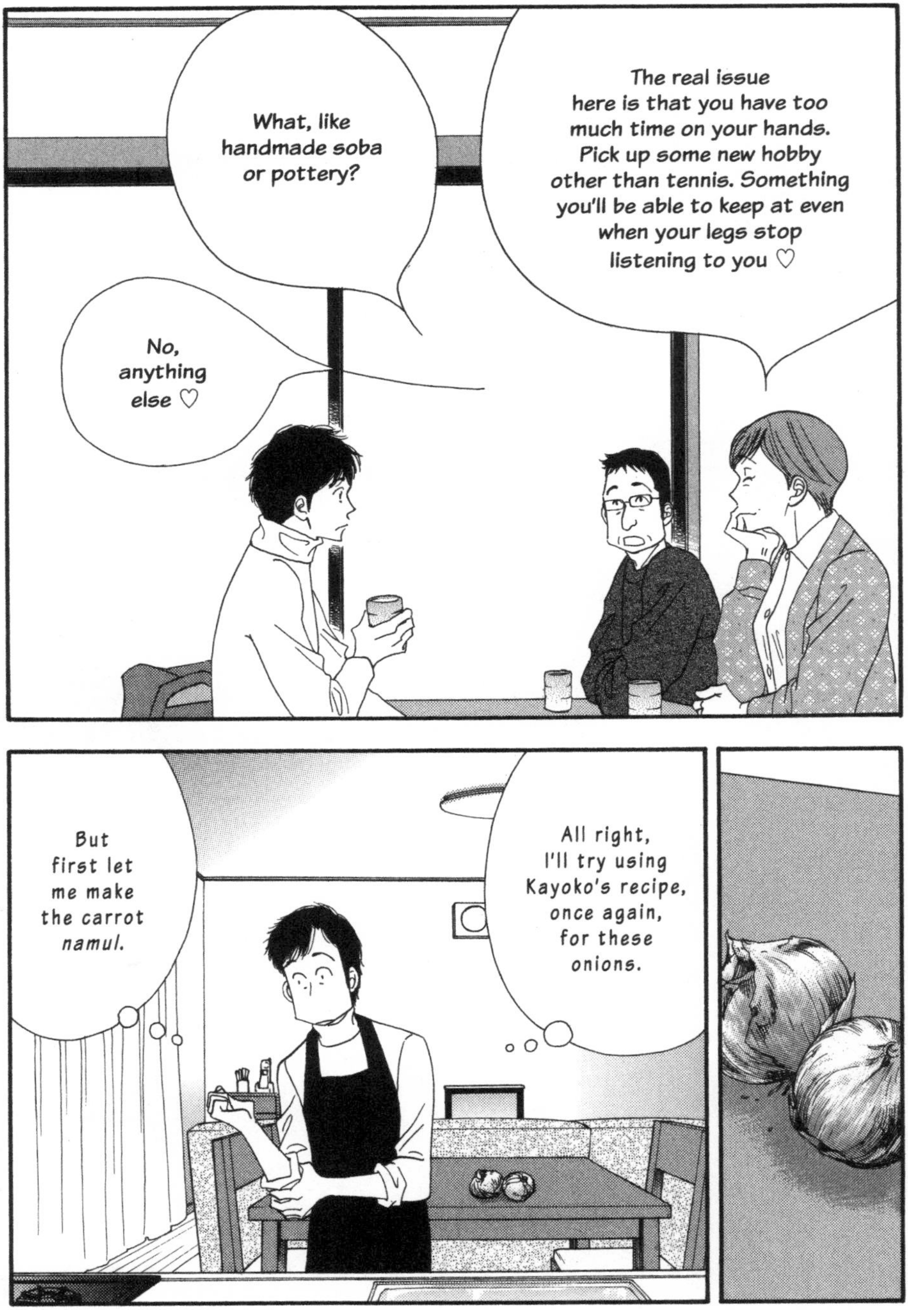
The real issue here is that you have too much time on your hands. Pick up some new hobby other than tennis. Something you'll be able to keep at even when your legs stop listening to you ♡
What, like handmade soba or pottery?
No, anything else ♡
All right, I'll try using Kayoko's recipe, once again, for these onions.
But first let me make the carrot *namul*.

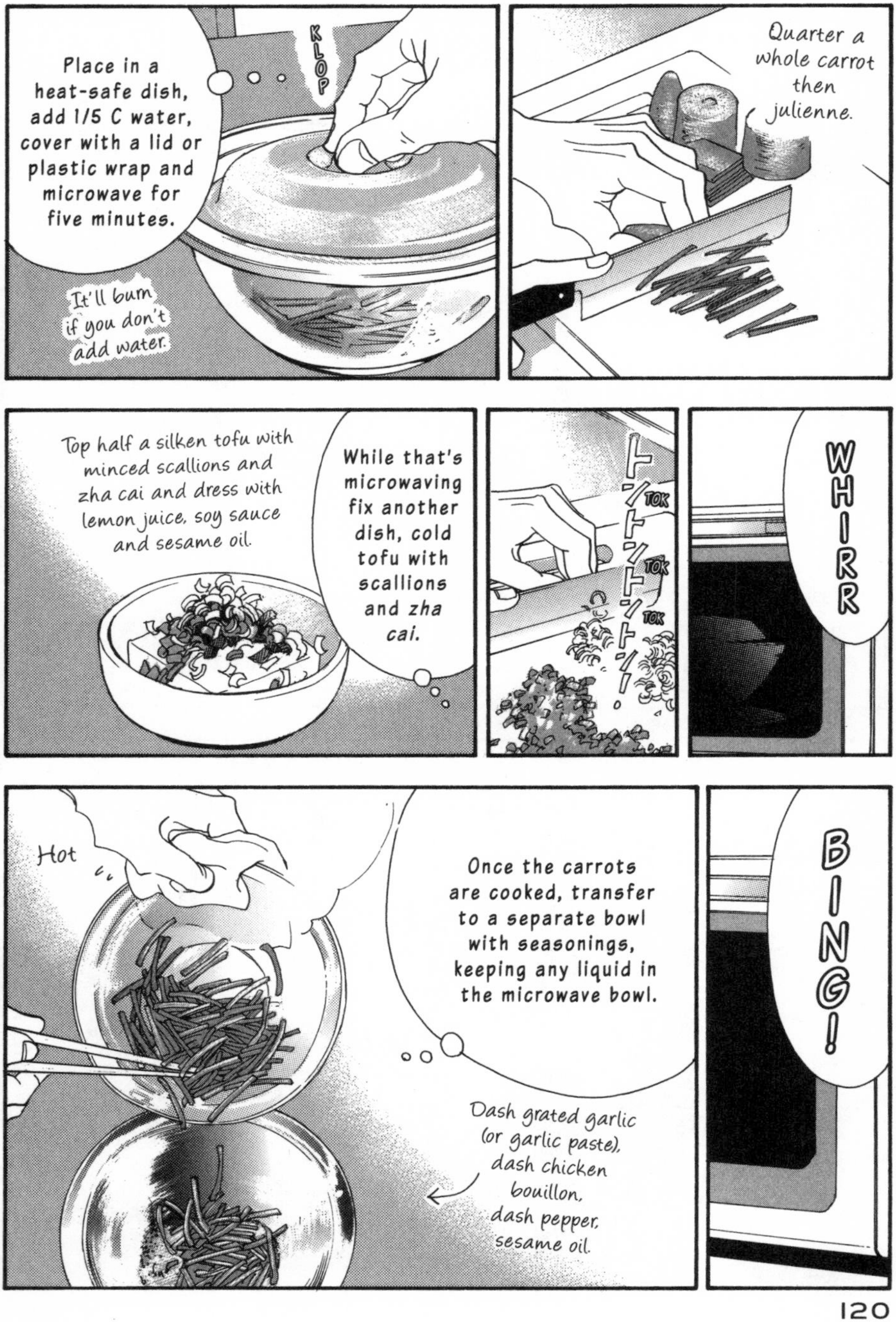
Quarter a whole carrot then julienne.
KLOP
Place in a heat-safe dish, add 1/5 C water, cover with a lid or plastic wrap and microwave for five minutes.
It'll burn if you don't add water.
WHIRR
TOK
TOK
TOK
While that's microwaving fix another dish, cold tofu with scallions and zha cai.
Top half a silken tofu with minced scallions and zha cai and dress with lemon juice, soy sauce and sesame oil.
BING!
Once the carrots are cooked, transfer to a separate bowl with seasonings, keeping any liquid in the microwave bowl.
Hot
Dash grated garlic (or garlic paste), dash chicken bouillon, dash pepper, sesame oil.

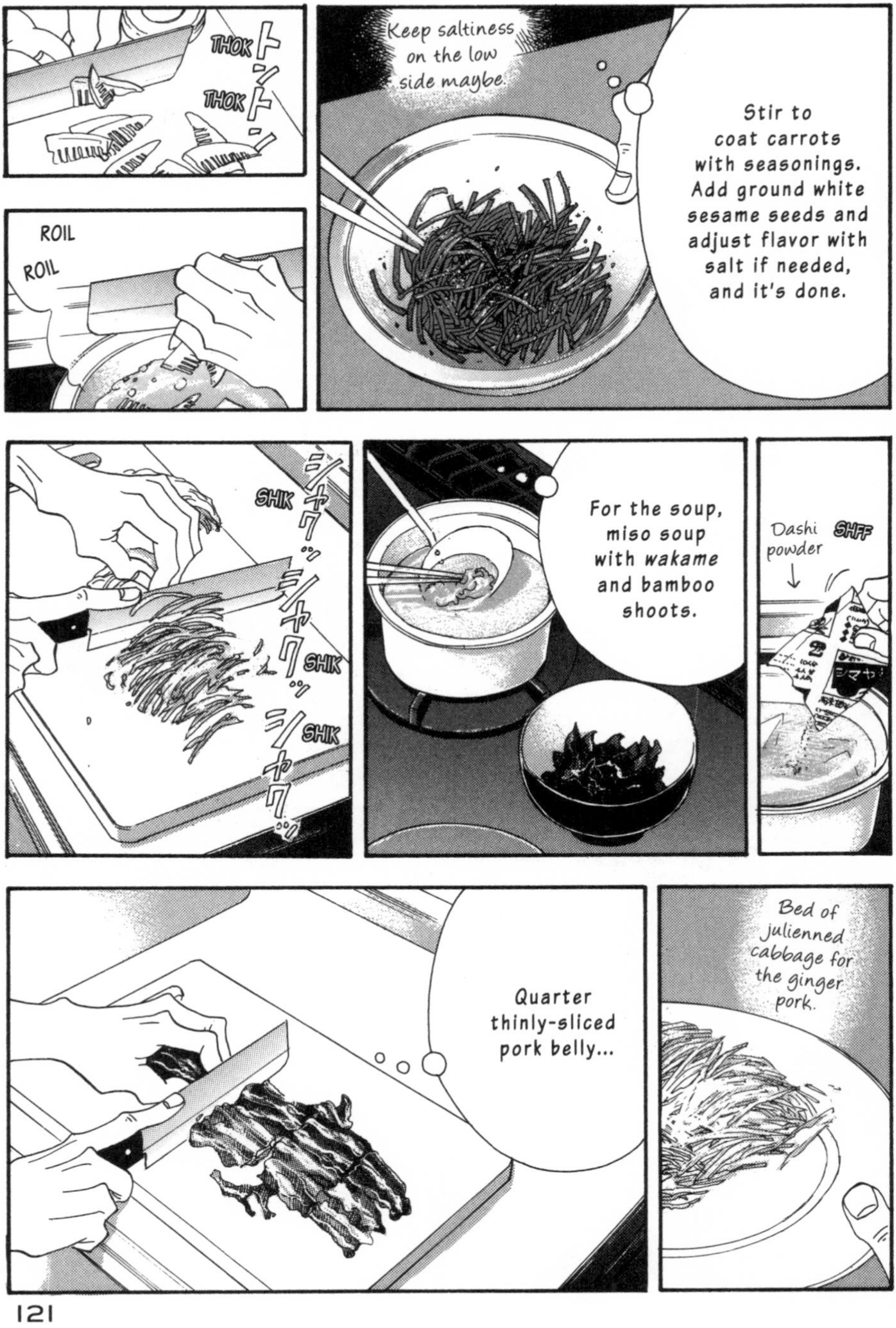
Keep saltiness on the low side maybe.
Stir to coat carrots with seasonings. Add ground white sesame seeds and adjust flavor with salt if needed, and it's done.
THOK
THOK
ROIL
ROIL
Dashi powder
SHFF
For the soup, miso soup with *wakame* and bamboo shoots.
SHIK
SHIK
SHIK
Bed of julienned cabbage for the ginger pork.
Quarter thinly-sliced pork belly...

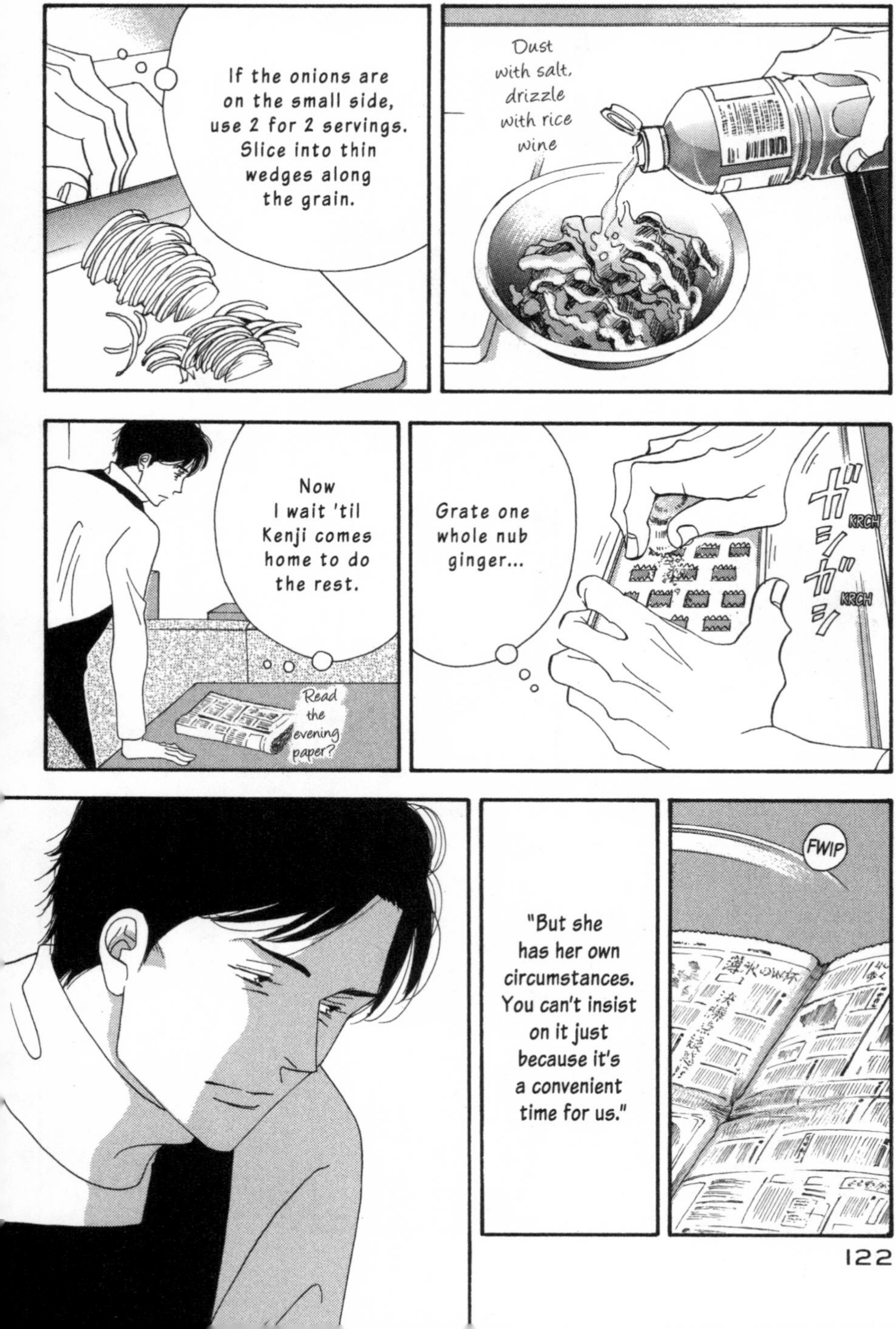
Dust with salt, drizzle with rice wine
If the onions are on the small side, use 2 for 2 servings. Slice into thin wedges along the grain.
KRCH
KRCH
Grate one whole nub ginger...
Now I wait 'til Kenji comes home to do the rest.
Read the evening paper?
FWIP
"But she has her own circumstances. You can't insist on it just because it's a convenient time for us."

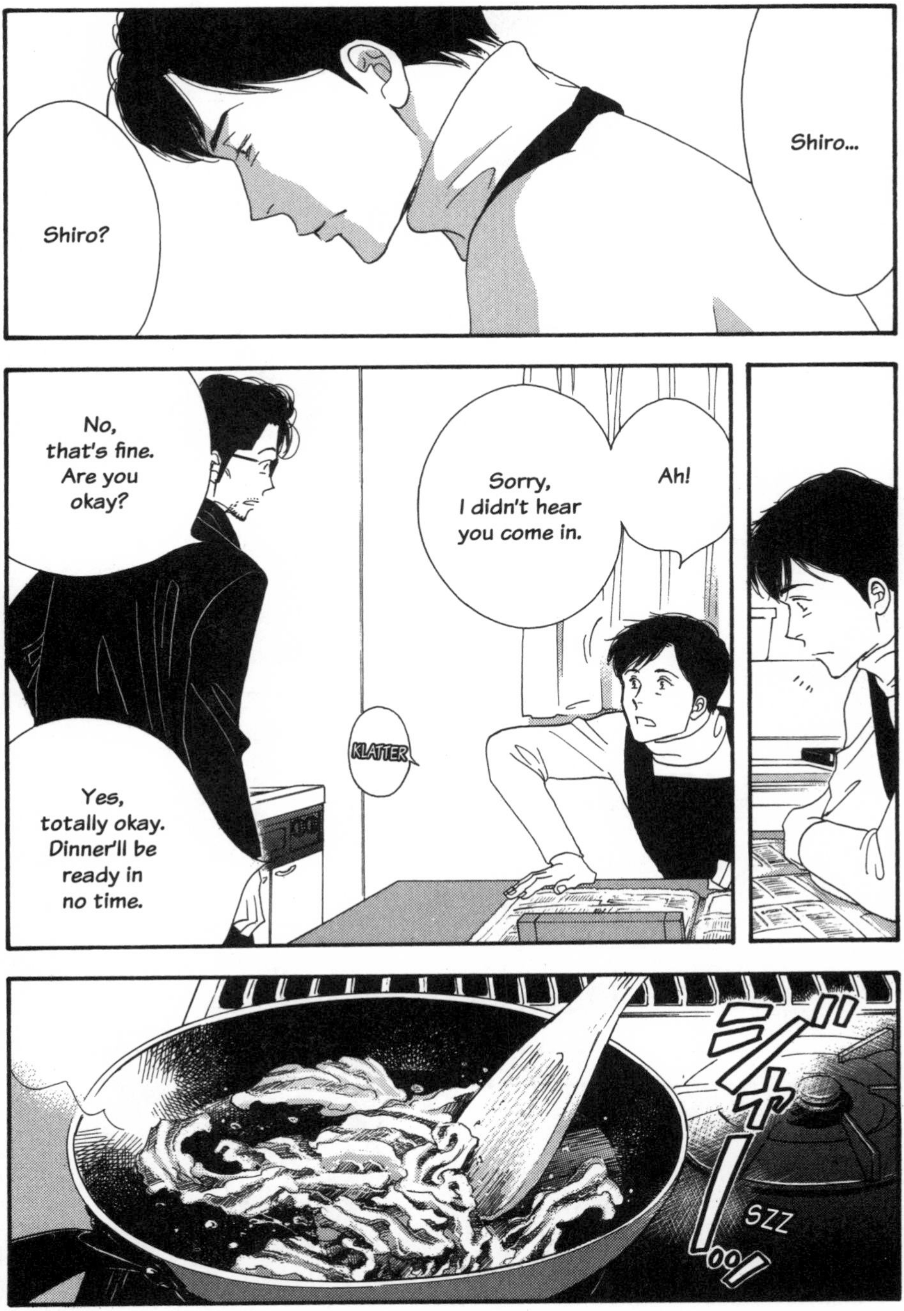

Shiro...
Shiro?
Ah!
Sorry, I didn't hear you come in.
KLATTER
No, that's fine. Are you okay?
Yes, totally okay. Dinner'll be ready in no time.
ジャー!
SZZ

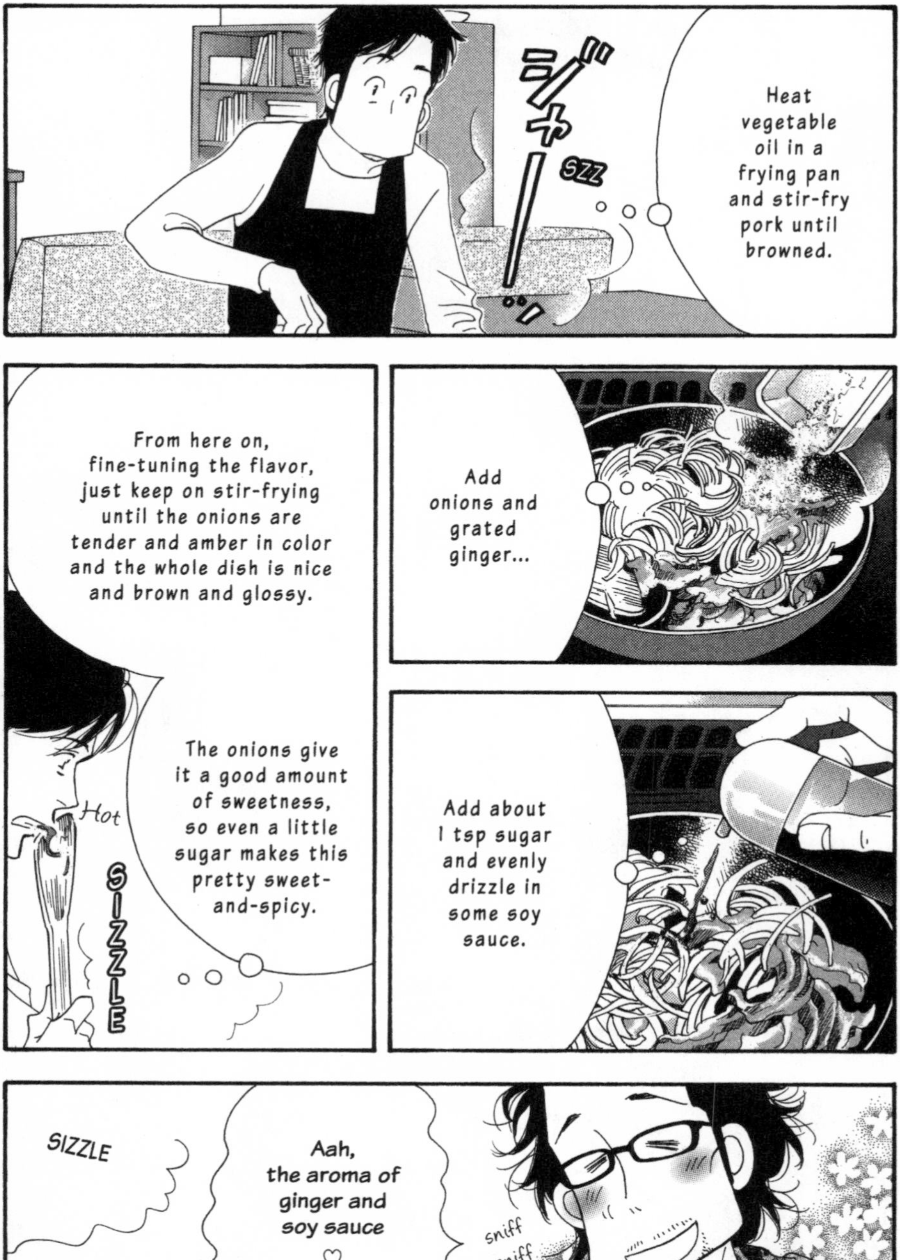

ジャー
SZZ
Heat vegetable oil in a frying pan and stir-fry pork until browned.
Add onions and grated ginger...
Add about 1 tsp sugar and evenly drizzle in some soy sauce.
From here on, fine-tuning the flavor, just keep on stir-frying until the onions are tender and amber in color and the whole dish is nice and brown and glossy.
The onions give it a good amount of sweetness, so even a little sugar makes this pretty sweet-and-spicy.
Hot
SIZZLE
sniff sniff
Aah, the aroma of ginger and soy sauce ♡
SIZZLE

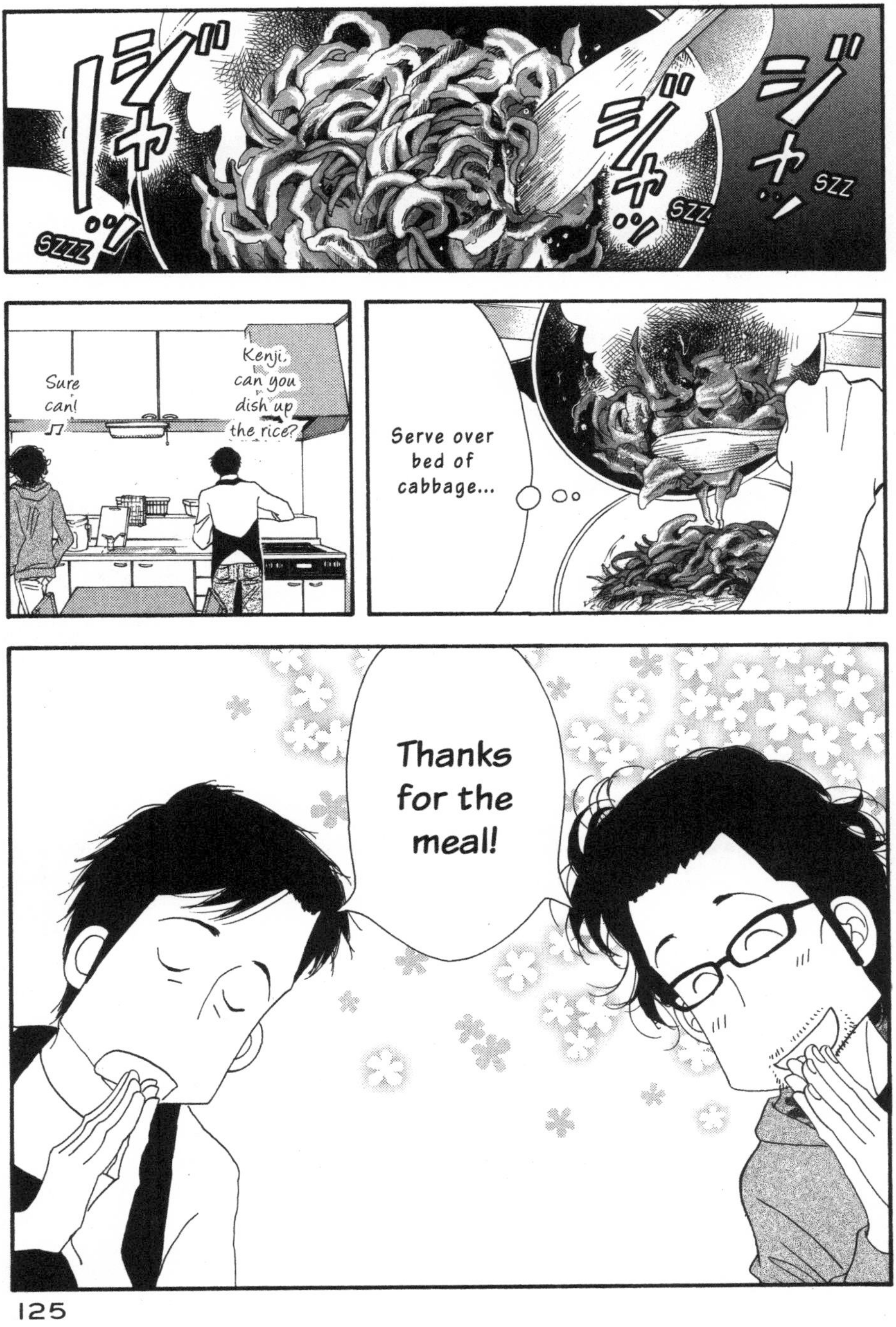
ジャッ
SZZ
ジャーッ
SZZ
ジャーッ
SZZZ
Serve over bed of cabbage...
Kenji, can you dish up the rice?
Sure can!
Thanks for the meal!

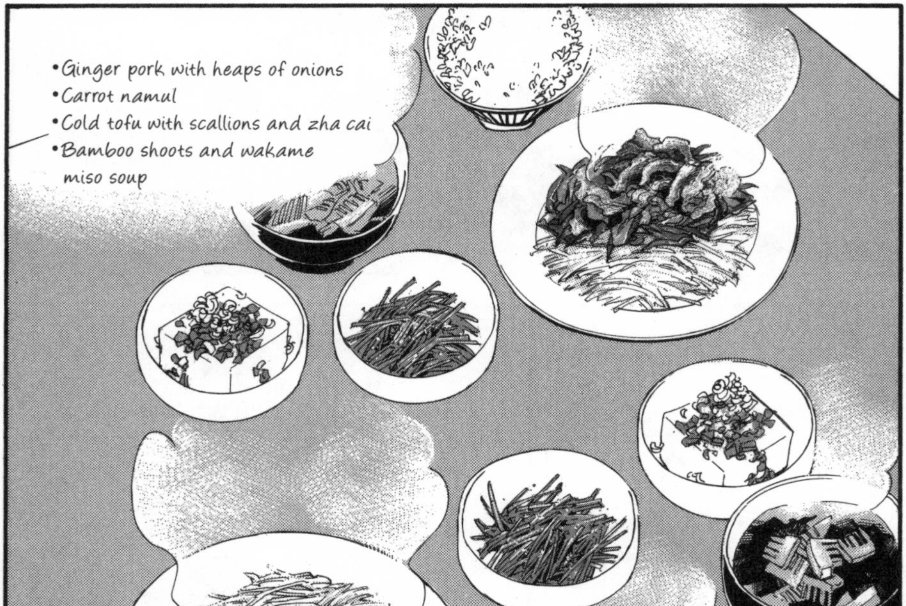
•Ginger pork with heaps of onions
•Carrot namul
•Cold tofu with scallions and zha cai
•Bamboo shoots and wakame miso soup

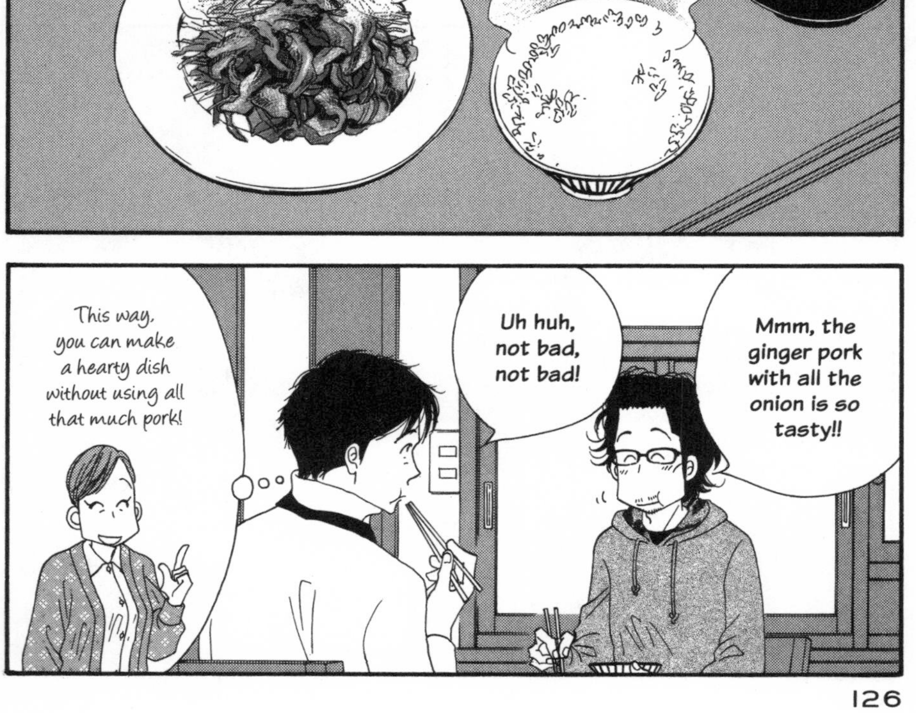
Mmm, the ginger pork with all the onion is so tasty!!
Uh huh, not bad, not bad!
This way, you can make a hearty dish without using all that much pork!

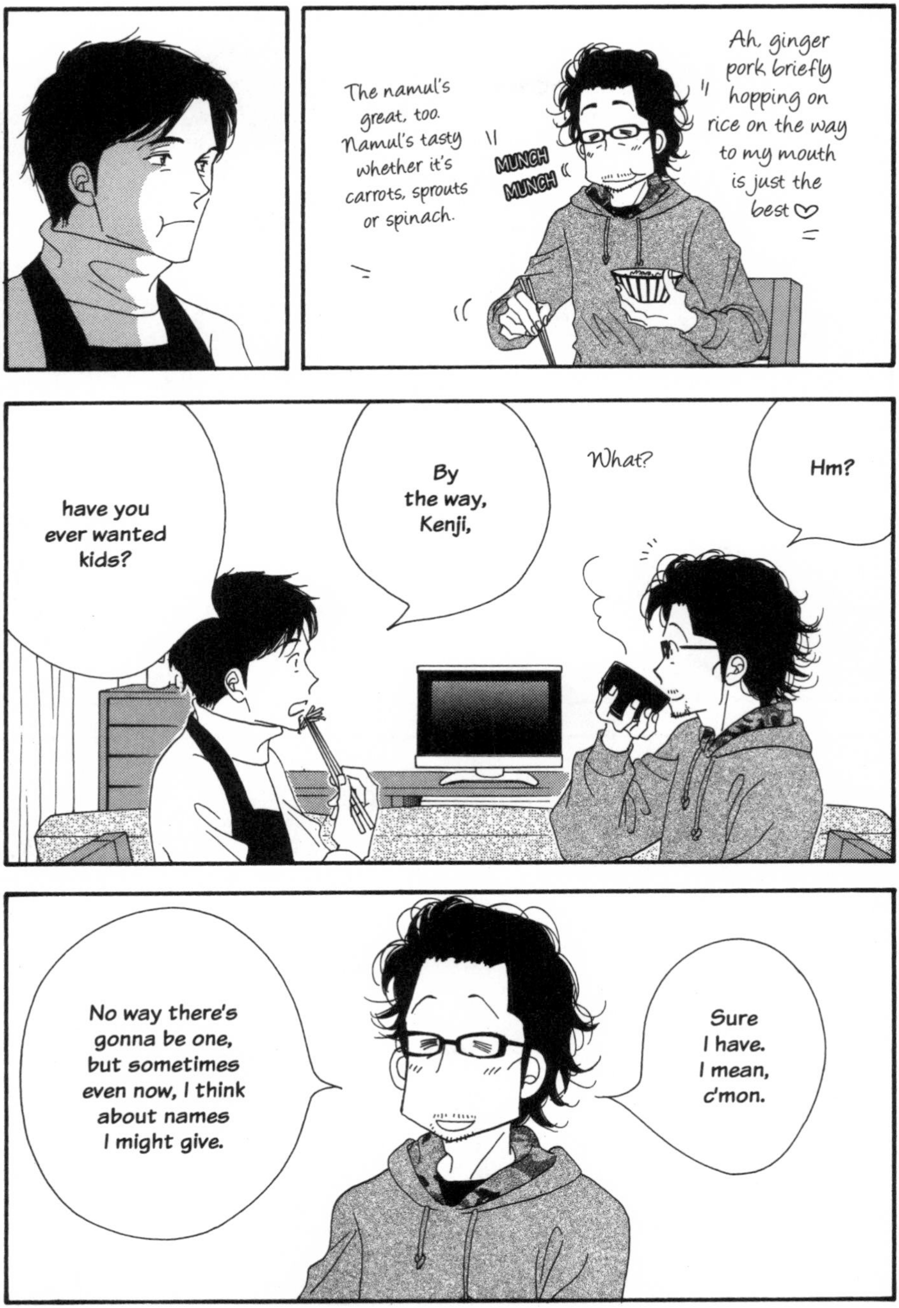
Ah, ginger pork briefly hopping on rice on the way to my mouth is just the best♡
MUNCH MUNCH
The namul's great, too. Namul's tasty whether it's carrots, sprouts or spinach.
Hm?
What?
By the way, Kenji,
have you ever wanted kids?
Sure I have. I mean, c'mon.
No way there's gonna be one, but sometimes even now, I think about names I might give.

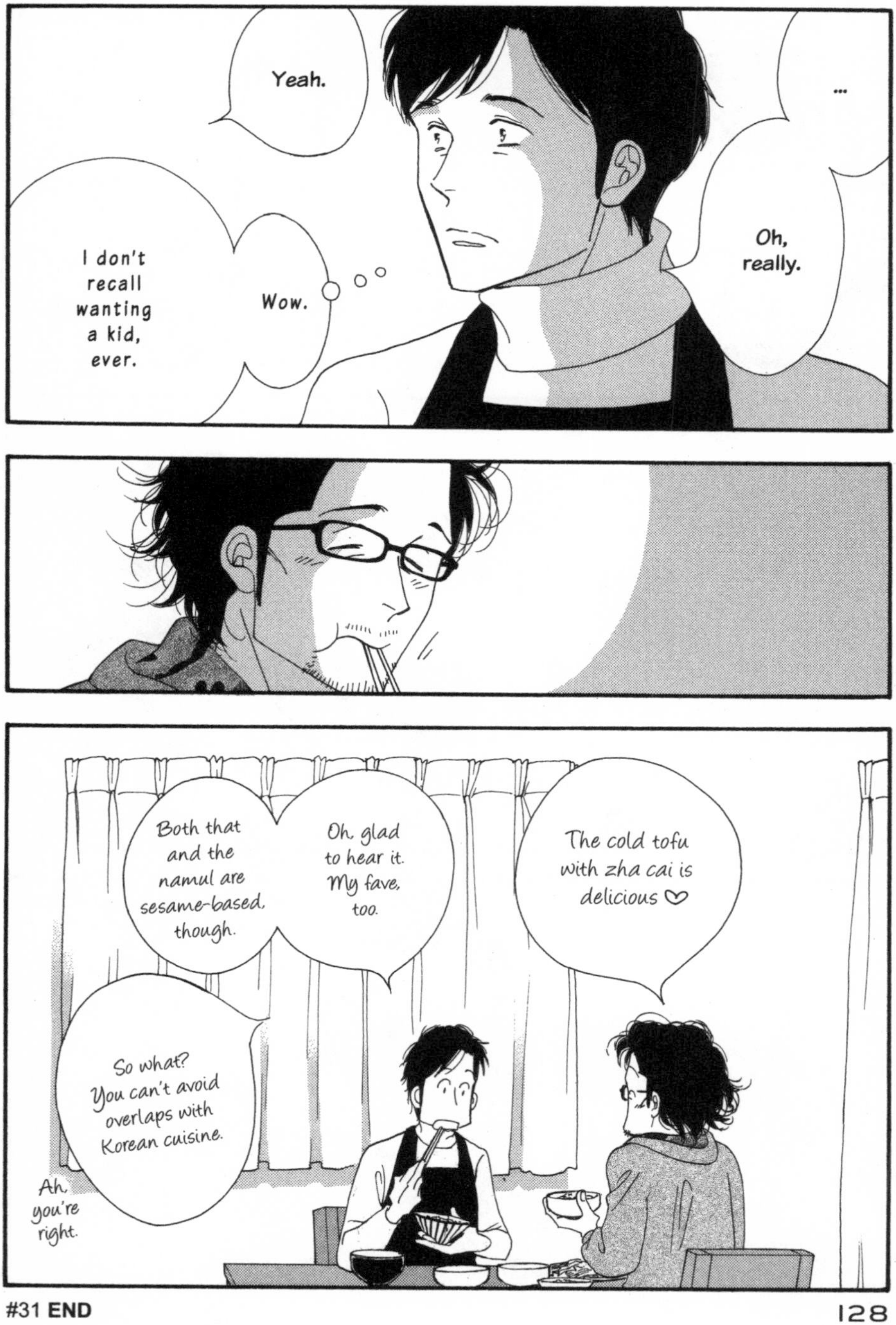
...
Yeah.
Oh, really.
Wow.
I don't recall wanting a kid, ever.
The cold tofu with zha cai is delicious ♡
Oh, glad to hear it. My fave, too.
Both that and the namul are sesame-based, though.
So what? You can't avoid overlaps with Korean cuisine.
Ah, you're right.

#31 END

In summer, try adding roughly minced tomatoes to the **cold tofu with scallions and zha cai.**

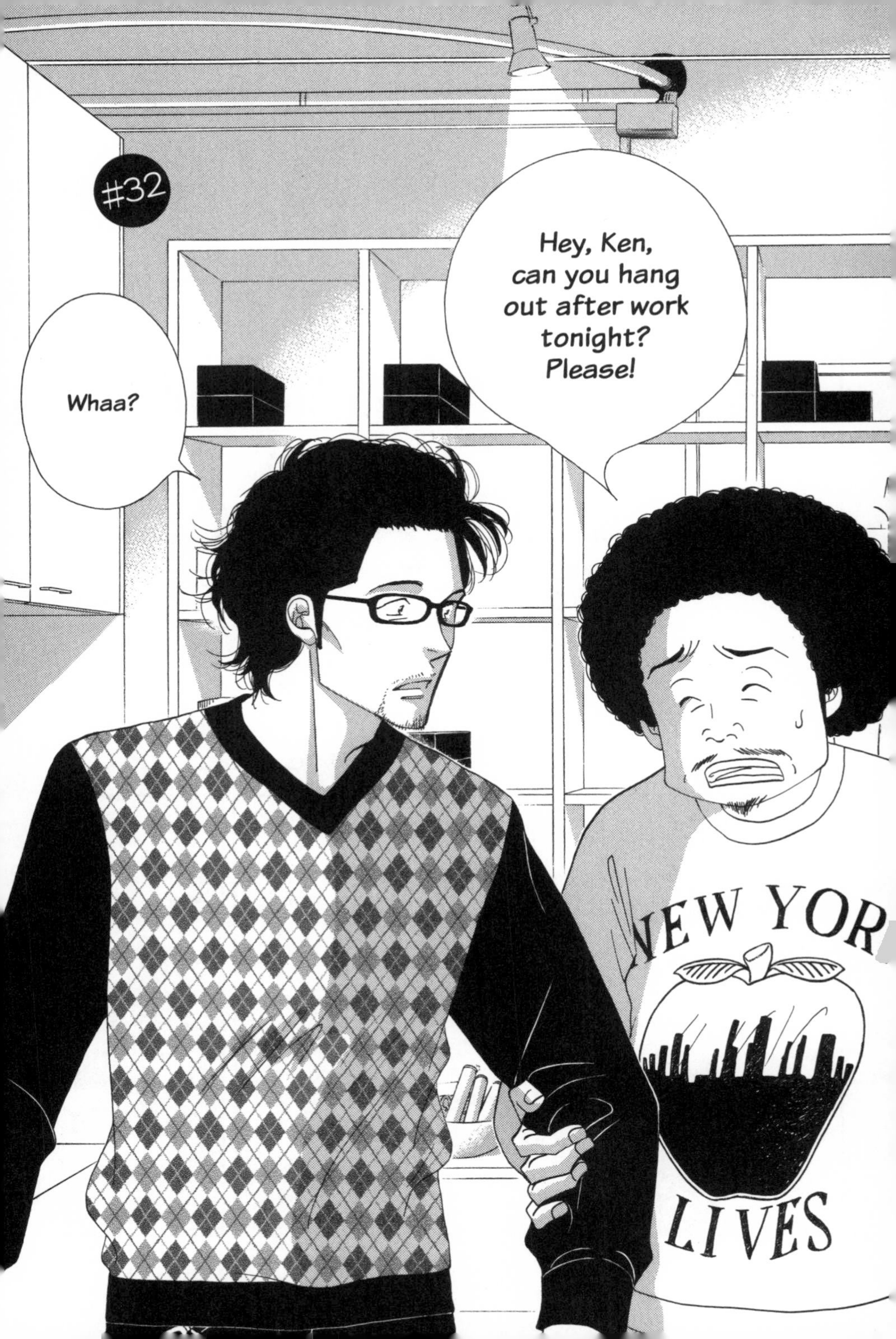
#32
Hey, Ken, can you hang out after work tonight? Please!
Whaa?
NEW YOR
LIVES

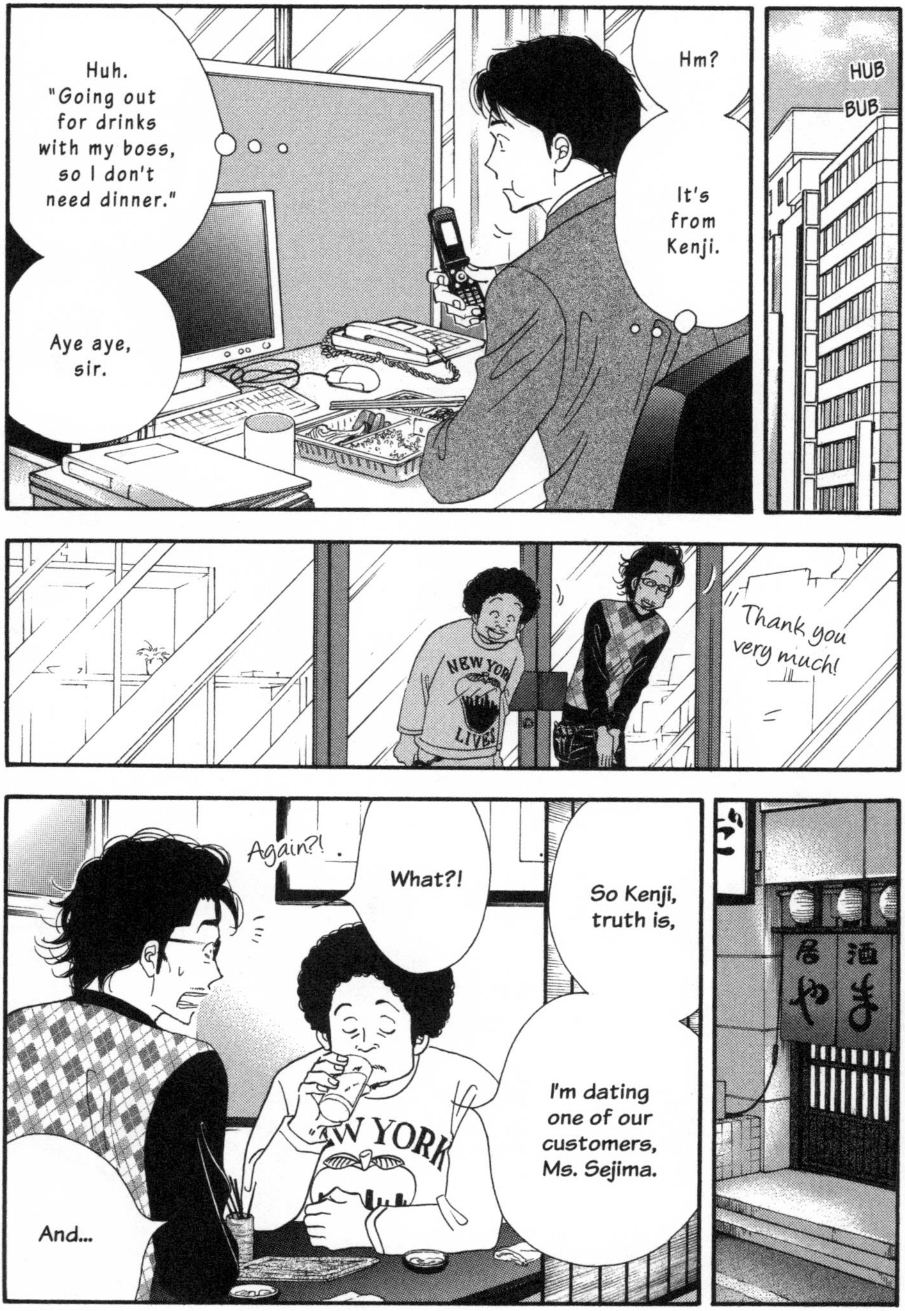
HUB
BUB
Hm?
It's from Kenji.
Huh. "Going out for drinks with my boss, so I don't need dinner."
Aye aye, sir.
Thank you very much!
So Kenji, truth is,
I'm dating one of our customers, Ms. Sejima.
What?!
Again?!
And...

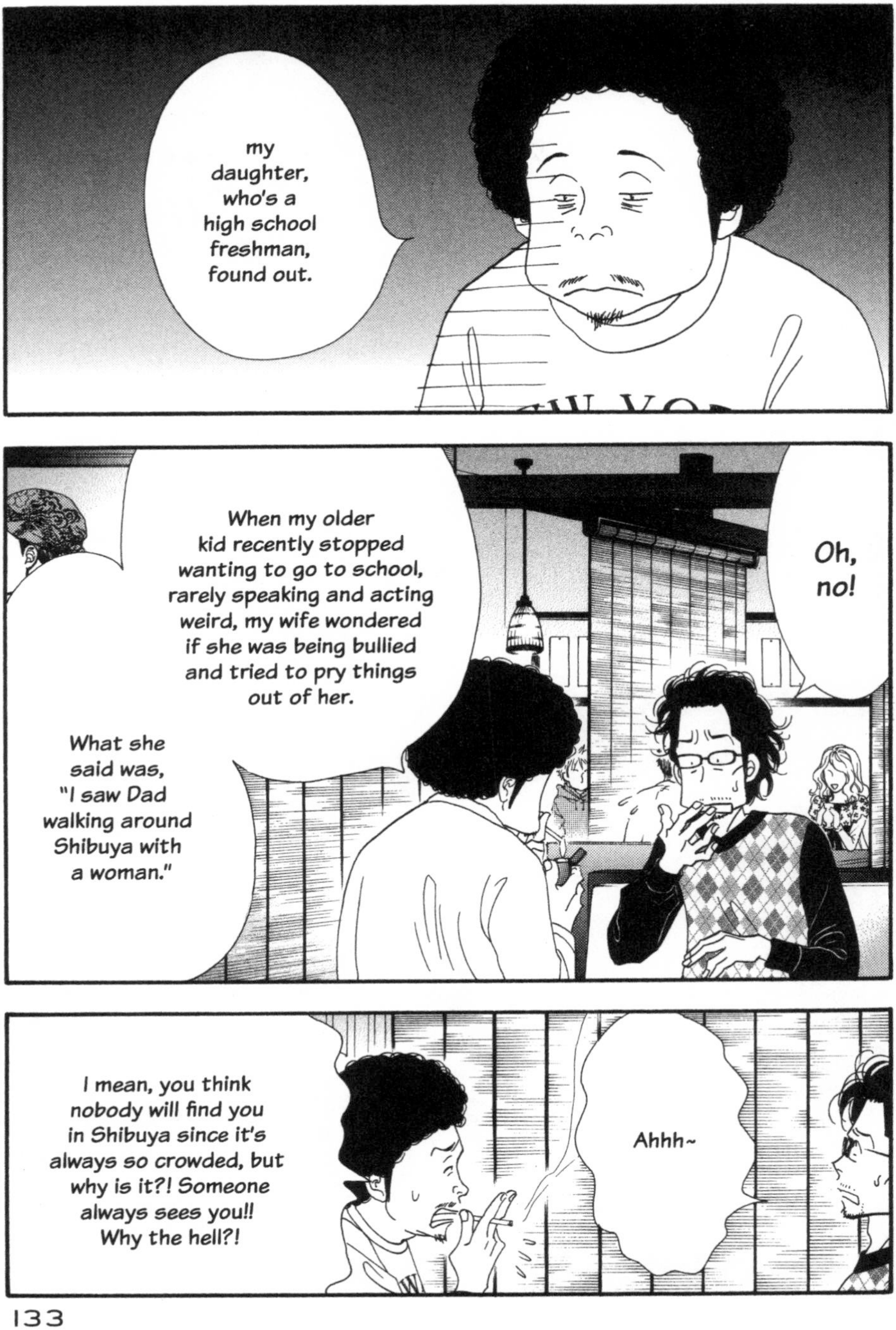
my daughter, who's a high school freshman, found out.
Oh, no!
When my older kid recently stopped wanting to go to school, rarely speaking and acting weird, my wife wondered if she was being bullied and tried to pry things out of her.
What she said was, "I saw Dad walking around Shibuya with a woman."
Ahhh~
I mean, you think nobody will find you in Shibuya since it's always so crowded, but why is it?! Someone always sees you!! Why the hell?!

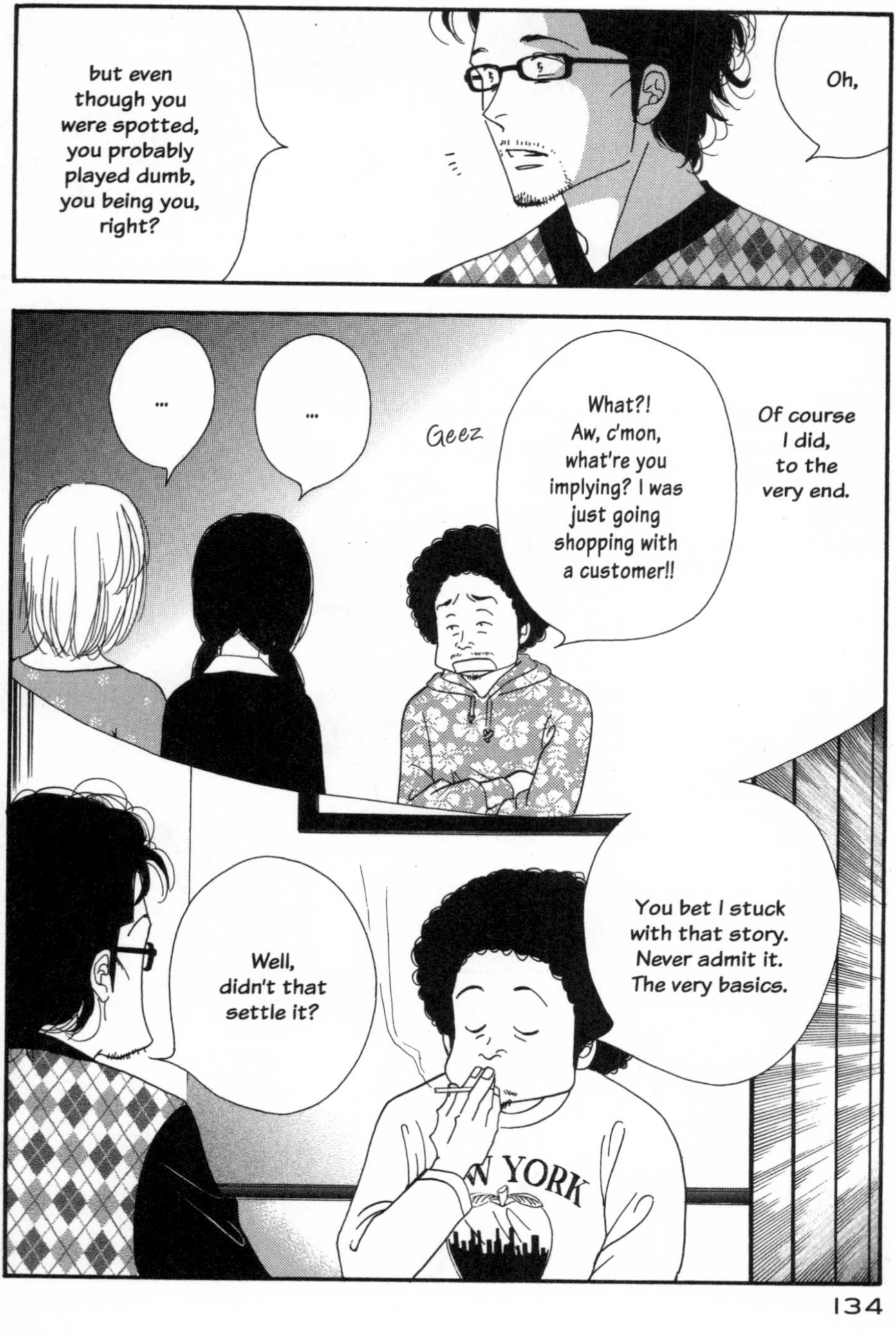
Oh,
but even though you were spotted, you probably played dumb, you being you, right?
Of course I did, to the very end.
What?! Aw, c'mon, what're you implying? I was just going shopping with a customer!!
Geez
...
...
You bet I stuck with that story. Never admit it. The very basics.
Well, didn't that settle it?
NEW YORK

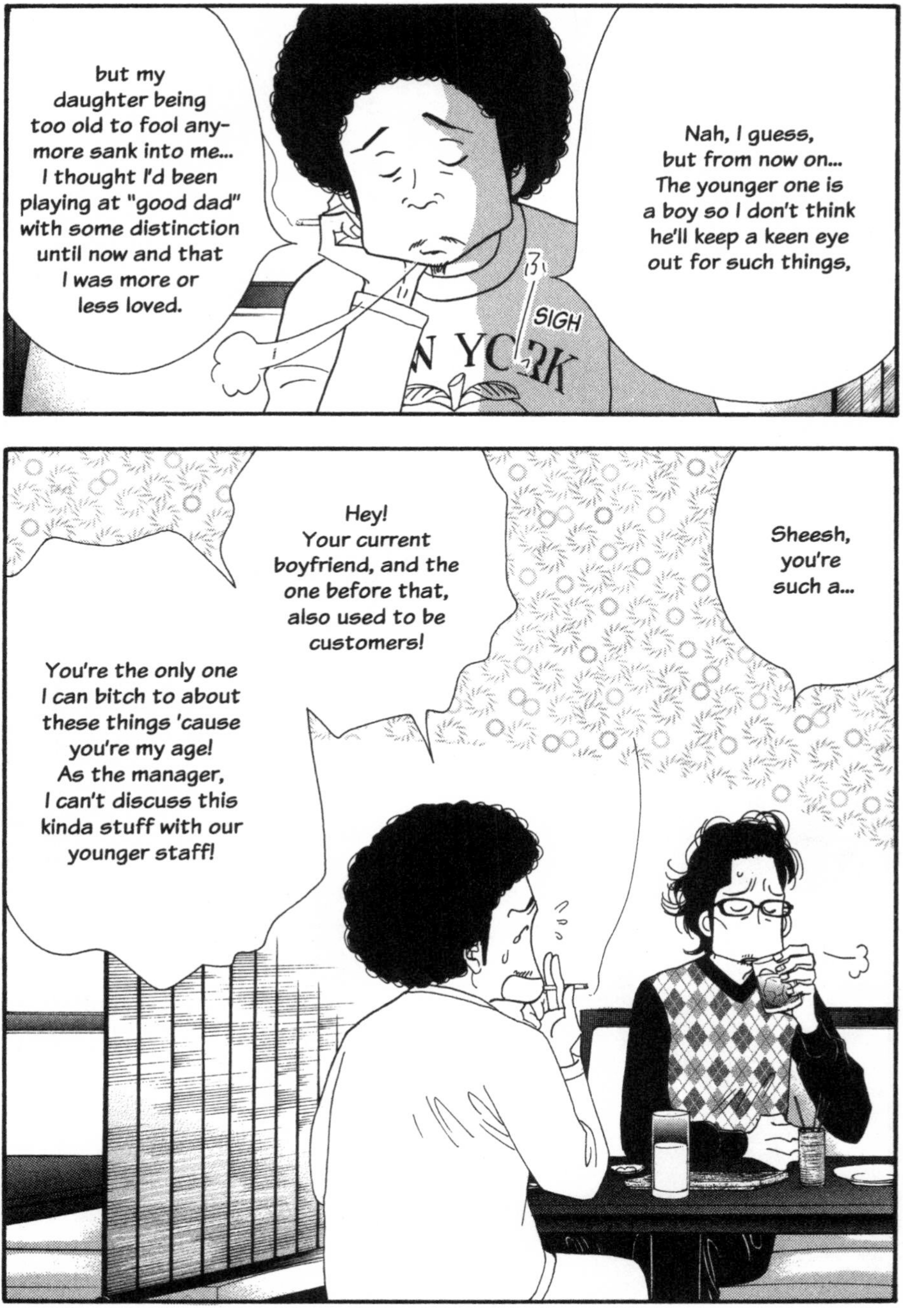

Nah, I guess, but from now on... The younger one is a boy so I don't think he'll keep a keen eye out for such things,
SIGH
but my daughter being too old to fool any-more sank into me... I thought I'd been playing at "good dad" with some distinction until now and that I was more or less loved.
Sheesh, you're such a...
Hey! Your current boyfriend, and the one before that, also used to be customers!
You're the only one I can bitch to about these things 'cause you're my age! As the manager, I can't discuss this kinda stuff with our younger staff!

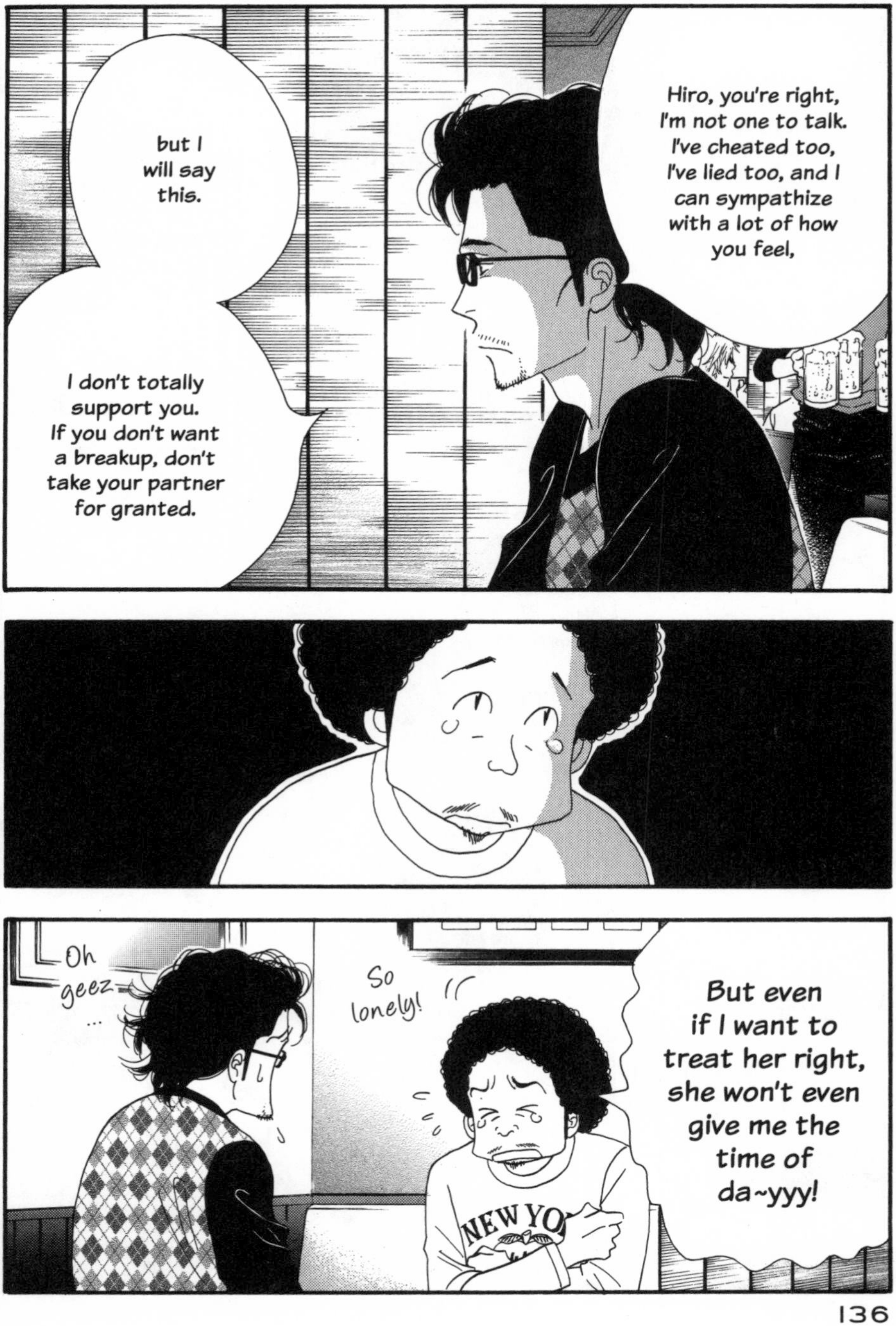
Hiro, you're right, I'm not one to talk. I've cheated too, I've lied too, and I can sympathize with a lot of how you feel,
but I will say this.
I don't totally support you. If you don't want a breakup, don't take your partner for granted.
But even if I want to treat her right, she won't even give me the time of da~yyy!
So lonely!
Oh geez...
NEW YO

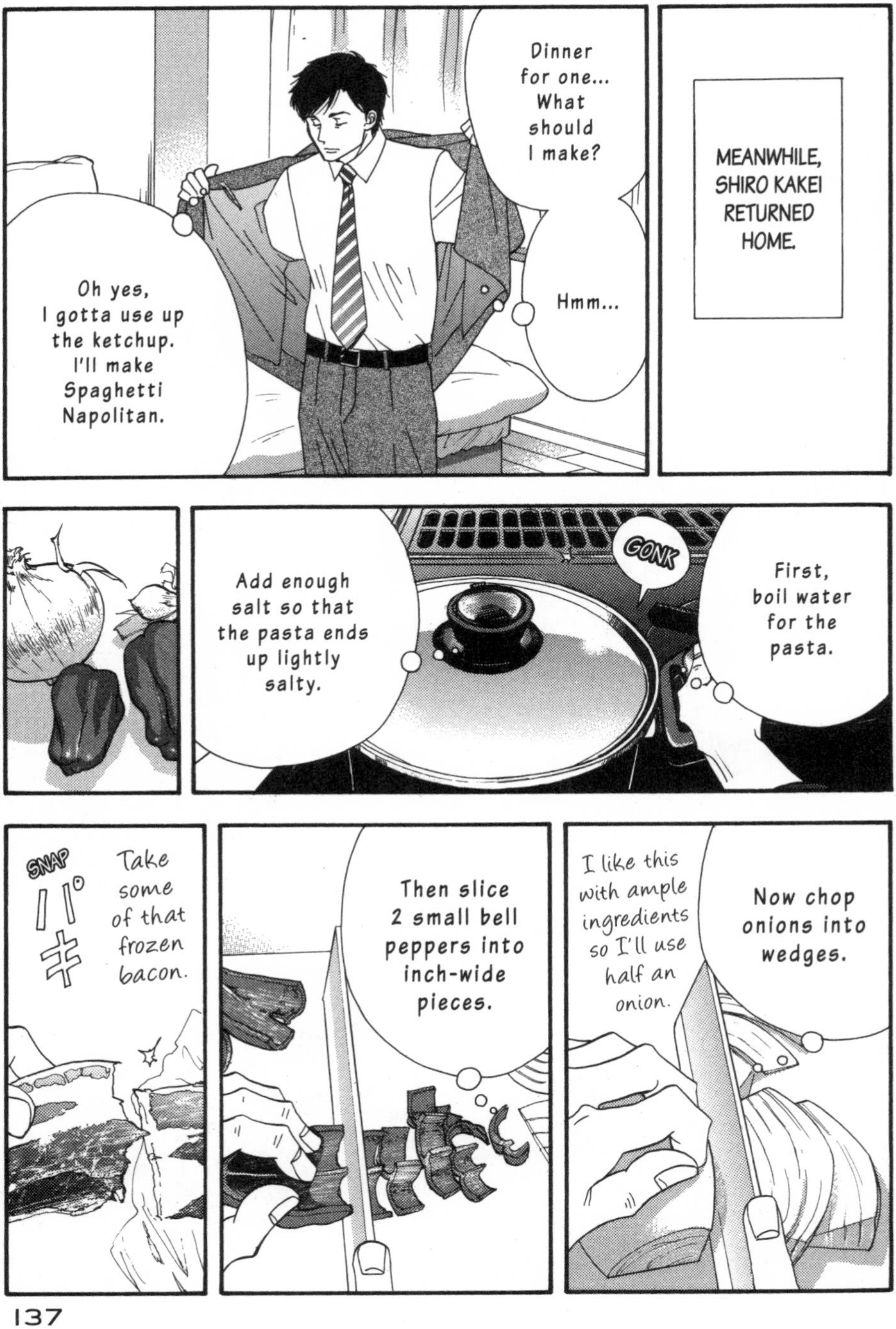
MEANWHILE, SHIRO KAKEI RETURNED HOME.
Dinner for one... What should I make?
Hmm...
Oh yes, I gotta use up the ketchup. I'll make Spaghetti Napolitan.
First, boil water for the pasta.
GONK
Add enough salt so that the pasta ends up lightly salty.
Now chop onions into wedges.
I like this with ample ingredients so I'll use half an onion.
Then slice 2 small bell peppers into inch-wide pieces.
Take some of that frozen bacon.
SNAP
パキ

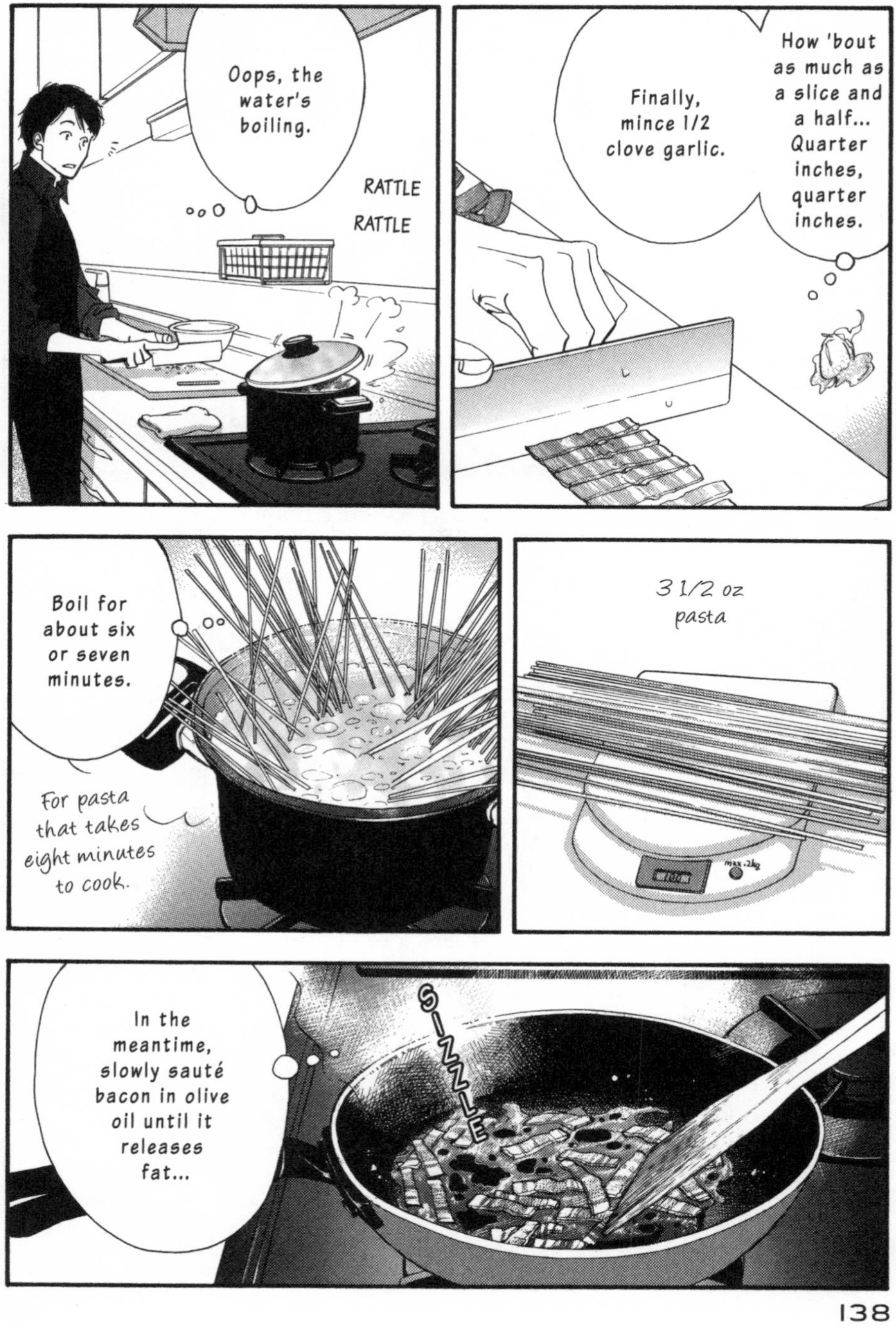
How 'bout as much as a slice and a half... Quarter inches, quarter inches.
Finally, mince 1/2 clove garlic.
Oops, the water's boiling.
RATTLE RATTLE
3 1/2 oz pasta
Boil for about six or seven minutes.
For pasta that takes eight minutes to cook.
SIZZLE
In the meantime, slowly sauté bacon in olive oil until it releases fat...

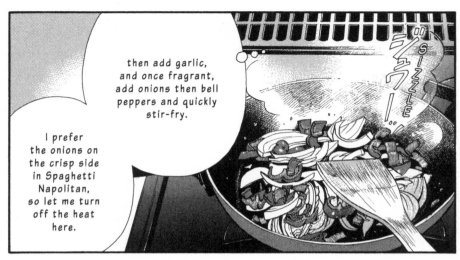

SIZZLE
then add garlic, and once fragrant, add onions then bell peppers and quickly stir-fry.
I prefer the onions on the crisp side in Spaghetti Napolitan, so let me turn off the heat here.
Okay, seven minutes!
FWSHH
Turn on heat again. Add ketchup, a little Worcestershire sauce, a drip of noodle sauce and pepper to season.
Well, the Worcestershire sauce I added just because I had some. I use bits of consommé or whatever other combination suits me then...
SZ
SZZ

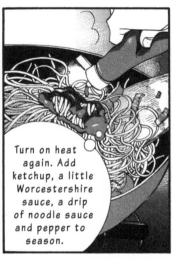

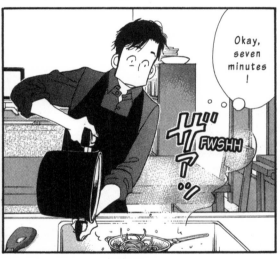

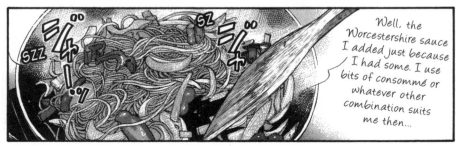

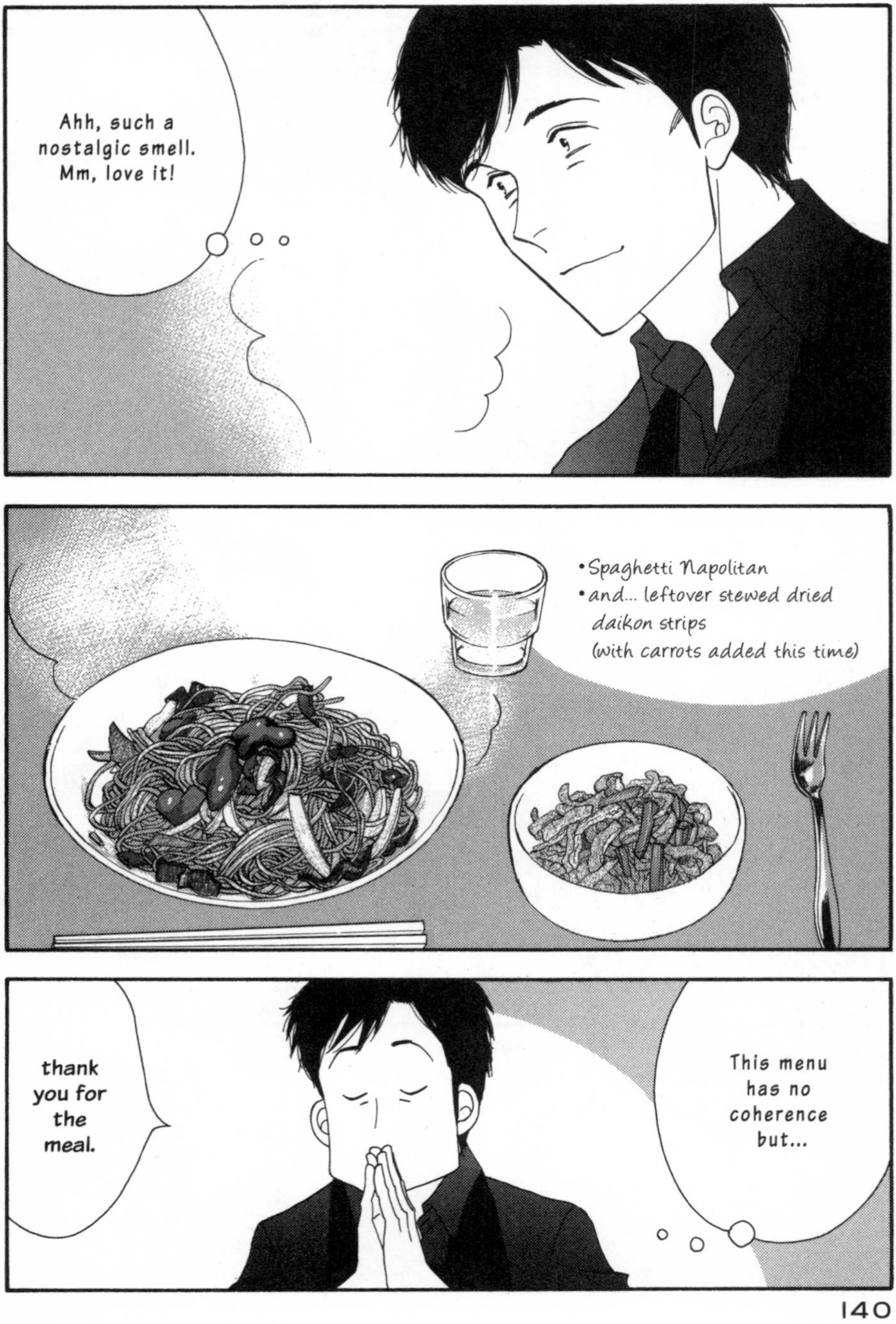

Ahh, such a nostalgic smell. Mm, love it!
•Spaghetti Napolitan
•and... leftover stewed dried daikon strips
(with carrots added this time)
This menu has no coherence but...
thank you for the meal.

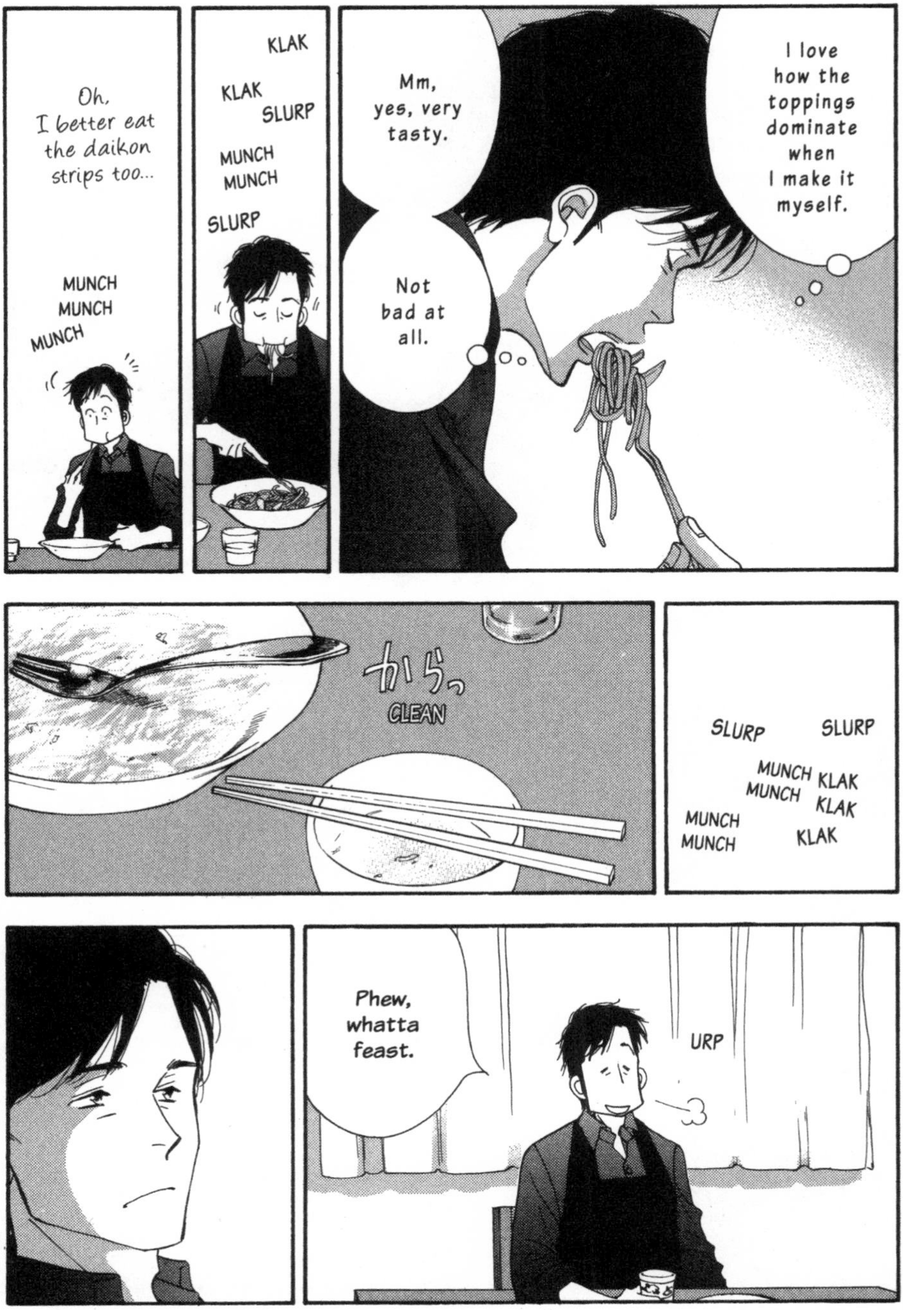
I love how the toppings dominate when I make it myself.
Mm, yes, very tasty.
Not bad at all.
KLAK
KLAK
SLURP
MUNCH MUNCH
SLURP
Oh, I better eat the daikon strips too...
MUNCH MUNCH MUNCH
SLURP
SLURP
MUNCH MUNCH
KLAK KLAK
MUNCH MUNCH
KLAK
からっ
CLEAN
URP
Phew, whatta feast.

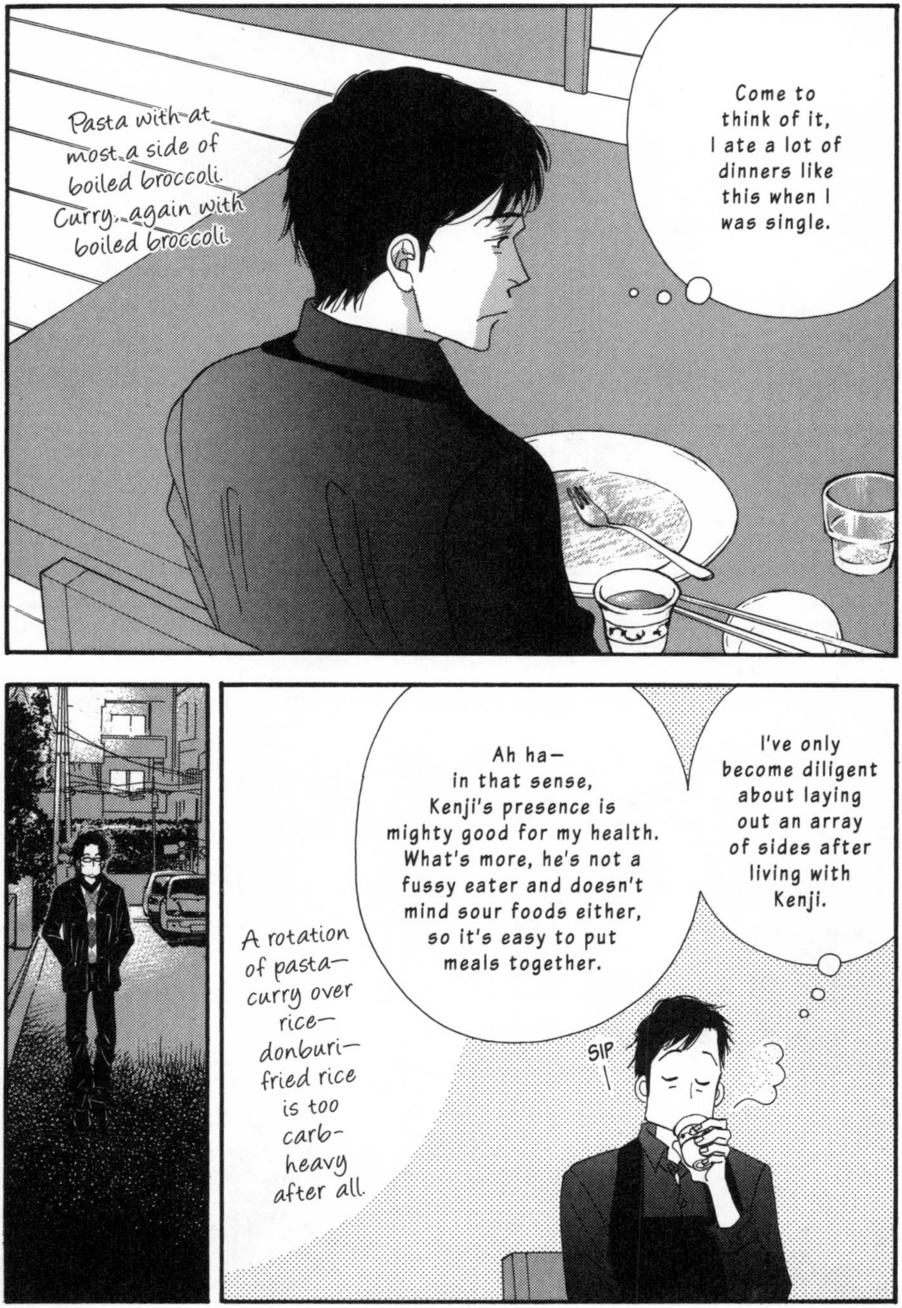
Come to think of it, I ate a lot of dinners like this when I was single.
Pasta with at most a side of boiled broccoli. Curry, again with boiled broccoli.
I've only become diligent about laying out an array of sides after living with Kenji.
Ah ha— in that sense, Kenji's presence is mighty good for my health. What's more, he's not a fussy eater and doesn't mind sour foods either, so it's easy to put meals together.
A rotation of pasta— curry over rice— donburi— fried rice is too carb-heavy after all.
SIP

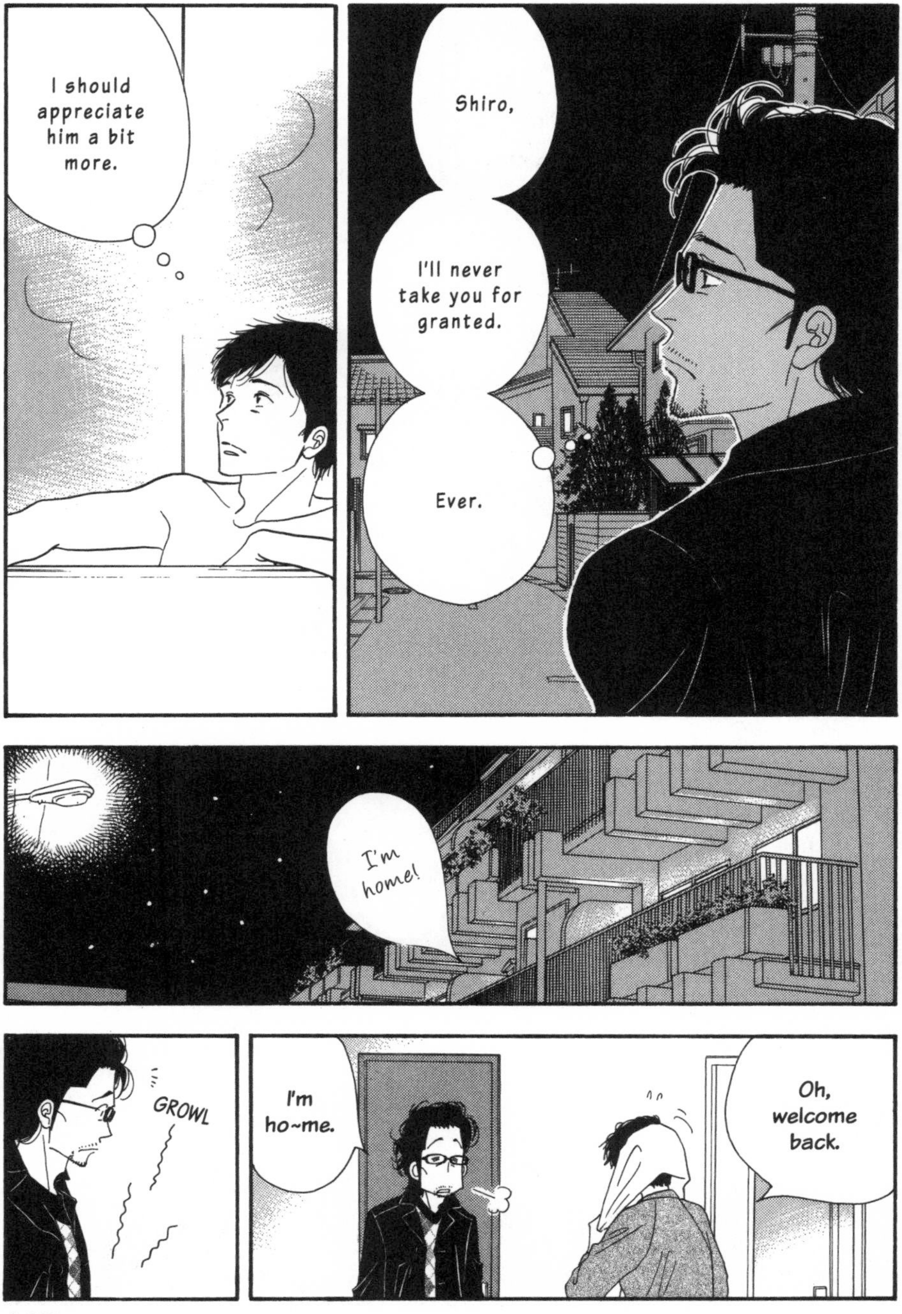
Shiro,
I'll never take you for granted.
Ever.
I should appreciate him a bit more.
I'm home!
Oh, welcome back.
I'm ho~me.
GROWL

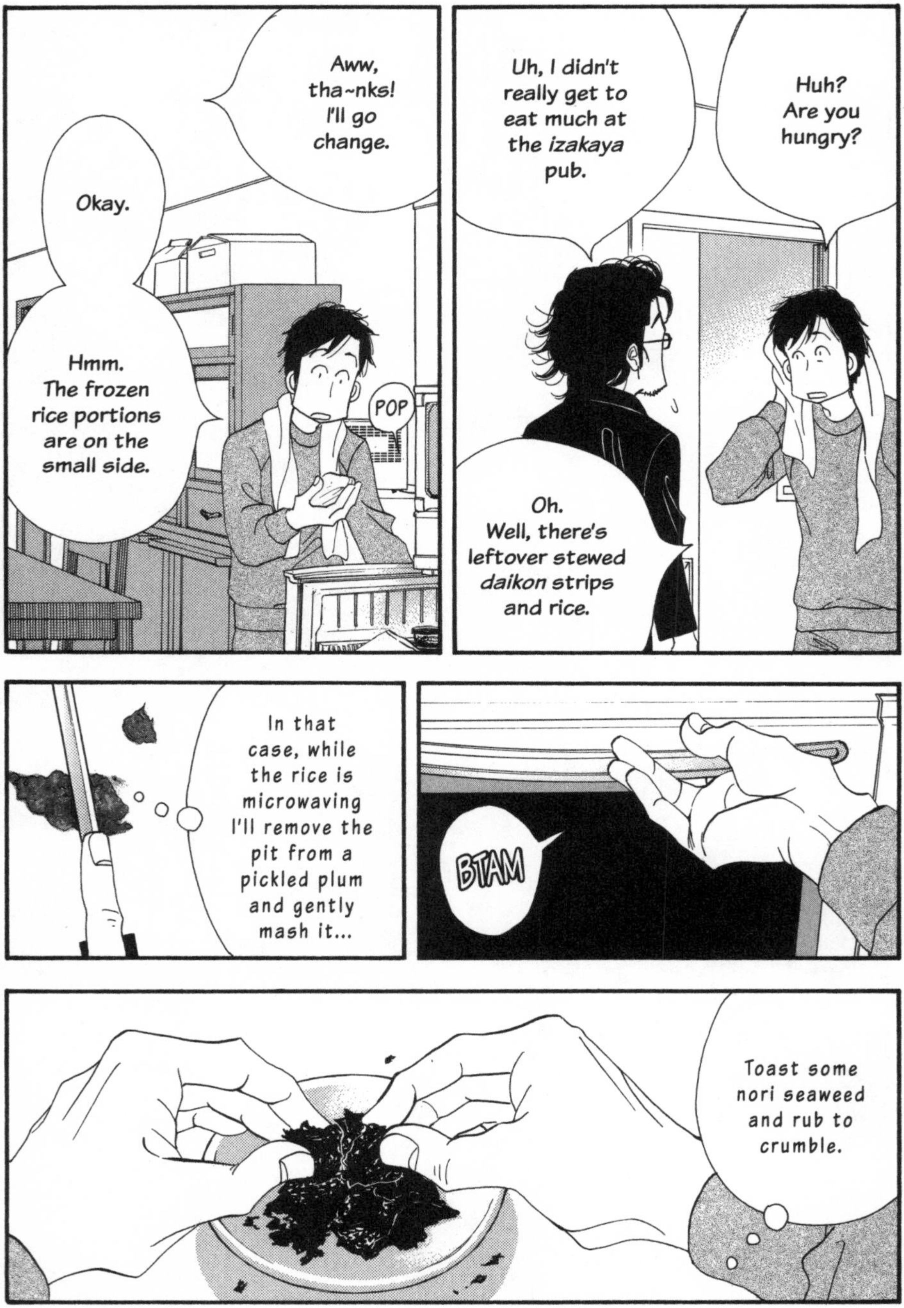
Huh? Are you hungry?
Uh, I didn't really get to eat much at the *izakaya* pub.
Oh. Well, there's leftover stewed *daikon* strips and rice.
Aww, tha~nks! I'll go change.
Okay.
POP
Hmm. The frozen rice portions are on the small side.
BTAM
In that case, while the rice is microwaving I'll remove the pit from a pickled plum and gently mash it...
Toast some nori seaweed and rub to crumble.

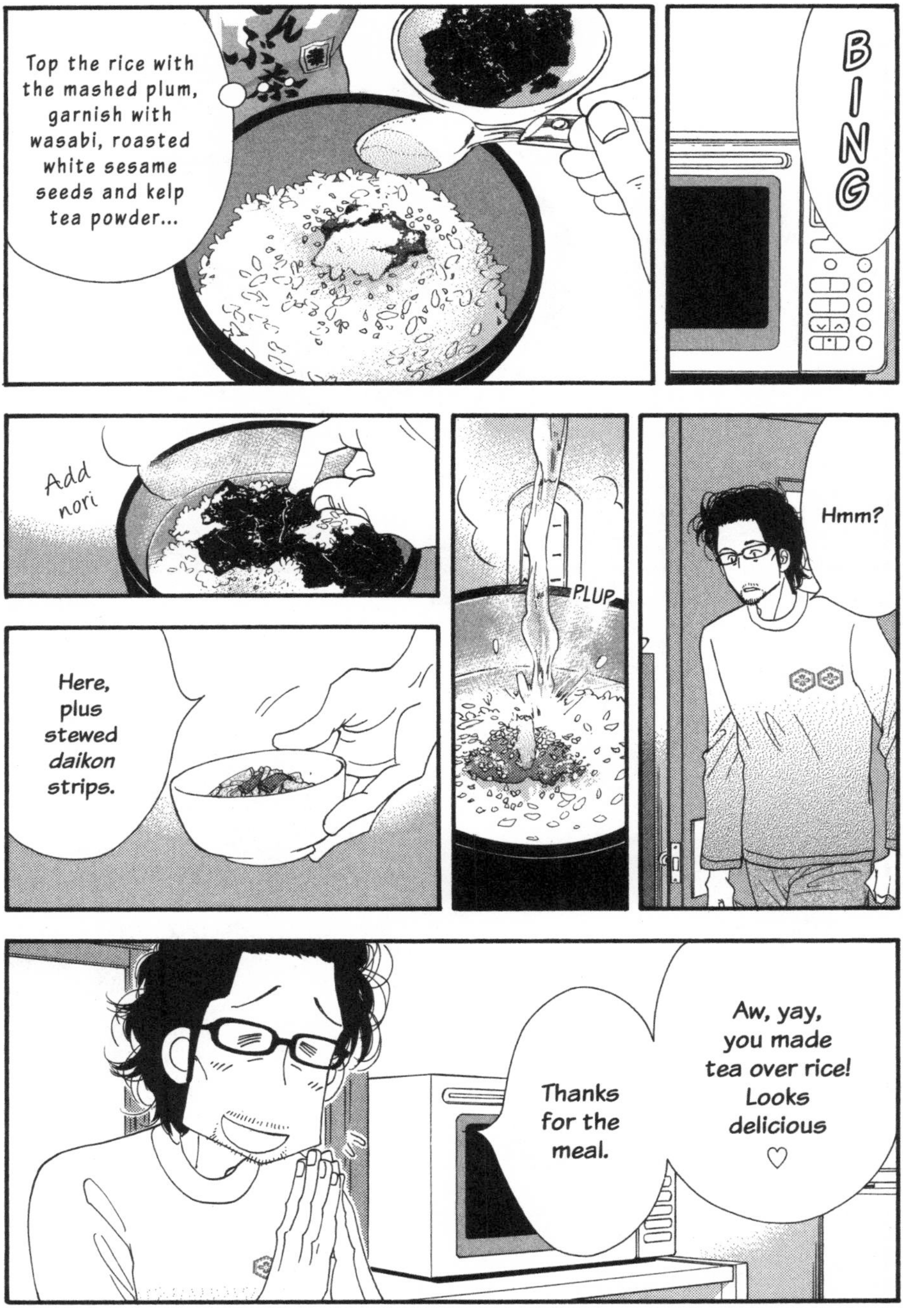
BING
Top the rice with the mashed plum, garnish with wasabi, roasted white sesame seeds and kelp tea powder...
Hmm?
PLUP
Add nori
Here, plus stewed *daikon* strips.
Aw, yay, you made tea over rice! Looks delicious ♡
Thanks for the meal.

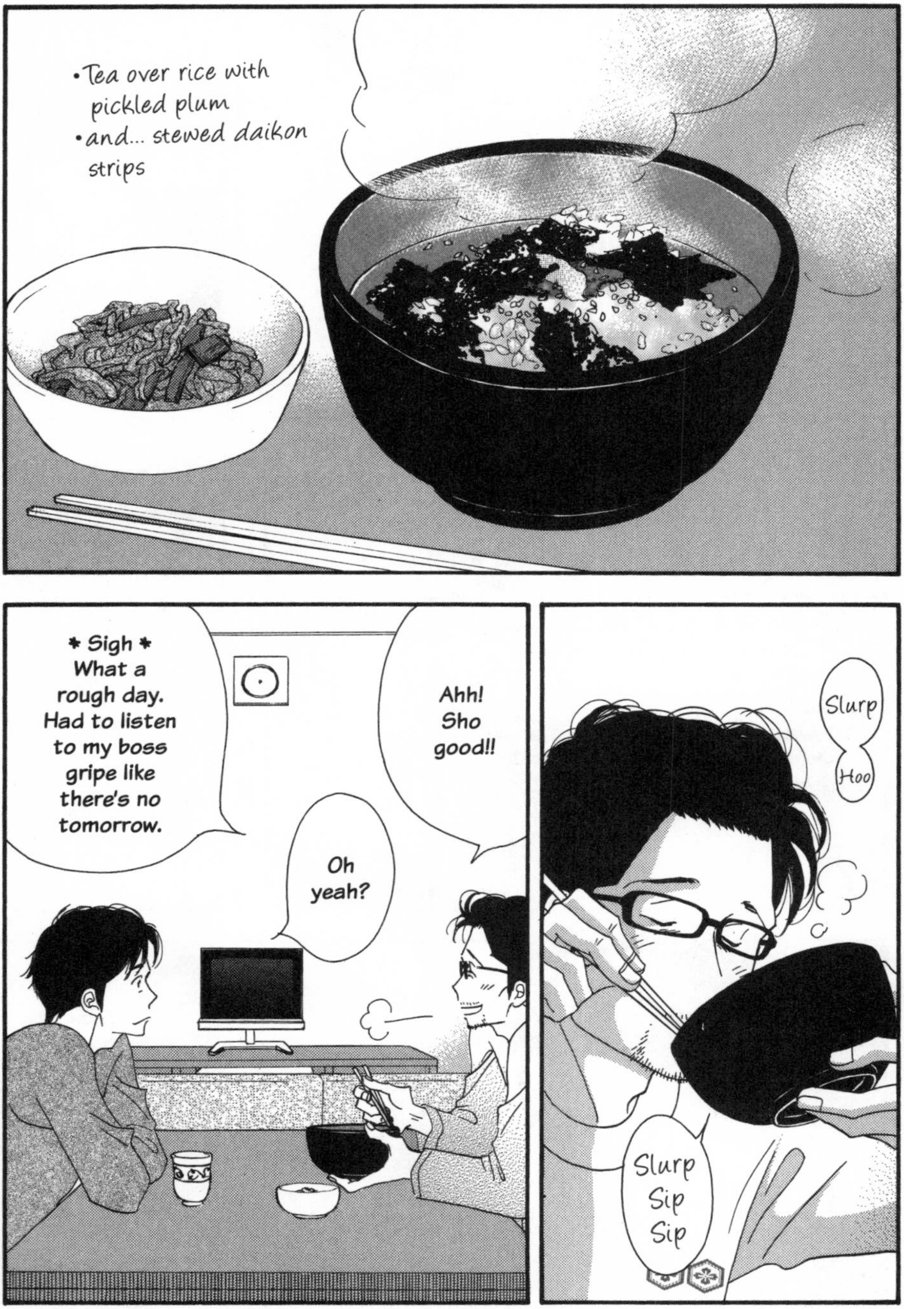

•Tea over rice with pickled plum
•and... stewed daikon strips
Slurp
Hoo
Slurp Sip Sip
Ahh! Sho good!!
* Sigh * What a rough day. Had to listen to my boss gripe like there's no tomorrow.
Oh yeah?

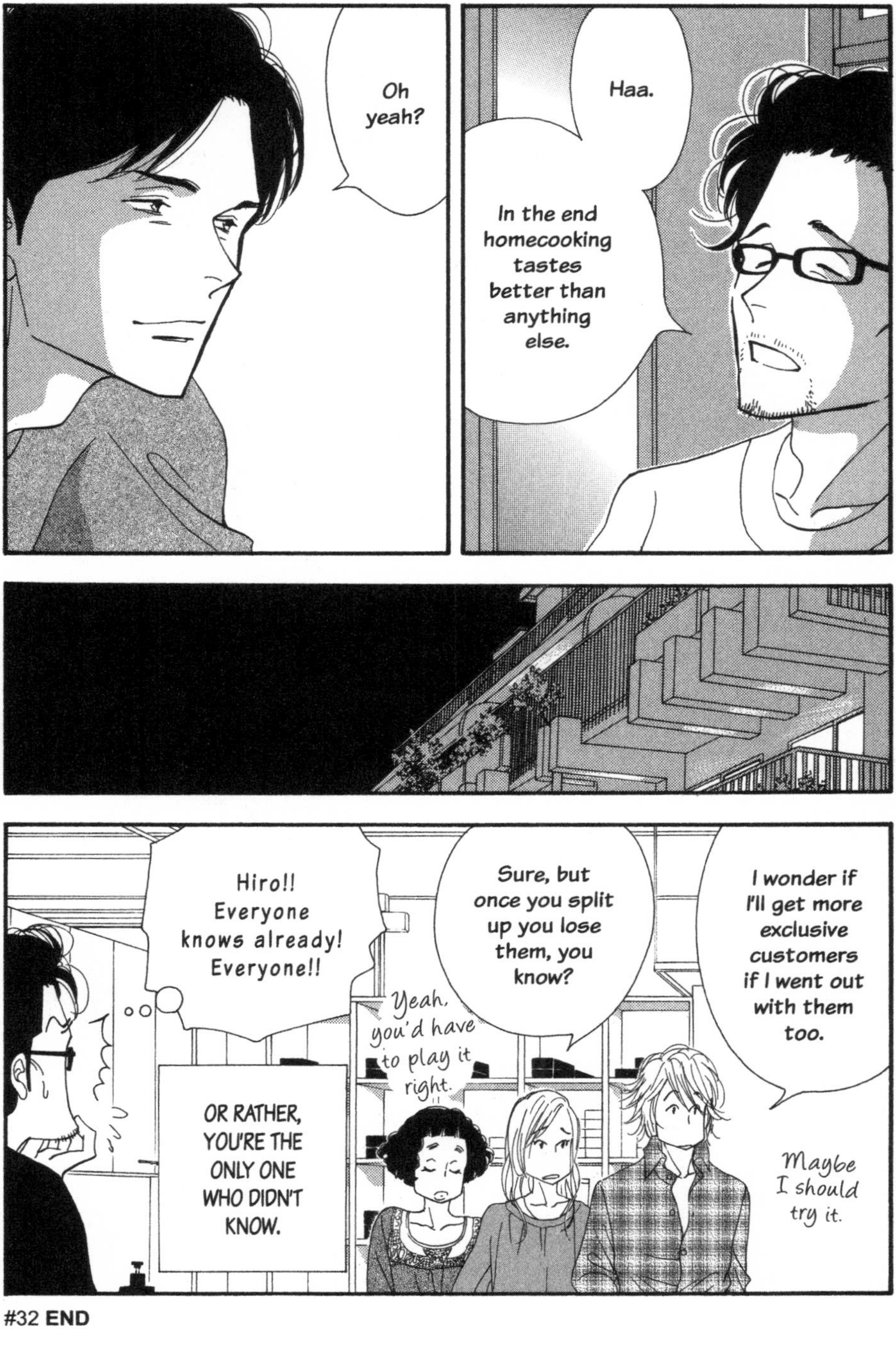
Haa.
In the end homecooking tastes better than anything else.
Oh yeah?
I wonder if I'll get more exclusive customers if I went out with them too.
Maybe I should try it.
Sure, but once you split up you lose them, you know?
Yeah, you'd have to play it right.
Hiro!! Everyone knows already! Everyone!!
OR RATHER, YOU'RE THE ONLY ONE WHO DIDN'T KNOW.

#32 END

Spaghetti Napolitan made with **hot dogs** is tasty too, but also try **canned tuna**. Use the juices in the can as well in that case (although making it with tuna might mean it's no longer "Napolitan").

in the next volume of
"what did you eat yesterday?"

bean rice

tomato-stewed chicken

cole slaw

seared mackerel

stewed cabbage and fried tofu

tomato and yam miso soup

etc, etc!

sharing seasonal gifts of happiness

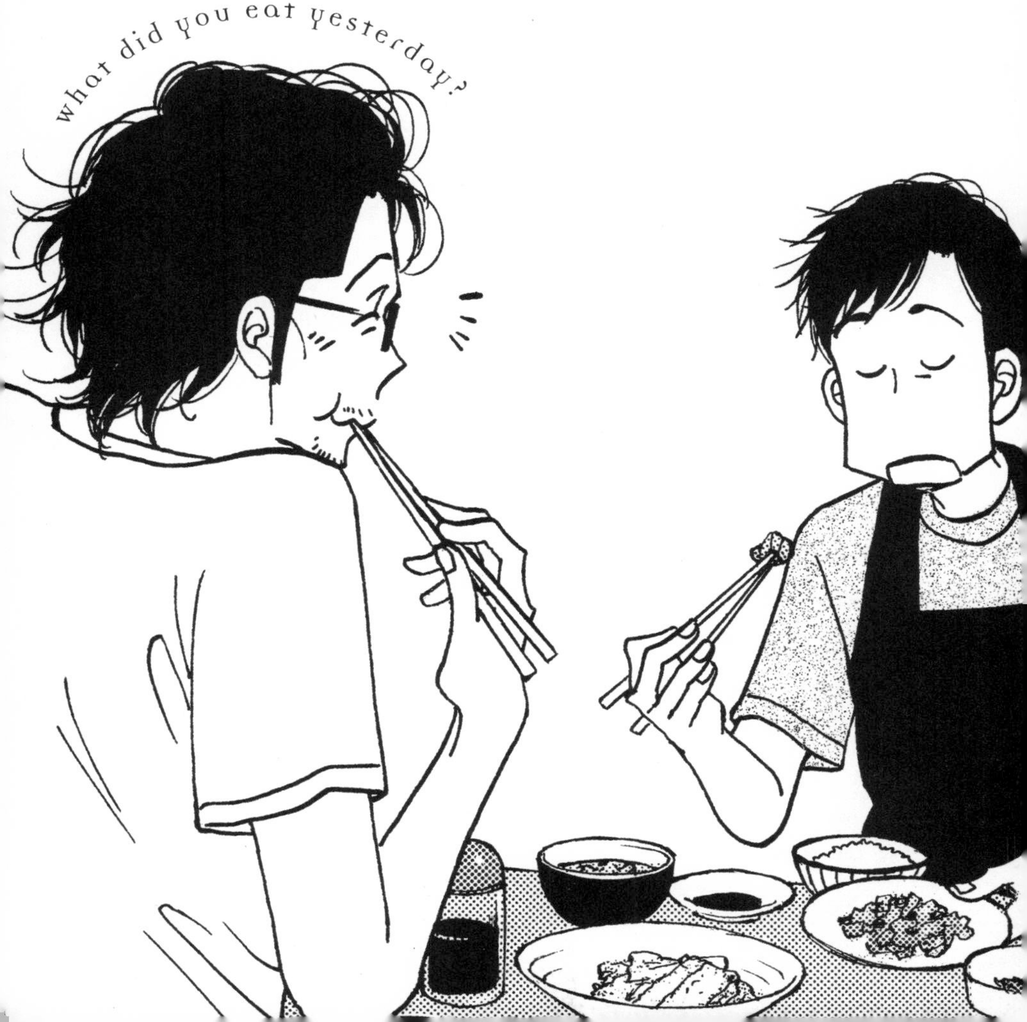
what did you eat yesterday?

FOPLAY2

what did you eat yesterday?, volume 4

editing: Yoshito Hinton
production: Risa Cho
Tomoe Tsutsumi

First published in Japan in 2010 by Kodansha Ltd., Tokyo.
publication rights for this English edition arranged
through Kodansha Ltd., Tokyo.
English language version produced by Vertical, Inc.

Translation provided by Vertical, Inc., 2014
Published by Vertical, Inc., New York

Originally published in Japanese as Kinou nani tabeta? 4 by Kodansha, Ltd.
Kinou nani tabeta? first serialized in Morning, Kodansha, Ltd., 2007-

This is a work of fiction.

ISBN: 978-1-939130-79-2

Manufactured in Canada

First Edition

Vertical, Inc.
451 Park Avenue South
7th Floor
New York, NY 10016
www.vertical-inc.com